322.109 Ros
Ross, Tara
Under God : George Washington
and
the question of church and state /

3402806815610⁹
KW $24.95 ocn182731433
            08/27/08

3 4028 06815 6109
HARRIS COUNTY PUBLIC LIBRARY

MIKE SULLIVAN
HOUSTON CITY COUNCIL MEMBER
DONATED AUGUST 15TH, 2008

WITHDRAWN

D0966161

Advance praise for

Under God

Ross and Smith restore George Washington's view of church and state to its proper place in history, which will inevitably change what we think and say in the present. Hint: he and Thomas Jefferson didn't see eye to eye.

RICHARD BROOKHISER

Author, *What Would the Founders Do?* and *Founding Father: Rediscovering George Washington*

Under God examines a subject that has long deserved careful attention. Ross and Smith present a thoroughly researched account of what the Father of our Country believed regarding the role of religion in American civic life, tracing the development of Washington's views over his lifetime of public service. The book is a must-read for every patriotic citizen.

EDWIN MEESE III

Former U.S. Attorney General

Ross and Smith's study of Washington illuminates the question of church and state in America in remarkable ways. Their book confirms the suspicion that the Father of our Country has been our most under-studied and under-appreciated Founder. And their discoveries and conclusions shed new light on a question about which one might have thought nothing more could be said. They have written a truly enlightening and thought-provoking book.

WILLIAM KRISTOL

Editor, *The Weekly Standard*

Under God examines, with clarity and brevity, Washington's vision for church-state relations and makes a compelling case that his perspective on this important topic deserves to be studied alongside those of other founders.

DANIEL L. DREISBACH

Professor, American University,
and author, *Thomas Jefferson and the Wall of Separation between Church and State*

Sidestepping the divisive issue of Washington's private beliefs, Ross and Smith have turned to his voluminous correspondence on the role of religion in the public sphere. Their fine work should prove enlightening and useful both to the general public and their fellow lawyers.

MARY THOMPSON

Research Specialist, Mount Vernon Estate & Gardens

Washington's political philosophy of church and state is not well understood and is severely underappreciated. All citizens interested in the American experiment in religious freedom should read this book.

VINCENT PHILLIP MUÑOZ

Assistant Professor of Political Science, Tufts University

Under God

Under God

George Washington and the
Question of Church and State

TARA ROSS

JOSEPH C. SMITH, JR.

SPENCE PUBLISHING COMPANY • DALLAS

2008

Copyright © 2008 by Tara Ross and Joseph C. Smith, Jr.

Many of the excerpts from Washington's writings in part two are from Washington, George. Theodore J. Crackel, Editor in Chief, The Papers of George Washington © 1976-2007 University of Virginia Press.

Cover illustration courtesy of the Anschutz Collection. Cover photo by Wiliam J. O'Connor.

All rights reserved. No part of this publication may be reproduced or transmitted in any form or by any means, electronic or mechanical, including photocopy, recording, or any information storage and retrieval system now known or to be invented, without permission in writing from the publisher, except by a reviewer who wishes to quote brief passages in connection with a review written for inclusion in a magazine, newspaper, or broadcast.

Published in the United States by
Spence Publishing Company
111 Cole Street
Dallas, Texas 75207

Library of Congress Control Number: 2007934523
ISBN 978-1-890626-73-0

Printed in the United States of America

*For my husband, Adam, and our
daughter, Emma, with much love.*

Tara

*For my wife, Mary, and our son, Joe,
who declared when he was three that he
wanted to meet George Washington.*

Joe

Contents

Authors' Note

PART TWO of *Under God: George Washington and the Question of Church and State* reprints many of Washington's writings touching on religion. Washington speaks best for himself, and the authors hope that readers will review his writings and evaluate them independently. *Under God* includes those letters, speeches, and military orders that the authors consider most important in evaluating Washington's perspective on the role of religion in civil life. A few other documents are included because they reflect the variety of contexts in which Washington invoked religion, even when acting in his public capacity. The authors would have preferred to make Part Two even more comprehensive; however, Washington's writings that touch on religion are simply too numerous to reprint, in full, in a book of this nature. Such a feat has therefore not been attempted here. Despite the limited scope of this reprinting, the authors hope that it is broad enough to reflect the degree to which religion was part of Washington's public statements. The nation's first president did not hesitate to discuss openly and to endorse the public benefits of religion, and he encouraged others to do the same.

Part Two presents Washington's writings chronologically, reprinting together the writings for each period of his life. No writings are reprinted for Washington's tenure in the House of Burgesses, as he did not write much about church-state matters during that period of his life (see chapter two). Where possible, the authors have reprinted a letter or speech in its entirety, enabling readers to see the full context of Washington's statements. Unfortunately, space considerations prevented a full reprinting in many cases, particularly in the case of Washington's military orders and letters. These latter documents often read like a bulleted list of tasks to accomplish. Thus, only those portions dealing with the religious matter in question are reprinted.

Interested readers may find more of Washington's writings in three easily accessible locations. First, the Library of Congress website has a searchable database that contains many of Washington's writings.[1] Second, many university libraries have a collection of Washington's writings that was published by the authority of Congress in the early 1900s: *The Writings of George Washington from the Original Manuscript Sources 1745-1799*, edited by John C. Fitzpatrick.[2] Finally, a more comprehensive edition of Washington's writings is currently being completed: *The Papers of George Washington*.[3] This latter project was established at the University of Virginia in 1969 with the cooperation of the Mount Vernon Ladies' Association of the Union. The editors emeriti of *The Papers* are W. W. Abbot and Dorothy Twohig. Its current editor-in-chief is Theodore J. Crackel. This book relies on the transcription of Washington's writings found in *The Papers of George Washington*, unless otherwise noted.

Acknowledgments

THE IDEA FOR THIS BOOK was Joe's. He first noted, more than a decade ago, the lack of attention to George Washington's views on church and state. Unfortunately, Joe's law practice did not leave much time for book-writing, so in January 2005, he recruited Tara to help him make the book a reality. *Under God: George Washington and the Question of Church and State* is the result.

We owe many thanks to our families, who sacrificed many hours that could otherwise have been spent with us, particularly Tara's husband, Adam, and Joe's wife and son, Mary and Joe III. Towards the end of the drafting process, Tara's daughter, Emma, had the privilege of making many trips back and forth to the library with her mother, *in utero*. Tara and Adam hope that Washington's wisdom seeped in by osmosis!

We owe a special debt of gratitude to the many academics who helped in the completion of this project. This book would not have been possible without them. Mary Thompson, research specialist at Mount Vernon Estate & Gardens, was very generous with her time early in the process, speaking with us at Mount Vernon, helping us with various questions, and reviewing a draft of our manuscript in late 2006. Philander D. Chase, senior editor at *The Papers of George Washington*, was equally generous with his time, helping us to track down answers to specific questions that we had about Washington's correspondence. Phil also read the draft of the manuscript when it was complete, and our book is significantly better for his contributions.

Several other historians and lawyers read our manuscript in late 2006 and early 2007: Richard Brookhiser, Daniel Dreisbach, Philip Hamburger, Vincent Phillip Muñoz, Patrick O'Daniel, and Samuel Bray. We have benefited from their many observations and suggestions, and we very much appreciate the time that they spent reading our manuscript, despite their own busy schedules.

Other academics took time to speak with us on the phone, in person, or by email about particular aspects of Washington's life: R. Don Higginbotham, Jeffry Morrison, Matthew Spalding, Mark Tabbert, Mark Hall, and J. Mark Thompson. We appreciate their helping us to refine our understanding of the specific historical matters that we discussed. We are also grateful to the Anschutz Collection, Edwin Meese, William Kristol, Eugene Meyer, Leonard Leo, Alice Starr, Jonathan Baron, and Cathy Hellier, all of whom helped in a variety of ways during the course of our project. Last but not least, we were fortunate to have two research assistants: Rachael Hendrickson and Lucas Newcomer. We have benefited tremendously from the help of all these individuals, and *Under God* is better for their input.

Finally, to our good and dear friends who have endured our many discussions of all things George Washington for more than two years: We hope you enjoy the book.

Introduction

WHAT IS THE PROPER RELATIONSHIP between government and religion? This question is among the most litigated in modern-day America. Headlines often trumpet news of the latest skirmish, as groups such as the American Civil Liberties Union (ACLU) ask judges to order that depictions of the nativity or the Ten Commandments be removed from government property.[1] One especially litigious atheist, Michael Newdow, has filed lawsuits arguing that schoolchildren should not be required to pledge allegiance to "one nation, under God" in public school and that the motto "In God We Trust" should be removed from U.S. currency.[2] And, of course, prayer in public schools has been the subject of intense litigation for as long as most Americans can remember.[3]

Conflicts over religion in the public sphere occur in every conceivable context.[4] Some cities and counties, for instance, have been forced to remove religious symbols, such as crosses, from their official seals. Many others do so voluntarily for fear of litigation.[5] In California, certain old mission buildings have faced opposition to their applications for earthquake restoration grants. Despite the immense historical value of some of these buildings, organizations such as Americans United for Separation of Church and State (AUSCS) claim that the religious nature of the buildings disqualifies them from government assistance.[6] Also in California, a public elementary school teacher was subjected to extra scrutiny by his school's principal because he used historical documents referencing God—including the Declaration of Independence—in his classes.[7] In Iowa, AUSCS filed a lawsuit arguing that government funds should not be used in support of prison counselors who include Bible teaching in their efforts.[8] One of Newdow's many lawsuits sought to prohibit the use of public prayer and a Bible at the presidential inauguration in January 2005.[9] The attempt failed: President Bush took his second inaugural oath with one hand on the Bible, concluding with the traditional phrase, "so help me God."[10]

On the other side of such battles are Americans who believe that religion should be welcomed in the public square, as it was for centuries.[11] They sometimes accuse their adversaries of being anti-religious or, specifically, anti-Christian.[12] They tend to support the legality of programs such as the White House Office of Faith-Based and Community Initiatives and school vouchers that allow parents to send their children (and government funds) to private, religious schools, rather than only public, secular schools.

Ironically, these legal battles rage alongside some religious traditions that continue virtually unnoticed and unchallenged in the daily operations of government. For instance, Congress still employs chaplains to open its daily proceedings with a public prayer, continuing a practice begun by the first Congress in 1789.[13] Members of Congress also have their own prayer room in the U.S. Capitol. This prayer room features a Bible and a stained glass portrait of the first American president, George Washington, kneeling in prayer. The text of Psalm 16 is prominently displayed next to Washington: "Preserve me, O God, for in Thee do I put my trust."[14]

The United States Supreme Court also acknowledges God and religion in its proceedings. A carving of Moses holding the Ten Commandments appears on the wall inside the Court's chamber.[15] Each time the Court convenes, the justices take their seats and the Court's marshal declares, "God save the United States and this Honorable Court!"[16] These official recognitions of God persist, despite the fact that many Americans consider the Court to be the branch of the federal government that most disapproves of religion in public life. Indeed, it is this Court's jurisprudence that has invited so many lawsuits over matters of church-state relations.

Such litigation, at its heart, boils down to a dispute over the meaning of the so-called "religion clauses" of the First Amendment to the United States Constitution. Those clauses are short— a mere sixteen words. They declare: "Congress shall make no law respecting an establishment of religion, or prohibiting the free exercise thereof."[17] Unfortunately, there is much disagreement—combined with a fair amount of confusion—over the meaning of these words.

Those who believe that religion should be excised from American civic life tend to argue for the strict "separation of church and state." They claim that the First Amendment's prohibition against an establishment of religion mandates such separation, as a matter of constitutional law. This argument is made so often, in fact, that many Americans doubtless believe that the phrase "separation of church and state" actually appears in the Constitution. It does not. To the contrary, the first notable appearance of the phrase "separation between Church & State" (with reference to the First Amendment) occurred in a letter written by the third president of the United States, Thomas Jefferson, more than a decade after ratification of the First Amendment.[18] Many Americans have come to equate this *post hoc* Jeffersonian statement with constitutional text. They do not question its validity, and they seem to assume that Jefferson spoke for all of the American Founders. He did not.

THOMAS JEFFERSON V. GEORGE WASHINGTON

Jefferson was an important leader in early American politics, and he was also a leader in the movement to establish religious freedom in Virginia. His views on the meaning of the First Amendment are certainly relevant when evaluating the founding generation's understanding of the religious freedoms guaranteed by the Constitution. But Jefferson also served as the American minister to France from 1785 to 1789. As such, he was not present at the Constitutional Convention when the Constitution was drafted, nor was he a member of the first Congress that debated and approved the language of the First Amendment.[19] His views on religious freedom are important, but his absence from these important founding events makes his views less than dispositive. As Chief Justice William Rehnquist once noted, Jefferson is a "less than ideal source of contemporary history as to the meaning of the Religion Clauses of the First Amendment."[20]

This fact makes it all the more puzzling that modern American discussion of the First Amendment's religion clauses has focused so narrowly on Jefferson's "wall of separation," nearly excluding the views of the other Founders. (The rare exceptions to this rule are James Madison and Benjamin Franklin, who have drawn some attention on church-state issues.)[21] If the views of Jefferson, Madison, and Franklin are relevant to understanding the meaning of the First Amendment, then the views of others in the founding generation are relevant as well. Certainly the views of the Father of the Country, George Washington, should be taken into consideration.

In many ways, Washington is among the most qualified to speak to the meaning of the Constitution, including the First Amendment. Washington was the most admired man of his age.[22] Unlike Jefferson, Washington was a key participant in the Constitutional Convention: he served as the Convention's president.[23] Moreover, Washington was the first man to take the presidential oath to "preserve, protect and defend the Constitution of the United States."[24] He served as president when the First Amendment was debated and ratified. Washington's involvement in founding events was so pervasive that one of his biographers, Joseph Ellis, has described him as the "central feature in every major event of the revolutionary era."[25]

Indeed, Washington's qualifications with respect to matters of church and state extend even further than his participation in these founding events. Washington confronted such issues throughout his time in public service, beginning with his service in the colonial military. Should he encourage the employment of government-paid military chaplains? Should he force Quakers to fight, despite their religious convictions to the contrary? Washington was confronted with these and other issues, and he had to consider the real-life consequences of his decisions. As he evaluated the issues and considered the implications of his actions, he developed a common-sense, practical approach to church-state matters. In this regard, he is unique among the Founders. His views developed over time, as the result of direct, everyday experience.[26]

The views that Washington developed differed markedly from Jefferson's "wall of separation." Washington's approach was, instead, for government to accommodate and even to encourage the practice of religion, albeit in ways that were typically non-denominational and tolerant of religious minorities. Religion, as Washington saw it, was a prerequisite for the virtue and morality that make self-government possible.[27] As Washington stated in his Farewell Address in 1796:

> Of all the dispositions and habits which lead to political prosperity, Religion and morality are indispensable supports. In vain would that man claim the tribute of Patriotism, who should labour to subvert these great Pillars of human happiness, these firmest props of the duties of Men & citizens. The mere Politician, equally with the pious man ought to respect & to cherish them. . . . And let us with caution indulge the supposition, that morality can be maintained without religion. Whatever may be conceded to the influence of refined education on minds of peculiar structure—reason & experience both forbid us to expect that National morality can prevail in exclusion of religious principle.[28]

In other words, even after passage of the First Amendment, Washington thought that the public good demanded that government at least accommodate, and in some circumstances support, religion. Yet Washington also recognized that the new nation was composed of people from a variety of religious backgrounds, and he cherished Americans' right to religious freedom. Particularly following his years at the head of a diverse American army, Washington knew the importance of protecting the religious liberty of all—even those in minority religious groups. Indeed, this attitude sometimes prompted Washington to exempt religious dissenters from laws of general applicability, assuming such accommodations could be made without undermining the common good. This practical approach endeared him to minority religious groups of the time, such as Jews, Baptists, and Quakers.[29]

Despite the tremendous amount of information available on Washington's approach to church-state relations, his views on this topic have, to date, been virtually ignored. Most of his biographers focus, instead, on other aspects of his career, particularly his military accomplishments.[30] Indeed, the problem is so pervasive that the thirty-nine-volume *The Writings of George Washington from the Original Manuscript Sources*, completed in 1944, does not include many of Washington's letters to religious organizations. Instead, the editor of *The Writings* relegates much of this correspondence to footnotes. For instance, Washington's remarkable letter to the Hebrew Congregation in Newport, Rhode Island (discussed in chapter five), merits only a brief mention in the fifth paragraph of one such note.[31] The result of such widespread inattention to Washington's perspective is that his approach to church-state issues remains unknown to most modern Americans.

Surely Washington's views on this important aspect of American life deserve at least as much attention as Jefferson's. His position on the subject was well-considered, self-consciously exemplary, and born of his practical experiences as an officer in the Virginia Regiment, a member of the Virginia House of Burgesses, commander-in-chief of the Continental Army, and first president of the United States. During this lifetime of public service, Washington developed a perspective that was more accommodating and encouraging toward religion than the "separation between Church & State" advocated in Jefferson's letter to the Danbury Baptists and, more than a century later, adopted by the United States Supreme Court. This book explores Washington's example as an alternative to Jefferson's separationism.

WASHINGTON'S PERSONAL V. PUBLIC RELIGIOSITY

Historians agree on a few basic facts about Washington's personal religiosity. He was a life-long member of the Anglican church, in which he was baptized and married.[32] He served not only as a vestryman in Truro and Fairfax Parishes, but also as the godfather of several children.[33] Moreover, Washington was a member of the Freemasons, which would have entailed a general vow of belief in a divine entity and an afterlife.[34] Washington's private letters reveal a man who knew, without question, that Providence was protecting him, and he often alluded to the need for divine guidance. Other than these basic facts, however, very little is known with certainty about Washington's personal beliefs. Washington was an intensely private man under normal circumstances, and his reserved approach was even more in evidence when it came to his religious convictions. Indeed, presidential scholar Paul F. Boller, Jr. concludes: "[W]hen it came to religion, Washington was, if anything, more reserved than he was about anything else pertaining to his life."[35]

The questions surrounding Washington's personal religiosity are complicated by the fact that his private statements regarding religion, like his public statements regarding religion, were usually nonspecific or nondenominational. Interestingly, however, to the degree that Washington made specifically Christian comments, he was marginally *more* Christian in his public statements than in his private statements. As one historian, Peter Henriques, observes: "A striking fact emerges from a study of George Washington's private correspondence. Not once in the myriad of letters that he wrote does he ever use the words 'Jesus,' 'Christ,' 'Jesus Christ,' or any synonyms for him such as 'savior' or 'redeemer.'"[36] But, Henriques observes, "there are a few references to Christ, either implicit or explicit, in Washington's *public* papers."[37]

A great deal of modern scholarship has speculated about Washington's personal religiosity. Some scholars argue that he was probably a devout Christian, while others believe that he was a Deist.[38] His reserved attitude makes it difficult to know what his convictions were with any degree of certainty. Ironically, though, Washington's private reticence actually makes it *easier* to discern his views on public matters of church and state. Because he was so reserved about his personal beliefs, it is fair to consider his public expressions of religiosity to be more than his personal religiosity inadvertently spilling over into his public life. To the contrary, there must have been some measure of deliberateness in his decisions to be publicly religious. They reflect a considered determination that such behavior was appropriate, even necessary, for a man in his position. Moreover, if Washington was irreligious, as some historians have argued, then it would make his public references to God and religion even more significant. Under this latter circumstance, such references would demonstrate that Washington spoke of God precisely because he thought a public man—a general or a president—should do so, not because his private beliefs motivated him.

Indeed, while historians do not agree on Washington's personal religiosity, they do agree on another Washington characteristic that is much more relevant for purposes of this book: Washington was always extremely conscious that his actions would set precedents for those who followed him.[39] His official uses of religion are thus particularly relevant in indicating that he believed such uses to be proper and (later) constitutional.

THE FOCUS OF THIS BOOK IS NARROW. It does not attempt to exhaustively interpret the religion clauses of the First Amendment, relying upon a Washingtonian perspective, rather than a Jeffersonian one. Instead, it works from the premise that Jefferson is not the only Founder with a viewpoint worth discussing in the context of church-state relations: Washington's views are also important. This book describes the development of those views throughout Washington's public life, culminating in his service as president both before and after ratification of the First Amendment.

Finally, the second half of the book reprints a generous sampling of Washington's key speeches and other writings that implicate church-state issues. Washington speaks best for himself, and it is hoped that readers will review his writings and evaluate them independently. Washington's works are the best evidence of his beliefs regarding the appropriate role of religion in American civic life.[40]

These works, no less than Thomas Jefferson's "wall of separation" letter, deserve our attention.

PART ONE

Public Homage

ONE

≈

Commander of the
Virginia Regiment

1755–1758

I am still in the land of the livg by the miraculous care
of Providence, that protected me beyond all human
expectation; I had 4 Bullets through my Coat, and two
Horses shot under me yet escaped unhurt.

Letter to John Augustine Washington,
July 18, 1755[1]

GEORGE WASHINGTON KNEW that the "miraculous care of Providence" had enabled him to survive the French and Indian War.[2] He could not possibly doubt the existence of special and divine care. The memory of one particular incident in 1755 stood out in his mind, forever convincing him that providential intervention in military affairs was a real and tangible force that should be respected, both publicly and privately. This unforgettable event occurred during the second year of the war.

On July 9, the twenty-three-year old Washington found himself riding with a column of about 1,300 British and Virginian

3

troops.[3] Washington was serving as aide-de-camp to British Major General Edward Braddock, and he accompanied the general in the procession.[4] Braddock was moving his troops toward Fort Duquesne, near the Monongahela River, which he had been ordered to attack and take from the French. Washington was heartily in favor of the mission, believing it to be important to the security of the colonies. Indeed, though he had been sick and away from Braddock's troops for weeks, Washington had gone to great lengths to be present for the conclusion of this campaign. He sat on his horse now only with the assistance of pillows that helped him to sit upright, despite his temporary weakness.

Suddenly, the crash of weapons firing and the horrifying sound of an Indian war whoop pierced the air. The French, aided by their Indian allies, had turned the tables on Braddock's men. The British and Virginians were no longer the aggressors. They were under attack.

Washington watched as chaos broke out in the ranks. The troops fired wildly, sometimes even shooting their own comrades. Braddock himself was mortally wounded, leaving a heavy weight of responsibility on the shoulders of his aide-de-camp, Washington. In the midst of it all, Washington fought gallantly, despite his recent sickness. As Braddock's forces retreated, Washington loaded the still-breathing Braddock into a cart so he could be carried off the field of battle. Later, Washington buried Braddock where his body could not be found and desecrated by the Indians.

When the battle was over and the dust had settled, more than nine hundred British and Virginian troops had been killed or wounded.[5] Only a handful of French and Indians had been so much as injured. Washington was one of the few officers to emerge virtually unscathed. He would later tell his brother Jack in a July 18, 1755, letter that Braddock's troops were "scandalously beaten by a trifling body of men."[6]

But the bulk of this letter to Jack focused on a different matter. Washington believed that Providence had protected him. He told Jack, "I am still in the land of the livg by the miraculous care of Providence, that protected me beyond all human expectation; I had 4 Bullets through my Coat, and two Horses shot under me yet escaped unhurt."[7] Washington soon discovered that many of his fellow Virginians also believed that God had protected him. They were impressed by his bravery and noted that he was one of the few to emerge from battle uninjured.[8] Within a matter of weeks, their praise led to a new opportunity for Washington. He was asked to serve Virginia again, this time as commander of the Virginia Regiment. Washington accepted this position at the end of the summer of 1755.[9]

As commander, Washington faced the daunting task of organizing a group of barely trained men into a professional military corps. Moreover, he had to do so in the face of constant supply and funding shortages. As if these challenges were not enough, he also found himself confronted with the question of how to address religious issues with his troops.

Washington probably had few reasons to focus on such church-state issues prior to his time as commander of the Virginia forces. But now he would need to develop his views in this area—and quickly. Two main issues presented themselves: first, the appointment of military chaplains; and second, the treatment of Quakers with religious objections to fighting. Washington responded to both of these issues in a similar fashion. Under his command, the regiment would be friendly toward religion, because religion was a necessary prerequisite to morality and discipline in the military.

On the other hand, Washington concluded that some accommodation could be made for those with differing religious views.

A CHAPLAIN FOR THE REGIMENT

On September 23, 1756, Colonel Washington wrote a letter to Virginia Governor Robert Dinwiddie. The letter was the first of several to mention a lack of chaplains for his troops. "The want of a Chaplain," Washington wrote, "does, I humbly conceive, reflect dishonor upon the Regiment, as all other Officers are allowed."[10] But the colonel didn't stop with merely noting the lack of a chaplain. This person, Washington felt, should be publicly appointed and publicly funded. "The Gentlemen of the Corps," Washington continued, "did propose to support one at their private expence—But I think it would have a more graceful appearance were *he appointed* as others are."[11]

Dinwiddie's response wasn't promising. It included only one quick comment about the possible appointment of a chaplain. "I have recommended to the Commissary to get one," Dinwiddie explained, "but he cannot prevail with any Person to accept of it."[12] Nevertheless, he concluded, "I shall again press it to him."[13] The governor thus declined to address the question of public funding, and he deferred responsibility for naming chaplains to the commissary of the Anglican church in Virginia.[14] Such opaqueness was typical of Dinwiddie and a source of frustration to the commander.[15]

Washington decided to try again. A few weeks later, he wrote two letters: another to the governor and one to John Robinson, speaker of the Virginia House of Burgesses. "As touching a Chaplain," he observed to the governor, "If the Government will grant a subsistance we can readily get a person of merit to accept of the place, without giving the Commissary any trouble on that point."[16] In a separate letter to Robinson, Washington continued with his plea: "A Chaplain for the Regiment ought to be provided; that we may at least have the show, if we are said to want the substance of Godliness!"[17]

Washington's pleas did not bear fruit. No record has been found of a response from the speaker, and the governor put the issue back into Washington's hands. Dinwiddie stated that he could not be expected to get the commissary's approval when no specific person had been proposed. He explained: "You shou'd know that it's necessary his Qualificat. & the Bishop's Letter of Licence shou'd be produc'd to the Commissary, & Self."[18] From Washington's perspective, however, finding a suitable chaplain and getting the commissary's approval were never the problems. Instead, he needed to know if public funds would be appropriated. Washington promptly wrote back, "I had no person in view, tho' many have offered and only said, if the country would provide a Subsistance, we cou'd procure a Chaplain: without thinking there was offence in the expression."[19] Washington's offer met with silence from Dinwiddie for several months.

Washington was not one to give up easily. In April 1757, he raised the subject again: "It is a hardship upon the Regiment, I think, to be denied a Chaplain," he told the governor.[20] Several weeks later, he renewed his appeal: "We shou'd also be glad if our Chaplain was appointed, and that a Gentleman of sober, serious and religious deportment were chosen for this important Trust!"[21] Yet no chaplain was forthcoming. Dinwiddie's only response was to note that "as yet, has no Clergiman offer'd to be Chaplain, if not one of good Character, better have none."[22]

In early 1758, poor health caused Dinwiddie to resign and return to England. The president of the Virginia Council, John

Blair, temporarily took his place.[23] At about this time, for reasons
the historical record doesn't reveal, the legislature finally approved a government-funded chaplain.[24] Washington wrote Blair,
requesting that the appointment be made, as authorized by the
legislature. Washington concluded, "Common decency, Sir, in a
camp calls for the services of a Divine."[25]

It is fair to conclude that Washington would not have showed
such persistence unless he considered the appointment of a chaplain, at public expense, to be important. But if the regiment needed
a chaplain so badly, why did it take Washington so long to make
his request? He assumed command by September 1, 1755, but
did not write Dinwiddie about a chaplain until September 1756.
Washington did not publicly articulate his reasons for this delay,
but it seems likely that certain events of that first year led him to
believe that a government-paid chaplain would be beneficial to
his troops. There is no reason to believe that he postponed acting
on this conclusion once he reached it.

The relevant events began in early April 1756, when Washington, after commanding the troops for more than seven months,
received a letter from Governor Dinwiddie. "The Assembly," Dinwiddie revealed, "were greatly inflamed being told that the greatest
Immoralities & Drunkenness have been much countenanced and
proper Discipline neglected."[26] Washington was horrified. The
allegations were aimed at him, too, as if he deliberately allowed
such behavior. He immediately responded to Dinwiddie:

> How far any of the individuals may have deserved such in-
> vidious reflections, I will not take upon me to determine; but
> this I am certain of; and can call my conscience, and what I
> suppose will still be a more demonstrable proof in the eyes
> of the World, my orders to witness how much I have, both

by Threats and persuasive means, endeavoured to discountenance Gaming, drinking, swearing, and irregularities of every other kind. While I have, on the other hand, practised every artifice to inspire a laudable emulation in the Officers for the Service of their Country; and to encourage the Soldiers in the unerring exercise of their Duty.[27]

No sooner had Washington posted his letter to Dinwiddie, than he received another letter from Speaker Robinson. The speaker's letter referenced similar allegations of impropriety.[28] Internally, Washington was fuming at the unjustified stain on his reputation. He dashed off a quick response to Robinson, but he did not have time to stew over the problem.[29] For the moment, he had his hands full dealing with the threat of Indian raids, more supply shortages, and his continuing inability to recruit more troops. The allegations over immorality would remain on the back burner for months.[30] But on September 3, 1756, they were abruptly brought to the fore again.

On that day, an anonymous writer, known as the "Virginia Centinel," wrote a piece that appeared on the front page of the *Virginia Gazette*.[31] The article was lengthy, occupying nearly the entire page. It alleged that the troops and officers of the Virginia Regiment were immoral and corrupt. Worse, the Centinel alleged, the "officers give the men an example of all manner of debauchery, vice and idleness."[32] The writer concluded that the regiment was composed entirely of "dastardly debauchees."[33]

The charges were harsh, and Washington initially did not know how to respond. Should he resign his commission? Should he publicly demand a retraction? After soliciting advice from others, he decided to do neither. But he did take action on another front. At this point, he decided to make his first official request for a government-appointed chaplain. He submitted this request within three weeks of the *Virginia Gazette* article.

One could hypothesize that Washington's request was spurred merely by a momentary public relations crisis, rather than a genuine belief that a government-sponsored chaplain would benefit the troops. Washington himself left few clues as to his intentions, outside of the few scattered comments in his letters to Dinwiddie, Robinson, and Blair. While a definitive answer regarding Washington's underlying motivations may not be possible, three key facts suggest that Washington requested government-sponsored chaplains because he genuinely expected them to be valuable.

First, Washington personally believed that "Providence" had been actively involved in his military career, as he wrote to his brother Jack in July 1755.[34] Washington's private expression of belief in a letter to his brother suggests that his view of religion in military affairs was not purely, if at all, cynical or political. Second, the *Virginia Gazette* incident was just one in a series of problems that Washington faced during 1756. He was also confronted with stubbornly low recruitment numbers, desertion, and poor troop morale. Even without the *Virgina Gazette* controversy, Washington would have been looking for ways to improve morale and discipline among his troops. The man who believed that Providence protected him during Braddock's failed campaign reasonably could have concluded that religion would help his regiment through all these difficulties, too, and that the government could therefore support the regiment by providing a chaplain. Third, Washington continued in his efforts to procure a chaplain even after the *Virginia Gazette* incident was largely forgotten, indicating that he was motivated by more than purely political considerations. Indeed, Washington became a permanent advocate for military chaplains, requesting them not only for the Virginia Regiment, but again two decades later, when he served as commander-in-chief of the Continental Army.

Yet whatever Washington's motives, one fact is clear: Washington obviously did not consider government support of religion to be problematic, at least not in this context and not at this point in American history. Indeed, not only did Washington seek to obtain a publicly-funded chaplain for his troops, but he began consistently ordering his troops to attend prayer and divine services.[35] Washington's actions demonstrate the conclusion he reached during this period: government must foster religion and enforce moral discipline if troops are to operate effectively.[36]

QUAKERS

On May 1, 1756, the Virginia Assembly enacted a statute requiring each county to identify its "able-bodied single men."[37] These men were to gather together, and those whose names were drawn in a lottery would be expected to serve in the militia unless they were able either to pay a fee or find a replacement. Following the drawings in Hanover and New Kent counties, six Quakers were drafted to serve in the militia.[38] Unfortunately, these Quakers were pacifists, with religious objections to the military effort in which they were now expected to participate.

These men joined Washington's troops before the end of June, immediately creating a problem for their new commander. The Quakers, Washington told Dinwiddie, "will neither bear arms, work, receive provisions or pay, or do any thing that tends, in any respect, to self-defence."[39] Washington sought help: "I should be glad of your Honours directions how to proceed with them."[40]

Dinwiddie responded promptly, "If the six Quakers will not fight You must compell them to work on the Forts, to carry Timber &ca if this will not do confine them with a short Allowance of Bread & Water till You bring them to reason or provide others in their room."[41] Washington wrote no more on the subject for a month. Presumably, he was seeking to accommodate the Quakers by finding tasks for them that would not be directly related to defense. But the Quakers were determined. They would not help the troops in any way, shape, or form. Washington set pen to paper again: "I could by no means bring the Quakers to any Terms—They chose rather to be whipped to death than bear arms, or lend us any assistance whatever upon the Fort, or any thing of self-defence. Some of their friends have been security for their appearance when they are called for; and I have released them from the Guard-House until I receive further orders from your Honour—which they have agreed to apply for."[42]

At this point, both Washington and the governor seemed at a complete loss. "A great Body of Quakers waited on me in regard to their Friends with You, praying they may not be Whipped," Dinwiddie wrote Washington, "[use] them with lenity, but as they are at their own Expence I wou'd have them remain as long as the other Draughts."[43] Washington wrote back in agreement, commenting that "[t]he Quakers still remain here, and shall until the other Drafts are discharged."[44] Both Washington and Dinwiddie were trying to accommodate the Quakers' religious concerns to a practicable extent, but such an accommodation was difficult in a military structure that normally did not tolerate desertion or refusal to comply with orders. To modern ears, Washington's confinement of the Quakers until the end of their enlistment probably seems harsh. But in 1756, the treatment was quite lenient: those who deserted or who showed cowardice and disobedience could be whipped or put to death.[45]

Paul Boller discounts the relevance of this episode in assessing Washington's views on religious freedom, noting that the governor deserves at least equal credit for the treatment accorded to the Quakers.[46] Undoubtedly, Washington showed appropriate deference to the governor throughout this series of events. But two facts indicate that Washington probably agreed with the governor's decision to make adaptations in line with the Quakers' freedom of conscience.

First, Washington strayed from his normal procedure in trying and punishing misbehaving troops. Typically, Washington handled disciplinary matters without involving the governor unless a court martial had determined that death was warranted.[47] In this latter case, Washington would write Dinwiddie, as required by law, to procure confirmation that the death sentence could be carried out.[48] Dinwiddie was not typically involved in the earlier stages of determining and meting out punishment. With the Quakers, however, Washington changed his procedure: he involved Dinwiddie from the beginning. The change in procedure may have merely reflected Washington's uncertainty about what course of action to take. Or perhaps Washington was anticipating a problem that would recur and hence require a consistent policy with which the governor agreed. Either way, the change suggests that Washington recognized the validity of religious objections, at least in some circumstances, such that they would require some sort of exceptional attention.

Second, Washington made at least one additional accommodation without awaiting approval from Dinwiddie. During July 1756, Washington attempted to find non-defense tasks for the

Quakers, as requested by Dinwiddie. But as recounted above, the Quakers refused to help the troops in any manner. Washington eventually decided, of his own accord, to release the Quakers from the guard house without punishing them further. *After* he made this decision, he wrote Dinwiddie to see what steps should be taken.[49] In part, Washington's decision was probably driven by the impracticability of long-term imprisonment during the eighteenth century, but his actions also indicate that he already knew the Quakers would not be punished and that accommodations would be necessary.

The Quakers' defiance prompted Washington, perhaps for the first time, to think about the practical difficulties in applying laws of general applicability to those with religious objections. In concert with the governor, he concluded that some accommodations could be made, at least in this particular instance. He would be required to develop his ideas in this area even further in the coming years.

FREEMASONS

At about this time, Washington became a Freemason. He was initiated an Entered Apprentice into Fredericksburg Lodge No. 4 on November 4, 1752, when he was twenty years old. He took his next degree, Fellow Craft, on March 3, 1753. He was raised to Master Mason on August 4, 1753.[50]

Washington's membership in the Freemasons has been the subject of some controversy. Those who are Freemasons passionately defend their connection with the Father of the Country, the man who is their most revered Brother. They describe Washington as an active Freemason who greatly treasured the virtues of the Craft.[51] On the other side of the debate are anti-Masons who downplay the importance of Freemasonry in the life of Washington.

The degree to which Washington did or did not value the precepts of Freemasonry is not important for purposes of this book.[52] What *is* interesting is the apparent similarity between Washington's developing views on church-state relations and the foundational principles of Freemasonry, as they relate to the use of religion.

To join a Masonic Lodge, a candidate must believe in God. He doesn't have to believe in the God of any particular religion, but he must believe in a divine and superior being.[53] As a result, Freemasons hail from a variety of religious backgrounds, both Christian and non-Christian. Indeed, during Washington's day there were several Jewish Freemasons.[54] When Freemasons come together, they include prayers and religion in their meetings and rituals, but they do so in a way that is nondenominational.[55] Their belief in God is central to their membership, and religion is viewed as an important component of their activities. However, they strive to include religion in such a way that members from all religious backgrounds will feel comfortable and welcome.[56]

The nondenominational yet devoutly religious approach of Freemasonry is remarkably like the path Washington eventually chose as a political and military leader. Perhaps Freemasonry influenced his views. Perhaps Washington felt comfortable in Masonic Lodges because he had already reached conclusions about religion that were compatible with those of the fraternity. Regardless, the similarity between the approaches of the man and the organization is noteworthy.

WASHINGTON STEADFASTLY BELIEVED that he had survived the early years of the French and Indian War only with the aid of Providence. His experiences led him to conclude that it is proper and wise to seek divine assistance in military endeavors. When problems arose during his tenure as commander of the Virginia Regiment, he naturally turned to religion as one of many methods of resolving these issues and preserving order among his troops.

Washington's responsibilities as commander of the Virginia Regiment gave him new, compelling reasons to ponder church-state issues. His next set of public responsibilities, in the Virginia legislature, would present him with similar opportunities. The conclusions that he reached as an elected official would build upon the lessons that he learned as a military commander.

TWO

ꙮ

Member of the House of Burgesses

1759–1775

Went to Church & fasted all day.

*Diary entry of June 1, 1774, noting his observance
of a fast recommended by Virginia legislators*[1]

I N DECEMBER 1755, a few of Washington's friends nominated him for a seat in the Virginia House of Burgesses. Washington did not win the election. He was still serving as commander of the Virginia Regiment, and no canvass was made for his election prior to the day that ballots were cast.[2] Nevertheless, the colonel must have been encouraged when he learned that his nomination earned forty votes (compared to the winners' 271 and 270) despite the informal nature of his candidacy.[3] A few years later, Washington again threw his hat into the ring.

The 1758 election would not be a repeat of 1755. This time, Washington declared his candidacy early, and several of his friends worked hard on his behalf prior to the election. Late in July, the colonel was overwhelmingly elected a burgess from Frederick County with more than three hundred votes.[4] Washington completed one final military mission to the Ohio, but at the end of 1758, he resigned his commission.[5] On January 6, 1759, he married Martha Dandridge Custis.[6] At least for now, military life was behind him. He was now George Washington, Esquire—a husband, stepfather, plantation owner, and member of the House of Burgesses.

Being a legislator gave Washington the opportunity to see public policy matters from a different point of view. As a military commander, he had submitted his requests to the state legislature and awaited its decision. But as a burgess, he was a part of the decision-making process. Several years into his tenure, he was asked to sit on the Committee for Religion. When the burgesses called for a day of fasting and prayer, Washington participated. Later, he was asked to serve as a representative for Virginia in the Continental Congress. That newly-formed body decided to begin its first session with prayer.

These years were quiet ones for Washington in many ways, but they were also a time of personal growth. Historian Paul Longmore notes that these years "worked a remarkable change in him. Personal challenges constituted a kind of spiritual schooling. They caused him to mature emotionally, preparing him for his later public service."[7] Bernhard Knollenberg agrees, but emphasizes the importance of Washington's service as a burgess: "[H]is many years of working with fellow members of the House, especially the work in committee, probably contributed more than anything to his understanding, patience, and tact in later dealing with the Continental Congress."[8]

The young, ambitious adult who was learning to lead in 1758 would reenter the military service in 1775 as a mature leader with firmly established opinions. Washington couldn't then know it, but this period of his life, combined with his tenure as commander of the Virginia Regiment, would prepare him to lead an army against the British during the American Revolution.

THE HOUSE OF BURGESSES AND RELIGION

Washington served as a member of the House of Burgesses for nearly two decades. As a burgess, he was immediately appointed to the Committee of Propositions and Grievances, which handled business and government issues.[9] He also served on several special committees created to address various military and other matters.[10] Later, he was appointed to two additional standing committees, including the new Committee for Religion.[11] This latter committee was created partly in response to worries about corruption and immorality, and its stated purpose was to "meet and adjourn from day to day, and to take into their Consideration all matters and things relating to Religion and Morality."[12] The committee regulated vestries and parishes, and it considered legislation for the protection of religious dissenters.[13] "In short," Longmore states, "its actions were part of the effort to restore communal unity and public virtue at a time when both seemed in jeopardy."[14]

Washington was a burgess before disestablishment in Virginia. Taxes were still levied to support the Anglican Church, and it was common for the legislature to regulate many matters related to religious entities. The legislature divided and dissolved parishes, resolved disputes regarding vestry elections and boundaries, and considered requests to buy or to sell parish lands.[15] Even small requests were considered by the House, as when it approved reimbursement to an organist who played in a Williamsburg church throughout the legislative session, or when it agreed to let a parish pay its minister with money instead of tobacco.[16] The House routinely appointed and paid chaplains who opened legislative sessions with prayer.[17]

Unfortunately, many of these colonial-era deliberations are lost to history because the records preserving them were destroyed in the evacuation and burning of Richmond, Virginia, during the Civil War.[18] Moreover, Washington himself did not write about many of these church-state matters during his tenure as a burgess, so his thoughts on any particular legislative action are largely unknown, with one exception. The incident is interesting, at least in part, because it foreshadows actions that Washington would endorse later, after passage of the First Amendment.

Tensions had been rising between England and her American colonies for some time, but on December 16, 1773, matters took a turn for the worse. In the dead of night, a group of Bostonians boarded British merchant ships, dressed as Indians, and threw their cargoes of tea overboard. The Bostonians were angry about taxes that had been levied on them by the British Parliament.[19] When news of the "Boston Tea Party" reached England, Parliament decided to retaliate. In March 1774, it passed a bill closing the Port of Boston to all vessels, effective June 1. The port was to remain closed until such time as Boston made recompense for the tea that had been lost. The text of this legislation reached Boston on May 10, and it sparked alarm and outrage throughout the colonies. If Parliament could close one American port, the colonists feared, then Parliament could close any American port. Boston asked the other colonies to resist England's exertion of power: *all* trade with England and Ireland should be shut down until the law was repealed. The text of the Boston Port Bill did not reach Virginia until shortly before May 19. Less than a week later, on the 24th, the House of Burgesses approved a resolution calling for a

> day of Fasting, Humiliation, and Prayer, devoutly to implore the divine interposition, for averting the heavy Calamity which threatens destruction to our Civil Rights, and the Evils of civil War; to give us one heart and one Mind firmly to oppose, by all just and proper means, every injury to American Rights; and that the Minds of his Majesty and his Parliament, may be inspired from above with Wisdom, Moderation, and Justice, to remove from the loyal People of America all cause of danger, from a continued pursuit of Measures, pregnant with their ruin.[20]

Washington not only voted for this resolution, but he also, as one of his biographers notes, "determined to respect it literally and in spirit."[21] Within two days, on the 26th, Virginia's governor responded to the House action, declaring that the resolve "makes it necessary for me to dissolve you; and you are dissolved accordingly."[22] Washington wrote of his surprise at this outcome: "[T]his Dissolution was as sudden as unexpected for there were other resolves of a much more spirited Nature ready to be offerd to the House wch would have been adopted respecting the Boston Port Bill."[23] On June 1, the day appointed for the fast, Washington joined his fellow burgesses, who had agreed to attend church together. His diary entry for the day was simple: "Went to Church & fasted all day."[24]

An exhaustive analysis of Washington's views on church and state during his time in the House of Burgesses is probably impossible.[25] Historians can recount the final decisions of the entire House, but the record regarding Washington's personal thoughts

on any particular legislative item is scarce. Washington did, however, seem comfortable operating within the religious establishment of his day—an establishment that existed at the state, not
the national, level. He endorsed a public day of prayer and fasting
when presented with an opportunity to do so, and he seemed
enthusiastic about the proposal. Washington's support for an
officially established Anglicanism (even at the state level) seems
to have declined shortly before adoption of the Constitution (see
chapter four). Nevertheless, his support for other, nondenominational endorsements and accommodations of religion did not
end either with disestablishment in his home state of Virginia or
adoption of the Constitution and then the First Amendment. To
the contrary, Washington would continue to find days of fasting,
prayer, and thanksgiving permissible and appropriate, not only
as commander-in-chief of the Continental Army, but also as
president.

THE CONTINENTAL CONGRESS AND RELIGION

Virginia's day of fasting and prayer was only one of many colonial
responses to the Boston Port Bill. The day after the Virginia governor disbanded the House, the burgesses met at Raleigh Tavern,
near the capitol. By the time the burgesses adjourned from their
hastily called meeting, they had agreed to the "expediency of appointing deputies from the several Colonies of British America,
to meet in general congress, at such place annually as shall be
thought most convenient."[26] Within a matter of months, similar
agreements were reached in the other colonies and delegates were
selected to serve at such a meeting. Washington was elected, along
with six of his peers, to represent Virginia.[27]

　　The first Continental Congress was called to order on Monday, September 5, 1774, in Philadelphia. After initial proceedings had been completed, one delegate moved that Congress be opened with prayer.[28] According to John Adams' written account of the day, two delegates opposed the motion on the grounds that "we were so divided in religious sentiments."[29] But Samuel Adams, delegate from Massachusetts, arose and declared that he "was no bigot, and could hear a prayer from a gentleman of piety and virtue, who was at the same time a friend to his country."[30] The Reverend Jacob Duché, an Episcopal clergyman and the rector of Christ Church in Philadelphia, was nominated for the purpose.[31] He read Psalm 35 and then prayed a prayer that "filled the bosom of every man present," according to Adams.[32] Washington's thoughts on this series of events were, unfortunately, not recorded, but he was present and participated in the opening prayer without apparent objection. Congress later appointed Duché as its chaplain.[33]

　　From a church-state perspective, the Continental Congress took two additional actions of significance during Washington's tenure. The first resulted from American efforts to gain Canada, with its large Roman Catholic population, as an ally in its dispute with Great Britain. A letter to the inhabitants of Quebec, adopted by the Continental Congress on October 26, 1774, emphasized that Canadian rights were in danger, just as surely as American rights were. "These are the rights *you* are entitled to and ought at this moment in perfection, to exercise," the congressional missive noted, "And what is offered to you by the late Act of Parliament in their place? Liberty of conscience in your religion? No."[34] The letter concluded with an appeal for Canadians to join with Americans in opposing the tyranny imposed on both of them by their mother country. "We are too well acquainted with the liberality of sentiment distinguishing your nation, to imagine, that difference of religion will prejudice you against a hearty amity with us," the congress wrote, "You know, that the transcendant nature of freedom elevates those, who unite in her cause, above all such low-minded infirmities."[35]

The statement on behalf of religious liberty was a strong one, but church-state historian Anson Phelps Stokes has argued that the letter to Quebec was not driven purely by a desire to promote freedom of religious conscience across North America. "That political considerations were involved in the address cannot be doubted," Stokes writes in *Church and State in the United States*.[36] Mere days before the letter to Quebec inhabitants was approved, the Continental Congress approved a second letter, this one to the inhabitants of Great Britain. This congressional correspondence reveals the fear of some Americans that a strong Roman Catholic neighbor to the north could endanger their own Protestant communities. Congress wrote:

> [T]he dominion of Canada is to be so extended, modelled, and governed, as that by being disunited from us, detached from our interests, by civil as well as religious prejudices, that by their numbers daily swelling with Catholic emigrants from Europe, and by their devotion to Administration, so friendly to their religion, they might become formidable to us, and on occasion, be fit instruments in the hands of power, to reduce the ancient free Protestant Colonies to the same state of slavery with themselves.
>
> This was evidently the object of the Act:—And in this view, being extremely dangerous to our liberty and quiet, we cannot forebear complaining of it, as hostile to British America. . . . Nor can we suppress our astonishment, that a

British Parliament should ever consent to establish in that country a religion that has deluged your island in blood, and dispersed impiety, bigotry, persecution, murder and rebellion through every part of the world.[37]

"The Continental Congress," Stokes concludes, "in dealing with Catholic Canada showed real tolerance, but in dealing with the Protestant mother country it did not hesitate to express its fears that too much consideration might be given to a Roman Catholic population!"[38]

Washington signed his name to both of these letters, but did not otherwise leave a record of his thoughts on the matter.[39] We thus cannot know whether his approval of the correspondence was driven by political or religious considerations. Nevertheless, Washington's actions toward Roman Catholics during the Revolution, discussed in the next chapter, suggest that tolerance of religious diversity may have influenced Washington's decisions. Or perhaps the episode merely prompted him to continue giving thought to the issue of religious freedom, much as his experiences with the Quakers had done.

The next year, Washington was elected to serve in the second Continental Congress. He would serve only part of this term before being elected commander-in-chief. Shortly before his departure, Congress decided to recommend a fast day to the colonies. The resolution spoke in terms of unified, public action, and it was adopted without recorded dissent. It is "at all times, our indispensible duty devoutly to acknowledge his superintending providence," the resolve began, "as well as to implore his merciful interposition for our deliverance."[40] The colonies should therefore "with united hearts and voices . . . offer up our joint supplications to the all-wise, omnipotent, and merciful Disposer of all events."[41]

It was hoped not only that "virtue and true religion may revive and flourish throughout our land," but also that "civil and religious priviledges may be secured" to all. [42]

Washington was appointed commander-in-chief of the army three days after the resolution was adopted. By the time the day of fasting came, he was near Boston, leading the army. Among the first of his general orders were those of July 16, 1775, ordering his army to observe the "Day of public Humiliation, Fasting and Prayer" that had been called by the Congress.[43] This would be the first in a long series of such orders requiring that his troops participate in public religious observances.

WASHINGTON'S EARLY YEARS IN VIRGINIA were developmental ones for him. First as a colonel in the Virginia Regiment, then as an elected official, he was presented with opportunities to ponder and develop a set of personal convictions regarding the appropriate relationship between church and state. His next public role as commander-in-chief of the Continental Army would present him with new opportunites to implement these principles, but with a new twist.

The army presented unique challenges for Washington. Although religious diversity was present in the Virginia Regiment, it would be even more pervasive in the army. Instead of leading men from one colony with one religious establishment, he would be leading men from thirteen colonies and various religious backgrounds. Washington would be given the opportunity to refine his developing views on church-state matters in new contexts.

THREE

Commander-in-Chief
of the Continental Army

1775–1783

> [T]he Brigadiers and Commandants of Brigades [are]
> desired to give notice in their orders and to afford every
> aid and assistance in their power for the promotion of
> that public Homage and adoration which are due to the
> supreme being, who has through his infinite goodness
> brought our public Calamities and dangers (in all humane
> probability) very near to a happy conclusion.
>
> *General Orders, February 15, 1783*[1]

THROUGHOUT THE AMERICAN REVOLUTION, General Washington expressed his conviction that Providence was protecting his Continental Army.[2] He reported time and again that divine intervention appeared to prevent the army from being demolished by British troops.[3] Fogs and heavy rains had arrived just when the American troops most needed protection.[4] At times, British soldiers received warnings of American movements but inexplicably failed to use the information.[5] Benedict Arnold's treachery was discovered before great harm was done.[6] On more than one occasion, Washington asked his troops to undertake tasks that would have been difficult, even for better-trained soldiers. Amazingly, the American soldiers succeeded in accomplishing many of these feats.[7]

Washington frequently remarked upon this divine care, both in his personal correspondence and in his official military orders.[8] Several years into hostilities, he remarked to a signatory of the Declaration of Independence, "The hand of Providence has been so conspicuous in all this, that he must be worse than an infidel that lacks faith, and more than wicked, that has not gratitude enough to acknowledge his obligations."[9] He similarly told Major General John Armstrong that "[t]he many remarkable interpositions of the divine governmt. in the hours of our deepest distress and darkness, have been too luminous to suffer me to doubt the happy issue of the present contest."[10] To Thomas Jefferson he noted, "[H]ad we not been held up by providence and a powerful Ally, we must have submitted before this to the Yoke of bondage."[11]

Washington's trust in Providence was in many ways a matter of personal belief, not public business.[12] But Washington's experiences during the French and Indian War had taught him to value the influence of official religion among his troops. Indeed, he probably felt more strongly about this issue during his command of the Continental Army than he did while with the Virginia Regiment. In sharp contrast to his time with the Regiment, he implemented his religion-friendly approach early in the Revolutionary War. Immediately upon assuming his command, he ordered his troops, "The General most earnestly requires, and expects, a due observance of those articles of war, established for the Government of the army, which forbid profane cursing, swearing & drunkeness; And in like manner requires & expects, of all Officers, and Soldiers, not engaged on actual duty, a punctual attendance on divine service, to implore the blessings of heaven upon the means used for our safety and defence."[13] Indeed, throughout the Revolution, Washington strove to include religion in the military's public life, particularly when he thought it would further the public good.

A MORAL AND VIRTUOUS ARMY

Washington often referred to God as the ultimate arbiter of the war. "Divine Providence," he told Governor Jonathan Trumbull, "wisely orders the Affairs of Men."[14] He later wrote to British Lieutenant General Thomas Gage: "May that God to whom you then appealed, judge between America & you!"[15] Washington repeatedly referred to the American effort as being "under God," "under the Smiles of Heaven," or "under Providence."[16]

Washington spoke to one of his chaplains, Reverend Israel Evans, of fostering dependence on God among the troops. "[I]t will ever be the first wish of my heart," General Washington wrote, "to aid your pious endeavours to inculcate a due sense of the dependance we ought to place in that allwise & powerful Being on whom alone our success depends."[17] Washington surely desired such dependence, at least in part, to foster the morality and virtue he considered necessary to military success.[18] He wrote in October 1778 that "by a want of Virtue we ruin and defeat ourselves."[19] Such depravity, he concluded, "is infinitely more to be dreaded than the whole force of G. Britain."[20] For this reason, senior officers should refuse to tolerate "Diabolical practices," such as plundering and rioting.[21] Officers were to punish those who engaged in gaming, licentiousness and drunkenness.[22] Likewise, swearing was to be discouraged.[23]

But virtue, morality, and reliance on God were not enough. Washington's soldiers also had a duty to use the skills that they had been given. Early in the war, Washington told the Pennsylvania Associators: "If we make Freedom our Choice we must obtain it by the Blessing of Heaven *on our united* & *vigorous Efforts*."[24] To Jonathan Trumbull, he declared: "To trust altogether in the justice of our Cause, *without our own utmost exertions* would be tempting Providence."[25] In a letter to Samuel Parsons he lamented: "The lanquor & Supineness that have taken place, but too generally, of late, are truly mortifying, and are difficult to be accounted for. All agree our claims are righteous and must be supported; Yet all, or at least, too great a part among us, withhold the means, *as if providence, who has already done much for us, would continue his gracious interposition* & *work Miracles for our deliverance without troubling ourselves about the matter*."[26] God is certain to help, Washington argued, but men also have a duty to put forth their best effort. To do otherwise would be to "presumptuously wait[ ] for Miracles to be wrought in our favour."[27]

Washington often spoke to his troops of the need for divine help, but exhortations for vigorous effort almost always followed. A typical expression of the general's views occurred on September 3, 1776, shortly after the Americans made a daring midnight escape from Brooklyn Heights. All soldiers, Washington stated, should be inspired "with Firmness and Resolution . . . Ever remembring that upon the blessing of Heaven, and the bravery of the men, our Country only can be saved."[28] Another success prompted a similar statement on October 5, 1777. Washington noted his pride in the "spirit and bravery" of the troops.[29] They should remember their success, Washington declared, and "assure themselves that on the next occasion, *by a proper exertion of the powers which God has given them*, and inspired by the cause of freedom in which they are engaged, they will be victorious."[30]

This theme continued in his writings, even as the war neared its end. In 1781, Washington told the president of the Continental Congress: "Blessed as we are with the Bounties of Providence, necessary for our support and Defence, the Fault must surely be our own (and great indeed will it be), if we do not, by a proper Use of them, attain the noble Prize for wch. we have so long been contending, the Establishment of Peace, Liberty and Independance."[31] In sum, as the general wrote to the Reverend Samuel Cooper, "[I]t is our Duty . . . to exert our utmost powers to bring to a happy Conclusion . . . a Contest in which we have so long been engaged, and in which we have so often, and conspicuously experienced, the Smiles of Heaven."[32] Not only soldiers, but also the states, should give the cause every last ounce of effort. In a circular letter, Washington argued that the "bountifull hand of Heaven is holding out to us a Plenty of every Article, and the only Cause of Want, must be placed to the Acco. of our Want of Exertion to collect them."[33]

Washington's writings during the Revolution are remarkable for the amount of time and attention that he devoted to issues of morality, virtue, and religion. Of these factors, critical to military victory, Washington observed, Providence had certainly done its part. "If we are not free & happy," the general observed, "it will be owing to a want of virtue, prudence & management among ourselves."[34]

CHAPLAINS AND RELIGIOUS SERVICES

Implementing his vision of a virtuous army required Washington to address the issues of military chaplains and religious services for his troops—issues that were familiar because of his experiences in the French and Indian War. In the earlier conflict, Washington's writings did not speak to these issues until about one year after he assumed command. His tenure as commander-in-chief of the Continental Army would be quite different.

The general joined the army, then stationed outside Boston, on July 2, 1775.[35] Two days later, he had already issued his first orders to the troops "requir[ing] & expect[ing], of all Officers, and Soldiers, not engaged on actual duty, a punctual attendance on divine service, to implore the blessings of heaven upon the means used for our safety and defence."[36] This command was merely the first in a long series of orders that would require the American troops to regularly observe divine services and to respect the chaplains who would lead them.

Some might argue that Washington was merely maintaining policies originally implemented by others. Washington's predecessor, Artemas Ward, had issued similar commands to the army.[37] Moreover, General Washington's July 1775 order was consistent with the articles of war recently enacted by the Continental Congress, which "earnestly recommended to all officers and soldiers, diligently to attend Divine Service."[38] Perhaps Washington's order was a reflection of others' views rather than his own. But there is no evidence that Washington had any qualms about implementing religion-friendly policies. Indeed, there is evidence suggesting he agreed with them.

First, Washington sat on the committee that drafted the articles of war, before he was appointed commander-in-chief. He probably made some contribution to the rules that were eventually drafted.[39] Second, Washington almost certainly did not see the final version of the articles of war before he issued his own orders on July 4. The president of the Continental Congress, John Hancock, forwarded Washington the articles within days of their approval, but Washington did not receive Hancock's letter until July 10, nearly one week after Washington's initial set of orders to the troops.[40] The sequence of events makes it probable that Washington issued the orders at least partly on his own initiative, or at least did not seek to drag his feet while he awaited formal notice of congressional action. Moreover, throughout the course of the war, Washington repeatedly addressed matters related to military chaplains and divine services in his orders and other writings. His sustained attention to this issue was clearly more than a token or perfunctory gesture, suggesting that he, too, considered such activities appropriate and worthwhile.

Paul Boller has argued that "Washington seems never during his life to have questioned the relevance of organized religion to social order and morality. . . . [H]e looked upon religion as indispensable to the morale, discipline, and good conduct of the men under his command."[41] The general's military orders of July 9, 1776, confirm this analysis. Washington stated:

> The Colonels or commanding officers of each regiment are directed to procure Chaplains . . . To see that all inferior officers and soldiers pay them a suitable respect and attend carefully upon religious exercises: The blessing and protection of Heaven are at all times necessary but especially so in times of public distress and danger—The General hopes and trusts, that every officer, and man, will endeavour so to live, and act, as becomes a Christian Soldier defending the dearest Rights and Liberties of his country.[42]

Washington noted the connection between army morality and organized religion on another occasion when an army colonel wrote Washington to ask "whether you thought proper for us to have [a chaplain]."[43] The general responded (somewhat drolly), "A Chaplain is part of the Establishment of a Corps of Cavalry, and I see no Objection to your having One, Unless you suppose yours will be too virtuous and Moral to require instruction."[44] A later set of military orders linked the need for chaplains, religious services, and morality among the troops, even more unmistakably: "As a mean to abolish [swearing], and every other species of immorality—Brigadiers are enjoined, to take effectual care, to have divine service duly performed in their respective brigades."[45]

Washington took the duties of his chaplains seriously. These duties included counseling those who had been sentenced to death by courts martial or visiting with the sick and wounded.[46] By agreement between the American and British armies, chaplains could not be made prisoners of war.[47] A chaplain, Washington wrote, should be "a Man of Character & good conversation" who will "influence the manners of the Corps both by precept & example."[48] Washington praised one chaplain as a man "whose exemplary Life and Conversation, must make him highly esteemd by every person"; his "usefulness in this Army is great—he is employed in the glorious work of attending to the Morals, of a brave people who are fighting for their Liberties."[49] One of the primary duties of chaplains in Washington's army was to conduct regular divine services, which each soldier, not on duty, would be expected to attend.[50] Indeed, even when the logistical difficulties of war hampered the regularity of divine service on occasion, Washington instructed the chaplains to consult with each other and find a solution so that services might be resumed.[51]

Washington's general orders of June 28, 1777, outlined his expectations that divine service would be diligently observed in the army:

> All Chaplains are to perform divine service to mor-
> row, and on every succeeding Sunday, with their respective
> brigades and regiments, where the situation will possibly
> admit of it: And the commanding officers of corps are to
> see that they attend; themselves, with officers of all ranks,
> setting the example. The Commander in Chief expects an
> exact compliance with this order, and that it be observed in
> future as an invariable rule of practice—*And every neglect
> will be considered not only a breach of orders, but a disregard to
> decency, virtue and religion.*"[52]

Washington's language was strong. First, he left no doubt that attendance at divine services was a requirement, not an option. Second, he specified "a disregard to . . . religion" as an offense beyond merely breaching orders.[53] A year later, he urged his soldiers in similarly strong language: "While we are zealously performing the duties of good Citizens and soldiers we certainly ought not to be inattentive to the higher duties of Religion—To the distinguished Character of Patriot, it should be our highest Glory to add the more distinguished Character of Christian."[54]

During the course of the war, Washington and Congress often corresponded about the appropriate level of funding for, and the appropriate number of, chaplains for the army. Washington's views developed during the course of the war, as he sought to balance fiscal concerns, the utility of religion for his army, and matters of religious freedom. He became a proponent of more (and well paid) chaplains, but ultimately he always deferred to Congress.

His perspective is interesting because he, more than anyone, knew the army was underfunded and that soldiers sometimes lacked clothing and food. Yet he did not veer from his position that funds for chaplains were an important item in the military budget.

On July 29, 1775, the Continental Congress passed its first act regarding chaplains. In the act, chaplains' salaries were set at twenty dollars per month.[55] Washington soon sought to improve this situation. He wrote the president of Congress on December 31, 1775, arguing that the level of pay for chaplains was "too Small to encourage men of Abilities."[56] He encouraged Congress to either increase their pay or to appoint chaplains to two regiments, thereby allowing each chaplain to earn more. "I need not point out the great utility of Gentlemen whose Lives & Conversation are unexceptionable, being employed for that Service, in this Army," Washington wrote.[57] Congress responded affirmatively, and on January 16, 1776, it provided for the appointment of one chaplain to every two regiments. Each chaplain had more responsibility, but his pay was also increased to $33^{1/3}$ per month.[58] Washington notified his troops of this new provision on February 7, 1776.[59]

The system worked for a time, as the troops were stationed close together early in the war. Following the siege of Boston, however, regiments were often separated. As a result, the chaplains sometimes faced logistical difficulties in ministering to soldiers who were stationed so far apart.[60] Washington again wrote Congress on June 28, 1776, requesting new regulations for the chaplains. Only one means seems apparent to "remedy the evil," Washington stated, "by affixing one [chaplain] to each Regiment with Salaries competent to their support. no shifting, no change from one Regiment to another can answer the purpose."[61] Yet as Washington so often did, he ultimately left the policy issue to Congress, noting that the "propriety of an alteration" was for legislators to determine.[62] At least for the moment, Congress complied with Washington's wishes, allowing chaplains to be assigned, one per regiment, without a reduction in pay.[63]

Close to one year later, fiscal concerns caused Congress to reverse course, increasing chaplains' pay slightly, but also decreasing the total number of chaplains.[64] Under this new plan, one chaplain would be assigned to each brigade, rather than each regiment. (A brigade was a much larger unit of the army, typically composed of a number of regiments.) Washington confirmed his intent to comply with the congressional resolution, but he expressed dissatisfaction with the change. He remarked, "[W]hen One [chaplain] was assigned, in the course of last year, to Two Regiments, the prevailing Opinion was, and that founded on a variety of reasons, that it would not do, and the old mode of appointment was introduced again."[65] In other words, Washington was telling Congress, the system was changed the first time because one chaplain for every two regiments was spreading them too thin. How can the chaplains be effective if they are spread even thinner than they were before?

Ten days later, Washington wrote another letter, expounding on his reasons for preferring one chaplain for each regiment. He noted logistical difficulties, but his primary concern was religious freedom. Washington's statement is worth reading in full:

> Among many other weighty objections to the measure, It has been suggested, that it has a tendency to introduce religious disputes into the Army, which above all things should be avoided, and in many instances would compell men to a mode of Worship, which they do not profess. The Old Establishment gives every Regiment an Opportunity of having a Chaplain of their own religious Sentiments—is founded on a plan of a more generous toleration—and the

choice of Chaplains to officiate, has been generally in the
Regiments. Supposing One Chaplain could do the duties
of a Brigade (Which supposition However is inadmissible,
when we view things in practice), that being composed of
Four or five—perhaps in some instances Six Regiments,
there might be so many different modes of Worship. I have
mentioned the Opinion of the Officers and these hints to
Congress upon this subject, from a principle of duty, and
because, I am well assured, it is most foreign to their wishes
or intention to excite by any act, the smallest uneasiness &
jealousy among the Troops.[66]

Professor Vincent Phillip Muñoz further explains Washington's
discontent with the new system, noting that the general "not only
wanted chaplains, but chaplains of every denomination so that
each soldier could attend his own religious services."[67] Appointing chaplains at the regiment level, rather than the brigade level,
facilitated his goal. Regiments were relatively small units of the
army. Obtaining consensus among the soldiers in one regiment
was (naturally) easier than attempting the same at the larger
brigade level. Thus, the old system increased the likelihood that
soldiers would agree on the denomination of their chaplain. The
new system, by contrast, introduced opportunities for disagreement and religious discord.[68]

Despite Washington's exhortations, Congress remained stead-
fast in its determination to assign chaplains at the brigade level,
rather than the regiment level, for the remainder of the war. Indeed, Congress maintained this stance even when the army faced
logistical difficulties in completing the change.[69]

Nevertheless, Washington continued to use chaplains, and
he continued to order his troops to attend divine service. He did
this despite the fact that some soldiers might not have access to

a chaplain of their preference. It seems that Washington thought the overall benefits of religion to the army outweighed marginal encroachments on the religious preferences of individuals. Yet Washington felt strongly enough about religious freedom that he mentioned the need for regimental chaplains, rather than brigade chaplains, again after the Revolution, in the context of recommendations for future American armies.[70]

One last observation should be made about Washington's attitude toward chaplains during the Revolution. His actions indicate that he viewed the function of chaplains and religious services to be both public and private. As discussed above, he often argued that virtue was a prerequisite to victory, and he relied upon chaplains and divine services as one means to inculcate this virtue. Therefore, his reliance on religious assistance would have a public, as well as a private, benefit for the army. Washington explicitly made this connection at least once when he stated that the military chaplains "may depend upon [my] utmost encouragement and support on all occasions" as they are "*publickly and privately* engaged in performing the sacred duties of their office."[71] In addition, his repeated efforts to obtain public funding for chaplains and his frequent orders on religious matters to the troops confirm that Washington saw legitimate public functions for chaplains and religious services. Their presence among the troops was not merely a matter of individual or personal concern.

THANKSGIVING AND PRAYER

During his command of the army, Washington occasionally issued orders requiring his troops to formally observe days of thanksgiving, prayer, or fasting. He issued the first of these orders just two weeks after assuming his command. This observance was to be one of "public Humiliation, Fasting and Prayer" that the troops may "with united Hearts & Voice, unfeignedly confess their Sins before God, and supplicate the all wise and merciful disposer of events, to avert the Desolation and Calamities of an unnatural war."[72] Washington issued the order to his troops, but the idea originated with Congress, which had recommended that such a day be observed.[73]

Such an order was not unusual during Washington's tenure as commander of the Continental Army. Most of these calls for special religious observances were initiated by Congress, which recommended both days of thanksgiving and days of fasting and prayer to the states at various times throughout the war.[74] On a few occasions, Washington chose to observe a prayer or thanksgiving day that had been called by a single state.[75] Yet Washington did more than simply observe those days that had been called by Congress or a state legislature: he instigated a handful of these observances on his own.[76] The fact that Washington added extra religious observances indicates that he supported efforts to publicly foster dependence on, and gratitude toward, God.

When Washington instructed his troops to observe religious days that had been recommended by a legislative entity, the terminology of his orders suggests that he took the duty very seriously. The troops were "strictly enjoined to pay all due reverance" and to observe the day "with the most unfeigned Devotion" or with an "unfeigned, and pious observance of their religious duties."[77] "[A]ll recreations and unnecessary labor" were "strictly forbid[den]."[78] Washington's orders generally made clear his desire that such days "be most religiously observed by the army."[79]

Those religious observances that were ordered by Washington, on his own initiative, were more likely to be thanksgiving celebrations than days of fasting and prayer. For instance, one success in 1777 prompted Washington to declare: "Let every face brighten, and every heart expand with grateful Joy and praise to the supreme disposer of all events, who has granted us this signal success—The Chaplains of the army are to prepare short discourses, suited to the joyful occasion."[80] When France agreed to fight beside America against Great Britain, Washington made a similar declaration: "It having pleased the Almighty ruler of the Universe propitiously to defend the Cause of the United American-States and finally by raising us up a powerful Friend among the Princes of the Earth to establish our liberty and Independence upon lasting foundations, it becomes us to set apart a day for gratefully acknowledging the divine Goodness & celebrating the important Event which we owe to his benign Interposition."[81]

Washington's thanksgiving observances sometimes included orders for celebratory military maneuvers as well. On one occasion, he ordered the firing of "*[t]hirteen* pieces of cannon . . . followed by a *feu-de-joy* with blank cartridges, or powder, by every brigade and corps of the army."[82] Another time, he ordered the firing of fifteen cannon, followed by several rounds of artillery fire.[83] Given the constant shortage of powder and other supplies, Washington's suggestion that any portion of it might be used for this purpose is interesting, indeed.

In addition to formally setting aside certain days for thanksgiving, Washington made less formal efforts to foster gratitude toward God among the troops. An early victory in the Revolution prompted Washington to declare: "The Commander in Chief is confident, the Army under his immediate direction, will shew their Gratitude to Providence, for thus favouring the Cause of Freedom and America; and by their thankfulness to God, their zeal and perseverance in this righteous Cause, continue to deserve his future blessings."[84] A few weeks later, he added his hope that "such frequent Favors from divine providence" would encourage vigorous efforts by the troops, "as it would now be the basest ingratitude to the Almighty, and to their Country, to shew any the least backwardness in the public cause."[85] In short, Washington noted, providential blessings "demand from us in a peculiar manner the warmest returns of Gratitude & Piety to the Supreme Author of all Good."[86]

If victories were cause for formal or informal expressions of gratitude to Providence, then setbacks or upcoming battles could be occasions for prayer and supplication, although Washington's encouragements toward prayer were typically more informal than his official thanksgiving days. For instance, as the Continental Army anticipated a British attack during the summer of 1776, General Washington declared: "[T]o be well prepared for an engagement is, under God, (whose divine Aid it behoves us to supplicate) more than one half the battle."[87] His words were similar to the exhortations that he made one year later, as he noted an outcome that was "not so favorable as could be wished," but nevertheless urged that "it becomes every officer and soldier humbly to supplicate" Providence, that they might be more successful in future.[88]

Washington did not designate official days for prayer or thanksgiving nearly so often as he encouraged his men toward religion in other ways; for instance, by regular attendance at divine service. Yet the fact that he *ever* issued such orders is telling. Washington's actions indicate that he found such official entreaties toward religion to be appropriate.

PUBLICLY FINANACED BIBLES

In 1777, the Continental Congress considered a request to finance an American edition of the Bible. A congressional committee determined that the costs of printing such an edition were too high. As an alternative, it proposed the importation of twenty thousand Bibles from "Holland, Scotland, or elsewhere."[89] Congress approved the project, but the planned importation was never completed. Several years later, a Philadelphia printer, Robert Aitken, offered to complete an American edition of the Bible and he asked for congressional support. In 1782, Congress endorsed Aitken's project, although it did not provide financing.[90]

In 1783, the Reverend John Rodgers wrote Washington with an idea: Congress should present each soldier with one of Aitken's Bibles. But by then the Revolution was drawing to a close and the troops were disbanding. "[I]t is now too late to make the Attempt," Washington observed, but "[i]t would have pleased me, if Congress should have made such an important present, to the brave fellows, who have done so much for the Security of their Country's Rights and Establishment."[91]

The episode, while brief, is significant. Washington's words indicate more than mere personal pleasure at the thought of his troops having access to Bibles. His letter takes an extra, critical step: Washington approved the concept of Bibles *distributed at public expense*. Although ultimately not tested in practice, Washington's position is not surprising. His statements are consistent with the support that he gave to chaplains and public religious observances throughout the war.

THE IMPORTANCE OF RELIGIOUS LIBERTY

The American Revolution was unique in many ways. At its heart, it was a civil war between Great Britain and her colonies in America. But there were other conflicts as well, many of which were internal. Regional and cultural differences sometimes led to a sense of unfamiliarity and distrust among the American troops. As commander-in-chief, Washington bore much responsibility for overcoming these conflicts and fostering unity among the soldiers, even as he recognized their differences.

Religious differences must have created special complications for General Washington. He relied upon religion to foster good morale and discipline among the troops, yet religion was simultaneously a tool that contained the potential to tear apart the army. One of Washington's great accomplishments as a military leader was finding a way to use religion for public purposes, even as he cultivated harmony and gained the respect and admiration of the religious minorities of his time.[92] He accomplished this difficult objective in two ways.

First, Washington's public expressions concerning religion were nearly always couched in terms that could be appreciated by individuals across a wide variety of religious denominations. He rarely referred to a Christian God, instead relying heavily upon such phrases as the "great Arbitor of the universe," the "Almighty ruler of the Universe," "that Being, in whose Hands are all human Events," and his favorite, "divine Providence."[93] Did Washington use such terms deliberately, in an effort to unify? Or was the result accidental, primarily a natural outgrowth of what some academics would call his "deist" attitude? Washington did not specifically address the matter in his writings; regardless, his nondenominational language seems to have contributed to his success in unifying people of varied religious beliefs.[94]

Second, Washington took action to protect specific religious minorities, at least to the degree that he could do so without compromising the public good. For instance, in September 1775, he appointed a Universalist, John Murray, as chaplain, and he immediately issued orders to the troops that Murray "is to be respected as such."[95] Washington took this action, despite apparent consternation among the non-Universalist chaplains.[96] Given his attitude regarding brigade versus regiment chaplains, Washington was presumably motivated by his desire to allow soldiers the chaplain of their choice whenever possible.

Washington exhibited a similar attitude, albeit in a different context, a month later. In October, Christopher French, a British prisoner of war, wrote Washington on behalf of several prisoners. "[W]e should esteem it as a particular favor," the captive wrote, "if you direct us to be remov'd to Middletown where there is [a Church of our Persuasion] and is but Fifteen Miles distant."[97] Washington responded favorably: "I have not the least Objection provided the Place is approved by Govr Trumbull."[98] Again, Washington acted on his instinct to allow anyone—even his enemy—the opportunity to worship freely, as long as no public harm resulted from the move.

These issues were minor and may have been relatively easy for Washington to solve. His greater religious challenges during the Revolution involved widespread harassment of Roman Catholics in the early part of the war and the Quakers' objections to fighting.

The best example of Washington's careful treatment of Catholics may be in his September 1775 letter and instructions to Colonel Benedict Arnold, whom General Washington dispatched on a mission to the predominantly Catholic Canada. As Arnold departed, Washington *twice* encouraged him to avoid showing disrespect for Catholicism in that country, first in a letter, then in an official set of instructions. In his letter, Washington urged Arnold to

avoid all Disrespect or Contempt of the Religion of the
Country and its Ceremonies—Prudence, Policy and a true
Christian Spirit will lead us to look with Compassion upon
their Errors without insulting them—While we are Contending for our own Liberty, we should be very cautious of
violating the Rights of Conscience in others; ever considering
that God alone is the Judge of the Hearts of Men and to
him only in this Case they are answerable.[99]

Washington's letter did not hide his disagreement with the
Catholic faith. Indeed, portions of his letter seem rather conde-
scending toward Catholics.[100] Nevertheless, Washington showed
concern that they be respected. The instructions accompanying
Washington's letter to Arnold were written in the same vein: "As
the Contempt of the Religion of a Country . . . has ever been
deeply resented—You are to be particularly careful to restrain
every Officer & Soldier from such Imprudence & Folly & to punish
every Instance of it."[101] Instead, Washington continued, "as far as
lays in your Power you are to protect & support the free Exercise
of the Religion of the Country & the undisturbed Enjoyment of
the Rights of Conscience in religious Matters with your utmost
Influence & Authority."[102]

Washington exhibited a similar attitude two months later
when he was faced with soldiers who wished to participate in anti-
Catholic demonstrations on Pope's Day.[103] His General Orders
of November 5, 1775, were harsh. "[The] Custom of burning the
Effigy of the pope," Washington declared, is "ridiculous and childish."[104] He expressed his "surprise that there should be Officers
and Soldiers, in this army so void of common sense, as not to see
the impropriety of such a step at this Juncture," particularly given
American efforts to obtain an alliance with Canadian Catho-

lics.[105] "[T]o be insulting their Religion," the general concluded, "is so monstrous, as not to be suffered, or excused."[106] According to Boller, Washington's attitude was one of the primary factors contributing to the permanent elimination of Pope's Day in the new country. If this anti-Catholic event was celebrated in America after 1775, there is no record of it.[107]

Washington's treatment of the Quakers during the Revolution was more inconsistent.[108] He was often kind to them and treated them well—despite their pacifist beliefs, which ran contrary to his military calling. For instance, early in the war, General Washington met with a group of Quakers who wanted to enter Boston (then held by the British) to help the poor and needy in the city.[109] With his assistance, the Quakers wrote a letter to British General Howe, and they were able to deliver assistance, as they desired.[110] Washington showed similar benevolence when several Quakers were arrested and exiled by Pennsylvania officials on suspicion of pro-British sympathies in 1777.[111] Although he lacked authority to free the Quakers, he was kind to the four exiles' wives who sought his assistance. He not only wrote the Pennsylvania governor on their behalf, but he also gave them a pass that would allow them to travel to Lancaster, Pennsylvania, to plead their case before state officials.[112]

Further, Washington exhibited his willingness to exempt those with religious objections from the draft, assuming they are "really conscientiously scrupulous."[113] For instance, in January 1777, he wrote that "it is absolutely Necessary, that Every person able to bear Arms (except such as are conscientiously scrupulous against it in every case) should give their personal service."[114] A few days later, he repeated that "every man who receives a protection from and is a subject of any State (not being conscientiously scrupulous against bearing arms) should stand ready to defend the same against every hostile invasion."[115] He thus seems to have assumed that Quakers would be exempted from any draft. Later that year, when a group of Virginia Quakers were drafted and marched to meet Washington's army, he immediately discharged them. Rather than keeping them with the army, as he had during the French and Indian War, he simply sent them home.[116]

On the other hand, Washington often mistrusted Quakers. In May 1777, he discussed the "evil intentions" of the "Quakers and disaffected" who are "doing all in their power to counteract your late Militia law."[117] Later, he denied the request of a group of Quakers to send food into British-occupied Philadelphia and would not so much as meet with the group.[118] At times, he ordered soldiers who were impressing supplies for the army to pay particular attention to the Quakers in the area.[119] These types of orders stand in sharp contrast to his defense, on at least one occasion, of a New York Quaker whose property had been wrongfully seized.[120]

Washington's distrustful attitude was again on display in March 1778, when he refused to let some Quakers enter Philadelphia to attend a meeting of the Society of Friends. He declared to Brigadier General John Lacey, "This is an intercourse that we should by all means endeavour to interrupt, as the plans setled at these meetings are of the pernicious tendency."[121] Lacey's response was harsh: "I have ordered [the troops], if they refuse to stop when hailed to fire upon them, and to leave their Corps laying in the Road."[122] Washington's letter to another brigadier general was similar to the instructions given Lacey: "I desire [the Quakers] may be stopped, and turned back and their Horses taken from them."[123] Washington's decision to disrupt attendance at the

Quakers' meeting, as Muñoz has noted, "clearly evinces his belief that religiously motivated actions could be prevented if they were antithetical to the interests of the nation."[124] In short, Muñoz notes, "Washington permitted or constrained Quaker religious exercises as the common good dictated."[125]

Why did Washington perceive the actions of some Quakers—but not others—as being against the public good? Boller has theorized that Washington's distrust was aimed primarily at the Pennsylvania Quakers, who were more uncompromising than their other Friends. They strictly adhered to the Quaker position that they should not only refuse to fight, but that they should also refuse to participate in the new government in any form or fashion, whether it was by paying taxes, holding office, or using its money.[126] "Like most patriots," Boller concludes, "[Washington] wrongly concluded from the intransigence of Pennsylvania Friends that the Quakers wanted the British to win the war and perhaps were even secretly aiding them. . . . His forbearance, under these circumstances, is surely impressive."[127] Impressive, indeed. But such an attitude was exactly what Washington expected from his officers and soldiers and, hence, himself.

Early in the war, General Washington encouraged his troops to remember that the "Honor and Success of the army, and the safety of our bleeding Country, depends upon harmony and good agreement with each other."[128] He concluded, "Let all distinctions of Nations, Countries, and Provinces, therefore be lost in the generous contest."[129] Washington's words were aimed at many differences, not merely religious differences. Yet his approach marked his view toward all matters of individual freedom, particularly when the nation had so much at stake.

THE END OF THE WAR

During the fall of 1781, American troops, with the help of their French allies, surrounded the troops led by British General Charles Cornwallis at Yorktown, Virginia. By the end of October, Cornwallis had surrendered.[130] This American victory marked the beginning of the end of the Revolution. As the prospect of American independence began to look more and more certain, Washington began wrapping up his affairs so he could return to Mount Vernon. This process included not only responding to congratulatory letters, but also writing farewells to an admiring army and a grateful citizenry.

Several congratulatory letters arrived even before the final peace treaty between the two nations was signed, and they continued to pour in as Washington prepared to submit his formal resignation to the Continental Congress.[131] Schools, churches, cities, and individuals were proud of their successful general, and many did not hesitate to say so. Washington worked diligently to respond to each of his well-wishers. This return correspondence often discussed the general's gratitude to Providence for the successful outcome of the war. His letter to the City of Albany, for instance, declared: "We may indeed ascribe these most happy and glorious Events to the Smiles of Providence, the Virtue of our Citizens, and the bravery of our Troops."[132] A missive to the the New Jersey legislature carried a similar theme. "[T]hat all-wise and most gracious Providence," Washington noted, "hath so conspicuously interposed in the direction of our public affairs and the establishment of our national Independence."[133] To Massachusetts legislators he declared: "I have ever turned my Eye, with a fixed Confidence on that superintendg. Providence which governs all Events: and the lively Gratitude I now feel, at the happy termination of our Contest, is beyond my Expression."[134] At times, Washington's letters turned to a hope that Providence would continue to care for the new nation. Notably, a letter to the Reformed Dutch Church at Albany concluded: "May the preservation of your civil *and religious* Liberties still be the care of an indulgent Providence; and may the rapid increase and universal extension of knowledge virtue and true Religion be the consequence of a speedy and honorable Peace."[135]

Many of these expressions of faith were somewhat personal, but Washington also occasionally referenced the need for public gratitude to God. He told the New York Reformed German Congregation, for example, that he was "[d]isposed, at every suitable opportunity to *acknowledge publicly* our infinite obligations to the Supreme Ruler of the Universe for rescuing our Country from the brink of destruction; I cannot fail at this time to ascribe all the honor of our late successes to the same glorious Being."[136] Indeed, he concluded, to the Learned Professions of Philadelphia, "[I]t is *our common duty* to pay the tribute of gratitude to the greatest and best of Beings."[137] Nor was Washington, in his more formal, public farewells, shy about mentioning the divine blessings that had been bestowed upon the new nation. "The singular interpositions of Providence in our feeble condition," Washington declared in his farewell orders, "were such, as could scarcely escape the attention of the most unobserving."[138] Indeed, the army's perseverance "through almost every possible suffering and discouragement for the space of eight long years, was little short of a standing miracle."[139]

Washington's most famous farewell letter was written as a circular to the states in June 1783. The letter repeatedly credits

Providence with the victory over Britain, an outcome described by Washington as the "glorious events which Heaven has been pleased to produce in our favor."[140] As a result of this victory, Washington noted in this circular, "[The Citizens of America] are, from this period, to be considered as the Actors on a most conspicuous Theatre, which seems to be peculiarly designated by Providence for the display of human greatness and felicity."[141] Americans are doubly blessed because "Heaven has crowned all its other blessings, by giving a fairer oppertunity for political happiness, than any other Nation has ever been favored with."[142] Characteristically, Washington noted the need for Americans to strive diligently on their own behalf. With all these providential blessings, Washington declared, if Americans "should not be completely free and happy, the fault will be intirely their own."[143]

As the letter concluded, Washington committed his fellow Americans to God's care. The paragraph has become popularly known as "Washington's Prayer":

> I now make it my earnest prayer, that God would have you, and the State over which you preside, in his holy protection, that he would incline the hearts of the Citizens to cultivate a spirit of subordination and obedience to Government, to entertain a brotherly affection and love for one another, for their fellow Citizens of the United States at large, and particularly for their brethren who have served in the Field, and finally, that he would most graciously be pleased to dispose us all, to do Justice, to love mercy, and to demean ourselves with that Charity, humility and pacific temper of mind, which were the Characteristicks of the Divine Author of our blessed Religion, and without an humble imitation of whose example in these things, we can never hope to be a happy Nation.[144]

Even as he "implore[d] the divine benediction upon [America]," Washington did not forget to mention the need for tolerance and understanding among the nation's diverse citizenry.[145] "[E]ssential to the [nation's] well being," Washington stated, is "that pacific and friendly Disposition, among the People of the United States, which will induce them to forget their local prejudices and policies, to make those mutual concessions which are requisite to the general prosperity, and in some instances, to sacrifice their individual advantages to the interest of the Community."[146]

Much of Washington's circular letter to the states is more specifically Christian than many of Washington's writings. The language has caused some academics to question whether Washington or a staff writer wrote the letter, particularly its closing prayer. If the latter, they question whether the Christian tone of the letter should be attributed to Washington.[147] But in this letter, as in his other writings, Washington bears ultimate responsibility for the ideas expressed in his name, especially given the constant care he took in setting what he knew would become precedents.

Washington's comfort with such religious expressions in official correspondence was confirmed again, several months later, in his resignation address to the Continental Congress, in which he stated: "I consider it an indispensable duty to close this last solemn act of my Official life, by commending the Interests of our dearest Country to the protection of Almighty God, and those who have the superintendence of them, to his holy keeping."[148]

CONTEMPORARY THINKING tends to view any official endorsement of religion, even if non-denominational, as an affront to religious liberty. George Washington did not share that view. To the contrary, while Washington clearly supported official endorsements of religion, he also considered religious liberty to be central to the very purpose of the American Revolution. "The establishment of Civil and Religious Liberty," he declared to the New York Reformed German Congregation in late 1783, "was the Motive which induced me to the Field; the object is attained, and it now remains to be my earnest wish and prayer, that the Citizens of the United States would make a wise and virtuous use of the blessings, placed before them."[149]

Certainly, issues such as economic and civil liberty prompted the Revolution as an initial matter, but Washington did not underestimate the value of the religious liberty that would result. He said as much to the Reformed Protestant Dutch Church in Kingston in November 1782. "Convinced that our Religious Liberties were as essential as our Civil," he told the church, "my endeavours have never been wanting to encourage and promote the one, while I have been contending for the other."[150] The "brave men" in the army should be proud of themselves, Washington continued in a set of April 1783 orders to the troops.[151] They have "assisted in protecting the rights of humane nature and establishing an Asylum for the poor and oppressed of all nations and religions."[152]

It was in service of that very goal that Washington developed and implemented his religion-friendly policies while commander-in-chief of the Continental Army.

༚

FOUR

Father of a
New Nation

1784–1789

Altho' no mans sentiments are more opposed to *any kind*
of restraint upon religious principles than mine are; yet I
must confess, that I am not amongst the number of those
who are so much alarmed at the thoughts of making people
pay towards the support of that which they profess, if of the
denominations of Christians; or declare themselves Jews,
Mahomitans or otherwise, & thereby obtain proper relief.

Letter to George Mason, October 3, 1785[1]

AFTER THE REVOLUTION, Washington retired to his beloved
Mount Vernon. He intended to resume life as a plantation owner, but the citizens of the new American nation
had other ideas. Throughout these early years of independence,
Americans continued to look to Washington as a role model and a
leader. They craved his attention, his company, and his advice, even
as Washington himself sought the peace and quiet of a planter's
life. The retired general was deluged with letters and guests.[2] These

visitors often stopped at Mount Vernon—uninvited—to eat at Washington's table or to spend the night. Indeed, Washington may not have dined alone with his wife, Martha, for more than a year and a half after he returned home from the war.[3]

Washington was not a public official for most of these years, but he nevertheless had opportunities to comment on church-state relations. When his home state of Virginia considered a statute that would impose religious assessments, he expressed his views on the matter in a letter. He also supported an effort to convert the Indians to Christianity, a project that was seen as part of an effort to civilize them and to curb violence on the frontier.

After only a few years at home, Washington was called upon to serve his country once more, this time as president of the Constitutional Convention. He did not speak often during the debates at the convention, but he was supportive of the proposed Constitution that emerged from the deliberations. This Constitution did not contain religious references, except to ensure that a religious test would never be required for any person to be elected to federal office. The First Amendment, specifically addressing issues of church and state, would not be added to the Constitution for several years.

By this time, Washington's attitude on church-state matters followed a fairly predictable pattern. To the degree that official uses of religion could be relied upon for the general good of the community, he was in favor of such measures. If such uses *harmed* the community, however, he was opposed. He continued to value freedom of religious conscience, and he sometimes supported accommodations for religious dissenters. The "public good" was the yardstick by which he measured the desirability of any legislative proposal concerning religion.

RELIGIOUS FREEDOM IN VIRGINIA

When Washington left for war in 1775, Virginians were subject to a state tax, the proceeds of which were used to support Anglican ministers. By the time Washington returned from war, the tax had been suspended; nevertheless, the subject was still the focus of much discussion.[4] In 1784, legislators proposed a modified tax, but this new assessment included a concession to non-Anglicans. Taxpayers would be allowed to designate which religious denomination was to receive their funds, although they could choose only among Christian denominations. Undesignated revenues would be given to "seminaries of learning."[5]

The bill was the subject of a long and intense debate. Proponents of the assessment argued that it would contribute to public virtue and morality in Virginia, while its opponents argued that any form of religious establishment was improper in a free society. Perhaps most notably, James Madison, who would later play a key role in promulgating the First Amendment, wrote a heated paper against the tax. His *Memorial and Remonstrance Against Religious Assessments* was widely circulated and helped turn public sentiment against it. As a result, the proposal died in the legislature in late 1785, and a Bill for Establishing Religious Freedom, long advocated by Thomas Jefferson, was enacted shortly thereafter. Jefferson's bill guaranteed that the citizens of Virginia would have the right to free exercise of religion. It also guaranteed that they would not be forced to support any religion with which they did not agree.

Washington was not actively involved in most of this decade-long battle because he was no longer a member of the Virginia House of Burgesses. Nevertheless, he expressed his view on the

1784 proposal on at least one occasion, when George Mason, an opponent of the tax, asked Washington to endorse Madison's memorial and remonstrance.[6] Washington refused to align himself, officially, with either side of the debate. But his response to Mason's request concisely explained the approach that he had developed for handling matters of church and state.

First, Washington was not opposed to compulsory, public support of religion. "Altho' no mans sentiments are more opposed to *any kind* of restraint upon religious principles than mine are," Washington told Mason, "yet I must confess, that I am not amongst the number of those who are so much alarmed at the thoughts of making people pay towards the support of that which they profess."[7] The idea of a religious assessment, in and of itself, did not alarm Washington. Perhaps he was remembering the ways in which official religion had supported order and discipline in his army during the Revolutionary War. Now, during the Virginia debates, he again expressed sympathy with the view that religion should be supported by government when it serves a public good.

Yet Washington's support of such assessments was not unconditional. In his letter to Mason, he immediately added a caveat. Compulsory support for particular denominations might be acceptable for those who profess such beliefs, but dissenters must not be forced to pay toward the support of others' religions. In this instance, if taxpayers do not profess the religion in question (Christianity), then they should "declare themselves Jews, Mahomitans or otherwise, & thereby obtain proper relief."[8]

Finally, Washington's response returned to a familiar objective: furthering the public good. He was not opposed to the idea of an assessment in principle, but he thought that, as a policy matter, this particular bill was a bad idea. Enactment, he noted, would "rankle, & perhaps convulse the State."⁹ Thus, any potential benefit from the religious activities themselves was undermined. Now, Washington wished the "Bill could die an easy death; because I think it will be productive of more quiet to the State, than by enacting it into a Law."¹⁰

In short, Washington's letter to Mason endorsed compulsory public support of religious groups to the degree that it could further the good of the community, provided that "proper relief" was given to dissenters.¹¹ To the degree that such actions undermined the public good, he was opposed to them. In the case of the proposed assessment, Washington's view was that the benefits simply did not outweigh the detriments. The proposed assessment was *permissible* in Washington's view (at least at the state level), but it was also *imprudent* because of the potential harm to the community.

CONVERSION OF THE INDIANS

In the early 1780s, Selena Hastings, the Countess of Huntingdon, formulated a plan whereby missionaries would be sent from Great Britain to settle on the American frontier. Their purpose would be to convert the Indians to Christianity, both through the example of their lives and by active evangelical efforts. The countess planned to finance the effort herself, but she also sought assistance from the states in the form of land grants.¹²

The countess first contacted Washington about this effort in 1783, while planning for the mission was still in its early stages. She informed Washington that he had been named "one of my Executors for establishing a foundation in America principally

intended as a college for a Mission to the Indian nations."[13] At
the time, Washington was still serving as commander-in-chief
of the Continental Army. He declined to serve as executor, but
stated that "so far as my general Superintendence, or incidental
Attention can contribute to the promotion of your Establishment,
you may command my Assistance."[14] His response was otherwise
favorable. "Your Ladyships benevolent Designs toward the Indian
Nations," he wrote, "claim my particular Attention, and to further
so laudable an Undertakg will afford me much pleasure, so far as
my Situation in Life, surrounded with many and arduous Cares
will admit."[15]

Lady Huntingdon's 1783 correspondence was general in nature,
and Washington did not receive details of the plan until January
1785.[16] When the specifics finally arrived on his desk, however,
Washington continued in his willingness to support this private-
public venture, declaring to Lady Huntingdon: "With respect to
your humane & benevolent intentions to-wards the Indians; & the
plan which your Ladyship has adopted to carry them into effect,
they meet my highest approbation; & I should be very happy to
find every possible encouragement given to them."[17] The primary
benefit of the plan, Washington told Sir James Jay (who was as-
sisting the countess), was that it combined the effort to convert
the Indians with efforts to civilize them:

> I am clearly in sentiment with her Ladyship, that chris-
> tianity will never make any progress among the Indians, or
> work any considerable reformation in their principles, until
> they are brought to a state of greater civilization; & the mode
> by which she means to attempt this, as far as I have been able
> to give it consideration, is as likely to succeed as any other
> that could have been devised, & may in time effect the great
> & benevolent object of her Ladyships wishes.[18]

Washington's letter to Jay continued at length, addressing the pros and cons of the measure from a policy perspective.[19] For instance, were the state legislatures or the Continental Congress in a better position to offer assistance? What financial considerations might be considered by the various legislative bodies? Implicit in Washington's extended discussion is an interesting assumption. He treated the proposal as a political matter, a policy decision to be made by a legislative body. Nowhere in his letter did he question the appropriateness of a private-public partnership for the purpose of converting the Indians to Christianity. To the contrary, he concluded his letter to Jay by offering to contact the president of the Congress, Richard Henry Lee, on behalf of Lady Huntingdon.[20] And he did just that several days later.

Washington's correspondence with Lee continued where the letter to Jay had left off. Washington did not allude to any potential impropriety in giving public assistance to a project with a religious purpose. Instead, the letter discussed the pros and cons of various legislative routes, as a matter of public policy. The decision, in Washington's view, was properly the province of Congress. He told Lee: "As the Plan contemplated by Lady Huntingdon . . . is not only unexceptionable in its design and tendency, but has humanity & charity for its object—and may, as I conceive, be made subservient to valuable political purposes, I take the liberty of laying the matter before you."[21]

Ultimately, neither Congress nor the states decided to grant land for Lady Huntingdon's project, but the episode is interesting for what it reveals about Washington's approach to church-state relations.[22] Washington again weighed the costs and benefits: if public support of religion brings about a public good, then such actions are worthwhile. In this instance, missionary efforts were combined with an effort to civilize the Indians, potentially lowering the threat of violence on the frontier. Moreover, locating British missionaries on the American frontier would serve as a buffer between ravaging Indian parties and American settlements.[23] All these benefits could accrue, as Washington told Lee, "without any expence to the Union."[24] The decision to be made was properly left to the discretion of legislators, and Washington was happy to leave the balancing of practical versus charitable priorities to them.

THE CONSTITUTIONAL CONVENTION

In the years immediately following the Revolution, before the Constitution was proposed, the states operated under a compact called the Articles of Confederation. These Articles gave the Continental Congress responsibility for certain matters requiring cooperation among the states. This Congress, however, was remarkably weak: its powers to tax, to pay for the common defense, and to regulate interstate commerce were very limited.[25] The fiscal and practical problems caused by this decentralized form of government eventually prompted a push for reform, and a convention to *"revis[e] the articles of Confederation"* was called.[26] Of course, this convention would ultimately do far more than merely revise the existing Articles. At the urging of men such as Alexander Hamilton and James Madison, it would draft and propose an entirely new constitution for ratification by the states.

Washington was asked to attend the Convention as a delegate for the State of Virginia, but he was reluctant to participate. He had already declined to attend a meeting of the Society of the Cincinnati, which was meeting in Philadelphia at about the same time as the Convention. He worried that the Society would take offense if he made the trip for another group.[27] Moreover, Washington may have been privately concerned that an unsuccessful convention might cause his reputation to suffer.[28] Eventually, however, patriotism and the urgent need for action caused Washington to put his concerns aside and attend the Convention.[29]

The Convention, which had been scheduled to convene in Philadelphia on May 14, 1787, was unable to begin work until May 25, when a quorum of seven states was finally obtained.[30] As it settled down to business in the State House, the first act of the Convention was to elect the former commander-in-chief as its presiding officer. Washington's election was unanimous.[31] Upon being elected, Madison reports, Washington "thanked the Convention for the honor they had conferred on him, reminded them of the novelty of the scene of business in which he was to act, lamented his want of better qualifications, and claimed the indulgence of the House towards the involuntary errors which his inexperience might occasion."[32]

The Convention met from May to September, hammering out the details of the Constitution it would eventually propose to the states. Washington deemed it inappropriate to express himself on pending matters because he was the Convention's president, and he remained silent during the Convention debates.[33] His interest in the proceedings, however, was "consuming," as described by his biographer, Douglas Southall Freeman, and he was an influential figure among the delegates.[34] "Washington showed himself firm, courteous, inflexible," historian Catherine Drinker Bowen writes, "When he approved a measure, delegates reported that his face showed it. Yet it was hard to tell what the General was thinking and impossible to inquire. In his silence lay his strength. His presence kept the Federal Convention together, kept it going."[35]

Washington did eventually speak, but not until the last day of the Convention. His plea then was on behalf of a last-minute amendment suggested by Nathaniel Gorham of Massachusetts. The proposed change would increase the number of representatives in Congress. Rather than one representative for every forty thousand inhabitants, Gorham proposed that there be one for every thirty thousand.[36] The question had previously provoked disagreement because it affected the strength of large versus small states in Congress. Yet once the general expressed his support for the change, the delegates quickly lined up behind him, unanimously approving it. Freeman explains that the vote was unanimous "not because all members agreed but because all of them wished to do what Washington desired."[37] This brief incident suggests that if Washington had expressed serious disagreement with any other aspect of the Constitution, including its approach toward religion, the delegates would have given his words great weight.

The Constitution that emerged from these debates did not explicitly mention God. "One of the most striking features of the United States Constitution of 1787," Professor Daniel L. Dreisbach has noted, "is the absence of an explicit acknowledgment of the Deity or the Christian religion."[38] Indeed, the Constitution's only explicit reference to religion, prior to passage of the First Amendment several years later, was the clause prohibiting a religious test for elected federal officials.[39] This "no religious test" clause was adopted in the Convention with limited debate, despite the fact that it departed from the then-common state practice of allowing such tests.[40]

Madison's records of the Convention show that Washington supported the prohibition on religious tests. He voted in favor of it, as did the entire Virginia delegation.[41] But conclusions regarding Washington's views on the lack of other religious references in the Constitution are necessarily limited by the fact that Washington was not heavily involved in the Convention debates. It is clear, however, that Washington's comfort with the proposed Constitution did not stem from a sudden opposition to any and all official support of religion. Indeed, his post-Convention statements offer two reasons to believe that his perspective on church-state relations had not changed significantly, if at all, in the years since he resigned as commander-in-chief.

First, the tenor of Washington's writings following the Constitutional Convention mirrors that of his letters prior to the Convention. The consistency of his language across these two periods of time suggests that Washington did not believe that any provision of the new Constitution contradicted his previous views on church-state relations. Of course, Washington was a private figure in the months immediately following the Convention, so to some degree his letters cannot be taken as a definitive statement regarding public matters. On the other hand, it is notable that the themes of Washington's letters in 1787-89 do not vary from the themes of his 1775-83 war writings. His letters continued to credit Providence for the successes of the new nation.[42] It is "little short of a miracle," he told Lafayette, "that the Delegates from so many different States . . . should unite in forming a system of national Government, so little liable to well founded objections."[43] As of old, he continued to express hope that the people of America would rely upon Providence in their endeavors to found a new nation, even including his old theme that "Nothing, however, on our part ought to be left undone."[44] He continued, on occasion, to speak of the need for virtue in the new nation.[45]

Second, Washington explicitly addressed the lack of religious references in the Constitution in at least two letters after it was ratified. These letters echo Washington's pre-Convention attitude toward matters of church and state. Two religious groups submitted addresses to Washington, having drawn opposite conclusions from the lack of religious terminology in the Constitution. The first address came from some Presbyterian ministers in Massachusetts and New Hampshire, who feared that the new government would not adequately support religion. The second address came from the United Baptist Churches of Virginia. The Baptists feared, to the contrary, that the Constitution was insufficient to protect their religious freedom.

The Presbyterians lamented the lack of "some Explicit acknowledgement of the *only true God and Jesus Christ, whom he hath sent* inserted some where in the *Magna Charta* of our country."[46] Washington's response to this concern first reflected his view that individual responsibility for matters of conscience was important in the new government. "[T]he path of true piety is so plain," Washington wrote, "as to require but little political direction. To this consideration we ought to ascribe the absence of any regulation, respecting religion, from the Magna-Charta of our country."[47] On the other hand, Washington affirmed that active governmental support of religion would still be permissible under the new Constitution. "[T]he ministers of the gospel," he wrote, "[are] to instruct the ignorant, and to reclaim the devious—and, in the progress of morality and science, *to which our government will give every furtherance*, we may confidently expect the advancement of true religion, and the completion of our happiness."[48] Interestingly, Washington omitted the specifically Christian terminology that had pervaded the Presbyterians' letter, even as he affirmed the prospect of government support for the "advancement of true religion."[49]

The Baptists interpreted the Constitution's lack of religious references in an entirely different manner from the Presbyterians. They feared that the lack of specific protections would undermine their liberty of conscience. "When the constitution first made its appearance in Virginia," these churches wrote Washington, "we, as a Society, had unusual strugglings of mind; fearing that *the liberty of conscience*, dearer to us than property or life, was not sufficiently secured."[50] But Washington had no such qualms, and he reassured them: "If I could have entertained the slightest apprehension that the Constitution framed in the Convention, where I had the honor to preside, might possibly endanger the religious rights of any ecclesiastical Society, certainly I would never have placed my signature to it."[51] Indeed, he continued, "if I could now conceive that the general Government might ever be so administered as to render the liberty of conscience insecure, I beg you will be persuaded that no one would be more zealous than myself to establish effectual barriers against the horrors of spiritual tyranny, and every species of religious persecution."[52]

Washington's correspondence with the Presbyterians and Baptists, taken together, reflects his long-standing view that religion should be supported by the government to the degree that it yields a public benefit. Nevertheless, he simultaneously respected the need for freedom of religious conscience in the new nation. The proposed Constitution, at least in Washington's view, did a good job of blending these two important principles.

❧

WASHINGTON WAS A STAUNCH SUPPORTER of the Constitution that emerged from the Convention in Philadelphia.[53] Knowledge of Washington's endorsement comforted many early Americans, including those who were worried about the Constitution's lack of explicit religious provisions. Indeed, Anson Phelps Stokes notes that many Americans were so interested in Washington's views that his 1789 letter to the Presbyterians was reprinted, in its entirety, by the *Massachusetts Centinel* on December 5, 1789.[54] This letter reveals that the lack of religious references in the Constitution neither bothered Washington nor caused him to believe that the new government would refrain from supporting religion. On the other hand, he continued to reassure minority religious groups that their religious freedom would be secure under the new government, as he did in his letter to the Baptists.

Washington's statements about the proposed Constitution, although few and brief, indicate that the proceedings at the Constitutional Convention had not altered his perspective on church-state relations. His views regarding permissible government action under the new Constitution appear to be the same as those that he developed and solidified during his years as commander-in-chief. As president, he would take many actions further confirming this interpretation of his views.

_ფ_

President of the United States
Before the First Amendment

_1789–1791_

[I]t would be peculiarly improper to omit in this first official
Act, my fervent supplications to that Almighty Being who
rules over the Universe, who presides in the Councils of
Nations, and whose providential aids can supply every human
defect, that his benediction may consecrate to the liberties
and happiness of the People of the United States.

First Inaugural Address, April 30, 1789[1]

THE CONSTITUTIONAL CONVENTION had been pervaded by an
unspoken assumption: Washington would be the nation's
first chief executive. Indeed, Madison told Jefferson, certain convention debates regarding the scope of executive power
were "peculiarly embarrassing" because Washington was in the
room.[2] Within days of seeing the draft Constitution, newspaper
reports began to speculate about the possibility of a Washington
presidency.[3] As the state ratification debates began, the reassur-
ing prospect of Washington's election pervaded the deliberations.

Who else could lead the nation in this new era? General Washington was the obvious choice.[4]

As the states began to ratify the Constitution, one by one, Washington could no longer ignore the probability that he would be asked to serve his country—again. He worried that accepting the presidency would undermine the gesture he made by retiring at the end of the Revolution. He had deliberately resigned his military commission and returned home, declining to take power as a conquering king would have done. If he emerged from retirement now, Washington told Hamilton, "the world and Posterity might probably *accuse* me of *inconsistency* and *ambition*."[5] Moreover, Washington was enjoying retirement, and he wanted to remain at his beloved Mount Vernon. But the appeals for a Washington presidency intensified.[6] As his election seemed more and more certain, Washington remained troubled. "May Heaven assist me in forming a judgment," he told Jonathan Trumbull, Jr., "for at present, I see nothing but clouds and darkness before me."[7] Ultimately, of course, Washington could not refuse the call to public service, and he was unanimously elected the first president of the United States by the presidential electors.[8]

Among the most notable aspects of Washington's administration was its concern for precedent. The new president was very mindful that future generations would look to his actions as a guide for their own. "As the first of everything, in *our situation* will serve to establish a Precedent," Washington wrote Madison, "it is devoutly wished on my part, that these precedents may be fixed on true principles."[9] When decisions came before him, he routinely solicited and considered advice from his cabinet members. He was particularly concerned about the constitutionality of his actions and often asked his advisors to elaborate on the arguments for and against the permissibility of the various options he was considering.[10]

Church-state matters were just one of many areas in which Washington was asked to make precedent-setting decisions.[11] The president knew that disputes among various religious sects were already brewing,[12] yet he still acted in a way that showed a marked desire to honor and to accommodate religion in the public realm. His statements reveal that he had no interest in being religiously provocative; his actions reflect his view that religion is vital for the moral health of the country. Importantly, Washington's public statements clearly showed the extent to which he believed it appropriate, even expected, for the president to invoke God and prayer in official ceremonies and correspondence.

THE FIRST INAUGURATION

April 30, 1789, was the congressionally appointed day for Washington's inauguration. On that morning, the citizens of New York awoke to a salute of thirteen guns and the peal of church bells. As New Yorkers hurried off to prayer services conducted by clergymen of various denominations, Washington finished his last-minute preparations for the day ahead.[13]

An inaugural procession to Federal Hall began at half past noon. Washington left the presidential residence in a coach drawn by four horses. Members of Congress, department heads, and military figures accompanied him, either in their own carriages or on foot. Once at Federal Hall, Washington followed the vice president, John Adams, to a balcony overlooking Wall and Broad Streets. Throngs of people looked up from the street below, and Washington could see a Bible awaiting him on a nearby table.

As he stepped forward, the secretary of the Senate picked up the Bible and presented it for the ceremony. Washington placed his right hand on the Bible and took the oath of office, as provided in the Constitution: "I do solemnly swear that I will faithfully execute the Office of President of the United States, and will to the best of my Ability, preserve, protect and defend the Constitution of the United States."[14] After Washington repeated the oath, he bent forward and kissed the Bible.[15] The newly inaugurated president then returned to the Senate chamber and delivered his inaugural address. Washington's delivery was imperfect, and at times his voice trembled. But the imperfections caused many in the audience to perceive sincerity in their war hero, and they loved him all the more. One great orator, Fisher Ames, later reported that he "sat entranced" during the address.[16] When the speech concluded, Washington and the members of Congress left Federal Hall and walked to a chapel nearby. Once there, divine service was performed by the chaplain of Congress.[17]

Religion was thus very much an official aspect of this first inauguration. Indeed, more than a dozen clergymen of varying denominations participated in various aspects of the day.[18] Of course, it is worth noting that Congress, not Washington, made most of the arrangements for the inaugural ceremony, but there is no evidence that Washington objected to the numerous religious references in this important public ceremony, of which he was the central participant.[19] To the contrary, he introduced religion into the day in his own way. Not only did he spontaneously kiss the Bible following his oath, but he also relied heavily upon religious references in the one aspect of the day that was indisputably and fully his own responsibility: his inaugural address.

The new president's inaugural address began in typical Washingtonian fashion: he lamented his want of abilities and expressed his hope that he would not fail in the important task that had been entrusted to him.[20] Given the great challenges of his new role, he continued, "*it would be peculiarly improper to omit in this first official Act,* my fervent supplications to that Almighty Being who rules over the Universe, who presides in the Councils of Nations, and whose providential aids can supply every human defect, that his benediction may consecrate to the liberties and happiness of the People of the United States, a Government instituted by themselves for these essential purposes."[21]

These sentiments, Washington thought, should be shared by all Americans. "No People," the president declared, "can be bound to acknowledge and adore the invisible hand, which conducts the Affairs of men more than the People of the United States. Every step, by which they have advanced to the character of an independent nation, seems to have been distinguished by some token of providential agency."[22] Because the founding of the United States was unique, Washington continued, it requires "some return of pious gratitude along with an humble anticipation of the future blessings which the past seem to presage."[23] Significantly, Washington took this, his first opportunity as leader of the new nation, to remind Americans that their freedoms came about only with the existence of divine assistance, and he led the way in publicly expressing gratitude for the blessings that Americans had so far received and would, he hoped, continue to receive.

Washington also expressed his expectation that future congressional action would lay the "foundations of our national policy" in the "pure and immutable principles of private morality."[24] Such a foundation is important, Washington stressed, because "there is no truth more thoroughly established, than that there exists in the œconomy and course of nature, an indissoluble union between virtue and happiness."[25] Indeed, he concluded, "the propitious smiles of Heaven, can never be expected on a nation that disregards the eternal rules of order and right, which Heaven itself has ordained."[26] Washington's conclusion is important. During his first moments in office, he emphasized the need to publicly observe and respect Heaven's "eternal rules."[27] In Washington's view, the new nation could not hope to prosper unless these eternal principles of "order and right" were respected.[28]

Washington then turned to other matters, but before closing, the president returned to the subject of divine Providence:

> I shall take my present leave; but not without resorting once more to the benign Parent of the human race, in humble supplication that since he has been pleased to favour the American people, with opportunities for deliberating in perfect tranquility, and dispositions for deciding with unparel-lelled unanimity on a form of Government, for the security of their Union, and the advancement of their happiness; so this divine blessing may be equally *conspicuous* in the enlarged views—the temperate consultations, and the wise measures on which the success of this Government must depend.[29]

With these words, Washington completed his first official act as president. Thus, his first public statement as the chief enforcer of the law under the Constitution clearly showed that he believed that it was appropriate for public officials to acknowledge and to praise God in official ceremonies—at least at this stage in the nation's pre-First Amendment history.

PUBLIC THANKSGIVING AND PRAYER

On Friday, September 25, 1789, Congressman Elias Boudinot of New Jersey introduced a resolution in the House of Representatives. A congressional committee, he suggested, should "be directed to wait upon the President of the United States, to request that he would recommend to the people of the United States a day of public thanksgiving and prayer."[30] The nation, Boudinot declared, should have the opportunity of "joining, with one voice" in "acknowledging, with grateful hearts, the many signal favors of Almighty God."[31] The resolution was adopted after a brief debate in which one congressman expressed concern about "this mimicking of European customs, where they made a mere mockery of thanksgivings," and another objected that it was not Congress' place to tell people to be thankful.[32] The Senate concurred in the House resolution one day later.[33]

Interestingly, Congress endorsed this resolution shortly after it approved a constitutional amendment prohibiting itself from making any law "respecting an establishment of religion" in the new nation.[34] The states would eventually ratify this amendment as the First Amendment to the Constitution.[35] Because the state ratification process was still incomplete in September 1789, Congress was of course not bound by the language of the First Amendment when the day of thanksgiving was proposed and approved. On the other hand, the congressmen at least knew what they thought the law in regards to church-state relations should be, and there is no reason to believe they acted to the contrary as they awaited ratification of the First Amendment.[36] Washington was in a similar position, as he received word of both congressional actions at about the same time. He was not required to take action on the proposed amendment, but he would have known of it when he evaluated the appropriate presidential response to the request for a day of public prayer and thanksgiving.[37]

If Washington thought that the congressional resolution presented him with a difficult decision regarding the appropriate boundaries between church and state, then there is no evidence of it. He complied with the congressional request in relatively short order. Congress submitted its request to the executive by September 28.[38] Washington issued his thanksgiving proclamation five days later, on October 3.[39]

As an official expression of religious faith, Washington's proclamation was not timid, despite the pending proposal of the First Amendment. To the contrary, Washington stressed the need for public, collective action:

> *Whereas it is the duty of all Nations* to acknowledge the providence of Almighty God, to obey his will, to be grateful for his benefits, and humbly to implore his protection and favor . . . .
>
> Now therefore I do recommend and assign Thursday the 26th day of November next *to be devoted by the People of these States* to the service of that great and glorious Being, who is the beneficent Author of all the good that was, that is, or that will be.[40]

In Washington's words, the gratitude due to God is more than a matter of individual duty or preference. The nation, as a whole, must act. Americans should "unite" in offering gratitude and prayers to God, the president twice declared.[41] Moreover, he encouraged the country to seek "pardon [for] our *national* and other transgressions—to enable us all, whether in public or private stations, to perform our several and relative duties properly and punctually."[42] Such joint action by the people, Washington concluded, will lead to public benefits. With God's help, Americans might "render our national government a blessing to all the people, by constantly being a Government of wise, just, and constitutional laws, discreetly and faithfully executed and obeyed."[43]

Notably, Washington did not find it contradictory to combine these official expressions of religious duty with references to the religious freedom newly enjoyed by all Americans. Indeed, his proclamation urged Americans to unite in thanking God, collectively, for the "civil and religious liberty with which we are blessed."[44] This fusion of concepts in Washington's proclamation—officially thanking God for religious liberty—echoed his other public correspondence from this era.

In the months following his inauguration, Washington's public letters often reminded the citizens of the new nation that their freedom and blessings were attributable to the "gracious interposition of Heaven" in human events.[45] "I trace, with infinite gratitude," he wrote the legislature of Maryland, "the agency of a Providence, which induced the People of America to substitute in the place of an inadequate confederacy, a general Government, eminently calculated to secure the safety and welfare of their Country."[46] When citizens gave their commander-in-chief credit for the nation's early successes, he reminded them that, instead, the "glory of the event, should be given to the great Disposer of events."[47]

The president's correspondence was apt to allude to the fact that a nation founded with divine assistance could continue forward only with continuing providential help.[48] For instance, he wrote to the citizens of Alexandria of the need to "commit myself and you to the protection of that beneficent Being."[49] To the citizens of Baltimore, he noted the extent to which he felt inadequate to complete the task before him "without the singular assistance of Providence."[50] When Rhode Island ratified the Constitution and joined the Union in 1790, he continued on this theme. He concluded to the governor of Rhode Island that "we have a right to expect, *with the blessing of a divine providence*, that our Country will afford us all those domestic enjoyments of which a free people only can boast."[51]

These official statements regarding the need for divine assistance were made even as Washington praised and espoused the importance of religious liberty in the new nation. In the president's writings, these two objectives are not at odds with each other. They are instead complementary.

A "GRAND" NATIONAL CHURCH

An early decision facing the First Congress was the necessity of establishing a "Seat of the Government of the United States."[52] The topic was the subject of intense debate, as many congressmen sought to obtain the new capital for their own parts of the country. Finally, a compromise was struck, and Congress approved an act that established Philadelphia as a temporary capital and gave the president responsibility for selecting a permanent site on the Potomac.[53] This Washington did, selecting a site near Georgetown. Today, this city is known as Washington, D.C.

The "Act for establishing the temporary and permanent seat of the Government of the United States" required the president to appoint commissioners and to oversee plans for the city.[54] Washington appointed Major Pierre Charles L'Enfant, his old comrade in arms, to design the new capital. Washington's confidence in L'Enfant stemmed not only from the latter's army service, but also from his work in converting New York's old City Hall into Federal Hall—the building in which Washington was inaugurated.[55]

L'Enfant's original plan for the "national city," as presented to the president, included provision for a "grand church."[56] This church, L'Enfant wrote, "is intended for national purposes, such as public prayer, thanksgiving, funeral orations etc. and assigned to the special use of no particular Sect or denomination, but equally open to all. It will be likewise a proper shelter for such monuments as were voted by the last Continental Congress for those heroes who fell in the cause of liberty, and for such others as may hereafter be decreed by the voice of a grateful Nation."[57]

In a letter accompanying the plan, L'Enfant further suggested that land be allotted to "each of the Individual states as also the making of a free donation to Every particular religious society of a ground for House of worship a mode from which Infinit advantages most result."[58] Washington gave initial approval to L'Enfant's plan, including its national church, a fact that Anson Phelps Stokes finds noteworthy. "It is not to be assumed that the president gave special attention to this particular proposal for a church," Stokes concludes, "but it is probable that if he had thought it inappropriate he would have asked for its elimination."[59] Ultimately, L'Enfant's original plan, including its provision for a "grand church," was not implemented in its entirety. Instead, the designer became embroiled in a series of disputes with the city's commissioners, and Washington eventually determined that L'Enfant must be fired.[60] At least one scholar has theorized that construction of a national church may have been further hindered by lack of funding.[61]

The currently existing National Cathedral is not the church of L'Enfant's original design. Construction on that cathedral did not begin until September 29, 1907, and it is not located in the central location originally envisioned by L'Enfant.[62] Nevertheless, the series of events by which a national church was first conceived is remarkable for one reason: when presented with the idea of an official, albeit non-denominational, national church sanctioned by the federal government, the nation's first president approved the concept. Washington found such a plan to be permissible.

CORRESPONDENCE WITH CHURCHES

Washington decided to tour as much of the country as possible during his presidency. He wanted to see those portions of the country that he had not yet visited, and he wanted to determine the "temper and disposition of the inhabitants towards the new government."[63] As Washington traveled, many civic entities, including religious congregations, wrote or otherwise formally welcomed the president to their cities. Other religious groups wrote Washington even without a presidential visit, simply to congratulate him on his election and, sometimes, to clarify their status in the newly formed nation. Washington was diligent in responding to these letters, and he made a priority of visiting with a variety of religious groups as he traveled around the nation. The new president was conscientious about visiting with religious groups, Michael Novak and Jana Novak argue, because he "was determined to bind religious people to the republic, and to give his support to religion, as the surest protector of the moral health of the republic."[64]

The Quakers, who had refused to fight in the Revolution, were among the first to address Washington. "[B]ut as we are a People whose Principles and Conduct have been misrepresented and traduced," they stated, "we take the Liberty to assure thee, that we feel our Hearts affectionately drawn towards thee."[65] They echoed Washington's own thanks to God for religious liberty: "The free Toleration which the Citizens of these States enjoy in the publick Worship of the Almighty, agreable to the Dictates of their Consciences, we esteem among the holiest of Blessings."[66]

Washington responded graciously. He agreed with the Quakers' statement that religious liberty was a blessing, but he went a step further, reminding them that it was also a right: "The liberty enjoyed by the People of these States, of worshipping Almighty God agreable to their Consciences," he wrote, "is not only among the choicest of their *Blessings*, but also of their *Rights*."[67] All that government can "with propriety demand or expect," Washington continued, is for its citizens to "perform their social Duties faithfully."[68] By and large, Washington described the Quakers as satisfying these duties of citizenship. Perhaps not surprisingly, though, the commander-in-chief added one caveat. "[E]xcept their declining to share with others the burthen of the common defence," Washington wrote, "there is no Denomination among us who are more exemplary and useful Citizens."[69]

Washington's letter to the Quakers was among the strongest expressions for religious liberty that he had written, to that point. The principle he articulated, however, would pervade many of his letters to religious groups during his presidency, particularly those written to minority religious groups. An equally strong statement for freedom of conscience soon appeared in his correspondence with the Hebrew congregation in Newport, Rhode Island.

The Jewish community in Newport presented Washington with an address during his 1790 Rhode Island tour. Echoing the Quakers, the Hebrew congregation referred to the "*Blessings* of civil and religious liberty."[70] The address praised the new American government, "which to bigotry gives no sanction, to persecution no assistance," instead "generously affording to All liberty of conscience, and immunities of Citizenship."[71] The congregation concluded with a wish that Washington might be conducted "through all the difficulties and dangers of this mortal life" by the "great preserver of Men."[72]

Washington's answer largely agreed with the Jewish address. "The Citizens of the United States of America," Washington concurred, "[a]ll possess alike liberty of conscience and immunities of citizenship."[73] But, once again, Washington emphasized to a religious group that had addressed him that its religious liberty was now protected as its right: "It is now no more that toleration is spoken of, as if it was by the indulgence of one class of people, that another enjoyed the exercise of their inherent natural rights."[74] In other words, Washington might have said, those in minority religious groups have as much right to practice their religion as do those in larger, more established religious groups. The religious freedom of minority groups does not result merely from the charity and goodwill of the majority.[75]

The president's next sentence returned to the language used in the original letter from the Jewish community, but he also tacked on his familiar requirement regarding good citizenship: "For happily the Government of the United States, which gives to bigotry no sanction, to persecution no assistance requires only that they who live under its protection should demean themselves as good citizens, in giving it on all occasions their effectual support."[76] Washington seemed satisfied with the efforts of American Jews to fulfill the requirements of citizenship, as he concluded with the wish that the "Children of the Stock of Abraham" will "*continue* to merit and enjoy the good will of the other Inhabitants."[77]

Many of Washington's statements regarding religious liberty were stronger or more straightforward at this time than at previous points in his life. Yet the president apparently did not view his statements in favor of religious liberty as being at odds with his view that the government should support religion generally. Indeed, Washington alluded to the desirability of public support for religion on multiple occasions during these early years of the Republic. An August 1789 letter to the Protestant Episcopal Church reassured the congregation that the "moderation, patriotism, and wisdom of the present federal Legislature, seem to promise the restoration of Order, and our ancient virtues; [and] the extension of genuine religion."[78] The following year, Washington responded favorably when the Roman Catholics praised him for the manner in which he "encourage[s] respect for religion, and inculcate[s], by words and actions, that principle, on which the welfare of nations so much depends, that a superintending Providence governs the events of the world, and watches over the conduct of men."[79] Washington was quick to agree with the Catholics that the nation would prosper "under the smiles of a Divine Providence" and the "protection of a good Government."[80] Finally, he promised the bishops of the Methodist Episcopal Church, "I shall always strive to prove a faithful and impartial Patron of genuine, vital religion."[81] The promise was made mere sentences after Washington had expressed his hope that he could contribute to the "preservation of the civil and religious liberties of the American People."[82]

As Washington made especially clear in his letters to the Quakers and the Newport Jews, however, this relationship between government and religious groups was not to be a one-way street. Religious groups, he believed, should inculcate a sense of patriotism and good citizenship in their members. Washington "readily" agreed with the Dutch Reformed Church in North America that "*while* just government protects all in their religious rights, true religion affords to government its surest support."[83] He thanked the German Reformed Congregations "for the promise that it will be your constant study to impress the minds of the

People entrusted to your care with a due sense of the necessity of uniting reverence to such a government and obedience to its' laws with the duties and exercises of Religion."[84] In Washington's estimation, the government should welcome the benefits that religion could confer on a self-governing nation, but religious groups should respond by supporting the government. There was not a strict "separation," but instead a mutually beneficial relationship.

Despite his general support for public religion, Washington also knew that a balance must be struck between public and private prerogatives. That balance was to be struck in favor of private conscience to the extent that it could be done without compromising the nation's "essential Interests."[85] As he wrote to the Society of Quakers in October 1789, "the Consciencious scruples of all men should be treated with great delicacy & tenderness, and it is my wish and desire that the Laws may always be as extensively accomodated to them, as a due regard to the Protection and essential Interests of the Nation may Justify, and permit."[86]

Consistent with that view, Washington continued as president to use non-denominational language when he addressed matters of religion. Indeed, on a few occasions, he pointedly declined to use language that could have been misconstrued as support for a particular denomination. For instance, shortly after his inauguration, Washington received a letter from the General Assembly of the Presbyterian Church. In their address, the Presbyterians praised their "chief Magistrate, a steady, uniform, avowed friend of the christian religion . . . [who] on the most public and solemn occasions devoutly acknowledges the government of divine Providence."[87] Washington agreed, in part, but he refused to go the extra "christian" step taken by the Presbyterians. His terminology regarding public religion remained nondenominational, even in the face of the specifically Christian language used by the General Assembly.[88] "I reiterate the possession of my dependence upon Heaven," Washington affirmed, "as the source of all public and private blessings."[89] His letter continued with a reminder that "all men within our territories are protected in worshipping the Deity according to the dictates of their consciences."[90]

Washington employed a similar adjustment in terminology when the establishment church in Connecticut addressed him. "As Ministers of the blessed Jesus," the Congregational Ministers of New Haven wrote, "we rejoice and have inexpressible pleasure in the demonstrations you have given of your sincere affection towards that holy religion, which is the glory of Christian States, and will become the glory of the world itself."[91] Washington again agreed, but clarified that one denomination would not be supported to the exclusion of others. Instead, public religion would be encouraged to the degree that it encourages virtue and, thus, self-government. "[T]hat deportment, which consists with true religion," he wrote the Congregationalist ministers, is the "best security of temporal peace."[92] Notably absent was the Christian terminology of the ministers. Instead, Washington continued more simply: "[I]t will be my earnest endeavor (as far as human frailty can resolve) to inculcate the belief and practice of opinions, which lead to the consummation of those desireable objects."[93]

Washington's nondenominational language was similar to that which he had used as commander-in-chief of the Continental Army. He sought the benefits of public religion, but he endeavored to do so in a manner that would minimize conflict among those with diverse religious backgrounds. Harmony was his goal. "It affords edifying prospects indeed," he told the Protestant Episcopal Church, "to see Christians of different denominations dwell together in more charity, and conduct themselves in respect to each other with a more christian-like spirit than ever they have done in any former age, or in any other nation."[94] He praised the Dutch Reformed Church for their efforts to "preserve that harmony and good will towards men which must be the basis of every political establishment."[95]

Many of Washington's addresses and letters to religious groups were written before the First Amendment became the law of the land. Hence, Washington was not bound by that amendment any more than he had been when he considered the prospect of a day of official thanksgiving. Regardless, many of his communications were written after the proposed amendment had been submitted to the states for ratification. It is unlikely that Washington would deliberately espouse views of church and state that were sure to be quickly contradicted by the new First Amendment. This interpretation of Washington's words is reinforced by the actions the president took during his final years in office, after ratification of the First Amendment (see chapter six).

Washington's writings in the early years of his presidency emphasize themes that were becoming familiar for him. He remained firm in his commitment to protect freedom of conscience for the citizens of the new republic. On the other hand, he often spoke of the public benefits of religion and urged his fellow citizens to rely on providential assistance. Without religion, self-government cannot hope to succeed. Religion and government must support each other to some degree.

ENACTMENTS OF THE FIRST CONGRESS

Drafting a Bill of Rights was a priority for the First Congress. By the time Washington had been in office for six months, Congress had already approved twelve proposed constitutional amendments and forwarded them to the states for approval. One of these amendments would eventually be ratified by the states as the First Amendment to the Constitution and would prohibit Congress from making any "law respecting an establishment of religion, or prohibiting the free exercise thereof."[96] The president himself was not involved in the amendment process.[97] He generally maintained a hands-off approach to any legislative matter that was pending in Congress, and the debates over the Bill of Rights were no exception. In Washington's view, separation of powers required him to abstain from such congressional debate, not making his views known until a bill was presented to him for signature or veto.[98] In the case of constitutional amendments, of course, the president was not given even this opportunity to be involved in law-making. Instead, the states themselves considered whether to amend the Constitution as recommended by Congress.

Other legislative decisions, however, required a presidential signature and thus presented Washington with an opportunity to make his views known. Several of these early bills implicated church-state relations. Neither Congress nor the president could be bound by the religious provisions of the First Amendment during this time, since they were not yet law. But the same Congress that drafted the First Amendment took these other legislative steps. They were unlikely to push policies that contradicted their own ideas of the proper relationship between church and state.[99] Similarly, Washington knew of the pending constitutional amendment. As he considered whether to sign or veto those items that were presented to him, he presumably sought to avoid signing legislation that would be rendered unconstitutional within a relatively short period of time by passage of the First Amendment. He also presumably sought not to undermine the ratification process by forcing the states to choose between the proposed amendment and legislation recently signed by their president.

The first of these legislative decisions occurred almost immediately after the new Congress convened in 1789. A joint congressional committee was named to "take under consideration the manner of electing chaplains."[100] Two chaplains of different denominations were appointed—one by the House and one by the Senate. These chaplains were to open sessions of Congress with prayer, and their salaries were to be paid with federal funds.[101] Washington's approval was not required for the initial appointments, but he later signed a law that provided for the chaplains' salaries.[102] Moreover, he invited chaplains to monthly dinners at the presidential residence when Congress was in session, a fact reported by Ashbel Green, the third chaplain of the House of Representatives.[103] Washington's decision was not insignificant, as he spent a fair amount of time early in his presidency evaluating the proper type of social engagements for a president to host or attend.[104] Indeed, his actions were in accord with his long support of publicly funded chaplains. Unsurprisingly, the president later signed additional legislation that authorized federally funded chaplains for the military.[105]

Appointing chaplains was just one of several measures taken by the First Congress to accommodate religion. As it debated the Bill of Rights during the summer of 1789, Congress also took time to renew the provisions of the Northwest Ordinance. Originally, this ordinance was adopted by the Continental Congress, the predecessor to the new U.S. Congress. The purpose of the ordinance was to regulate the settlement of certain lands on the frontier and to provide for the admission of additional states to the Union as the territories became more populated. After the

Constitution was ratified, the newly elected U.S. Congress decided to "adapt" the Northwest Ordinance to the Constitution, by enacting "An Act to Provide for the Government of the Territory Northwest of the River Ohio."[106] The act made logistical changes that would be necessary for the U.S. government to pick up where the Continental Congress had left off.[107] The other, substantive provisions in the ordinance were left unchanged.[108]

The ordinance included a few notable provisions regarding religious activity on the frontier: "No person, demeaning himself in a peaceable and orderly manner, shall ever be molested on account of his mode of worship or religious sentiments, in the said territory."[109] In the territories, then, freedom of religion was guaranteed. But two paragraphs later, the ordinance included a provision that encouraged public support of religious activity: "Religion, morality, and knowledge, being necessary to good government and the happiness of mankind, schools and the means of education shall forever be encouraged."[110] Under this provision, land in each township had been set aside for religious and educational use. The new Congress would continue this tradition.[111] Washington signed the bill without expressing any concern over its religious provisions. To the contrary, the bill echoed two sentiments that the president had been espousing for years: First, religion is necessary to morality and virtue, which, in turn, is necessary for republican government. Second, people are entitled to freedom of conscience in religious matters, but they also have a duty to be good citizens. In the words of the ordinance, an individual should "demean[ ] himself in a peaceable and orderly manner."[112]

Several weeks later, Congress passed an "Act to Establish the Judicial Courts of the United States."[113] Part of this organizational bill required justices, judges, court clerks, and court marshals to take oaths of office before entering upon their duties. These oaths, by the terms of the statute, were to conclude with the words "So help me God."[114] Washington signed this bill also. If he had any reservations about the religious component, there is no record of it. He seemed satisfied with the first congressional session and the organization of the new government. He told Gouverneur Morris that "national government is organized, and as far as my information goes, to the satisfaction of all parties."[115]

The First Congress enacted one last bill with religious ramifications. This piece of legislation was approved after the Bill of Rights had been proposed to the states, but before any constitutional amendments were ratified. In April 1790, Congress enacted a bill that would abolish what had been referred to as the "benefit of clergy" in certain criminal federal cases.[116] In colonial America, clergymen had often been given special rights in the legal system, including, in some instances, the right to an ecclesiastical trial instead of a civil trial.[117] Congress abolished this right in a statute that declared: "[T]he benefit of clergy shall not be used or allowed, upon conviction of any crime, for which, by any statute of the United States, the punishment is or shall be declared to be death."[118] Washington signed the bill. Stokes notes that passage of the act "virtually removed this ancient form of clerical privilege from use in Federal jurisprudence."[119]

The First Amendment, with its provisions regarding matters of church and state, was finally ratified by the states on December 15, 1791, giving the amendment the force of law. Washington's limited involvement in the events that led to passage of the First Amendment makes it virtually impossible to know if he would have drafted the amendment differently, left to his own devices. The most that can be known with any degree of certainty is what presidential actions Washington saw as permissible, following enactment of the First Amendment. His decisions in this regard will be discussed in the next chapter.

AS THE NATION'S FIRST PRESIDENT, Washington knew that his actions would set precedents for future generations. Areas of religious concern were no exception to this rule, and Washington worked diligently to identify and to conform to constitutional standards. The president's actions thus reflect his considered view that government support of religious activity was constitutional, at least prior to adoption of the First Amendment. As in his previous public roles, he supported public funding of chaplains, and he continued to embrace religion in his public actions and correspondence. However, he often did so in a nondenominational manner that would respect the religious diversity of the new nation.

Nearly three years into Washington's first term as president, the states ratified the First Amendment, with its protections for religious freedom. Washington's actions over the course of the next five years would demonstrate his view that the amendment did not change the propriety of the national government's support for certain religious activity. The views he had developed through the years regarding the permissible interaction between church and state do not seem to have changed significantly, if at all, as a result of the First Amendment.

SIX

President of the United States
After the First Amendment

1792–1797

Of all the dispositions and habits which lead to political
prosperity, Religion and morality are indispensable supports.
In vain would that man claim the tribute of Patriotism,
who should labour to subvert these great Pillars of human
happiness, these firmest props of the duties of Men & citizens.

Farewell Address, September 19, 1796[1]

ASHINGTON'S FIRST TERM AS PRESIDENT was coming to an
end, and he hoped that he might avoid a second one.
He was tired of public life and impatient with the in-
creasingly partisan nature of politics. His position, he told James
Madison in May 1792, was "scarcely tolerabl[e]."[2] He hoped that
now, finally, he might be able to retire to Mount Vernon. He
therefore asked Madison to draft a "plain & modest" farewell address.[3] He had every intention of retiring, he told Madison, unless
his "deriliction of the Chair of Government . . . would involve the
Country in serious disputes respecting the chief Magestrate."[4]

Washington's hopes were not to be fulfilled, as several of his advisors set out to convince him that he was still needed. His secretary of state, Thomas Jefferson, argued that only Washington could hold the new nation together. "North & South will hang together, if they have you to hang on," Jefferson wrote.[5] He told Washington that he was the "only man in the U.S. who possessed the confidence of the whole, . . . and that the longer he remained, the stronger would become the habits of the people in submitting to the government & in thinking it a thing to be maintained."[6] Madison concurred, noting that Washington's retirement would result in a "surprize and shock to the public mind."[7] For once, the secretary of the treasury, Alexander Hamilton, was in agreement with Madison and Jefferson, and he also sought to discourage Washington's retirement. The president's departure, Hamilton wrote, would be "deplored as the greatest evil, that could befall the country at the present juncture, and as critically hazardous to your own reputation."[8] Ultimately, Washington did not withdraw his name from consideration prior to the election, and he was unanimously (if reluctantly) reelected.[9] The man who had served his country for so long would continue to do his duty for four more years.

In respect to matters of church and state, one might expect Washington's second term (and even the last year of his first term) to differ in some respects from his early years as president, given the ratification of the First Amendment in December 1791. To the contrary, passage of the amendment had no perceptible effect on the manner in which Washington handled the interplay between religion and civic life. He continued to view public support of religion as both permissible and necessary in a healthy, self-governing society. He maintained his views regarding the importance of religious liberty and the accommodation of dissenters in some circumstances. From a policy perspective, he also always seemed to consider what would best serve the public good. Washington's continued support of religion in the public square shows that he did not view the First Amendment as erecting a "wall of separation" between governmental and religious entities, as was later advocated in Jefferson's letter to the Danbury Baptists.

DAYS OF PRAYER AND THANKSGIVING

President Washington issued two proclamations calling upon the country to observe days of prayer and thanksgiving. The first of these declarations was issued at the request of Congress in October 1789, before the First Amendment was ratified by the states (see chapter five). The second proclamation was issued much later, on January 1, 1795.[10] By this time, the First Amendment had been the law for more than three years. The president's decision to call for this second official religious observance was prompted by the successful resolution of an internal insurrection that came to be known as the Whiskey Rebellion.

The seeds of rebellion had already been sown when Washington took his second oath of office in 1793. The discontent began when Congress enacted an excise tax on whiskey in 1791. Unfortunately, the weight of the tax did not fall equally across the country, and some on the frontier felt that they were being treated unfairly. By the summer of 1794, a full-blown insurrection emerged in western Pennsylvania. Washington decided to act. He declared to the nation:

> Now, therefore, I, GEORGE WASHINGTON, President of the United States, in obedience to that high and irresistible duty, consigned to me by the Constitution, "to take care

that the laws be faithfully executed;" . . . [and] resolved, in perfect reliance on that gracious Providence which so signally displays its goodness towards this country, to reduce the refractory to a due subordination to the laws; do hereby declare and make known . . . [that a force] is already in motion to the scene of disaffection.[11]

Troops marched into the state, and the rebellion was defeated.[12] The successful end to the Whiskey Rebellion greatly relieved Washington. He knew that the federal government could not thrive if Americans felt they could disregard the law at will. The republic had survived a potentially fatal blow. Yet again, Washington observed an event that had gone well for the United States when it might have gone otherwise. He decided to designate February 19 as a "day of public thanksgiving and prayer."[13]

As had become typical for Washington, he used nondenominational language in his official directive. The proclamation was directed to "all religious societies and denominations, and to all persons whomsoever, within the United States."[14] Moreover, his references to God were not specifically Christian. Instead, the call to thanksgiving employed such terms as the "Great Ruler of Nations," the "Divine beneficence," and the "kind Author of these blessings."[15] The closest that Washington came to specific terminology was his single use of the term "Almighty God."[16]

Washington's proclamation began by reciting the national blessings that had prompted his call for a day of thanksgiving, including the recent "suppression of an insurrection."[17] The country has been given many "indications of the Divine beneficence toward us," Washington declared.[18] "In such a state of things," he noted, "it is in an especial manner *our duty as a people*, with devout reverence and affectionate gratitude, to acknowledge our many and great obligations to Almighty God and to implore Him to continue and confirm the blessings we experience."[19] Americans should "*meet together*," the president continued, and they should "render their sincere and hearty thanks to the Great Ruler of Nations" for the "prosperous course of our affairs, *public and private*."[20] Moreover, Americans should "beseech the kind Author of these blessings . . . to imprint on our hearts a deep and solemn sense of *our obligations* to Him."[21] Importantly, Washington's terminology repeatedly assumed joint, not individual, action on the part of Americans.

Washington's endorsement of official religious observances was echoed in at least two other contexts during this period. Washington participated in the laying of the cornerstone for the U.S. Capitol. The ceremony was conducted according to Masonic rites, and it included public prayer.[22] Moreover, Congress continued to pass, and Washington continued to sign, legislation authorizing government-paid military and congressional chaplains.[23] Washington's signature on this legislation ensured that official religious observances would be much more than merely an occasional occurrence. Such activities would occur on a regular basis, at least in the military and in Congress.

It is significant that Washington found public, collective gratitude to God permissible in these post-First Amendment years. Passage of the First Amendment had not changed his view on the constitutionality of the national government sponsoring religious observances. Perhaps much more interesting, however, is the fact that Washington saw public expressions of thanksgiving as more than merely *permissible*. America's first president continued to view such united, religious action as a *duty* incumbent upon the nation. His perspective differs starkly from the belief that the

Constitution requires a complete "separation between church and state," a view later espoused by America's third president.

CONTINUING MISSIONARY EFFORTS

As president, much of Washington's time was occupied by the necessity of improving relations with the Indians. His interest in the topic came naturally and could be traced back to his days as commander of the Virginia Regiment. Much of his time, then, was occupied with defending the frontier against Indian raiding parties. Perhaps not surprisingly, his early experiences led him to look favorably upon efforts to "convert[ ] the Indians to Christianity and consequently to civilization."[24] Such an event, he once told a Moravian bishop, has been "so long and so earnestly desired."[25]

Over the years, Washington's desire to civilize the Indians sometimes led him to sanction official religious activity in connection with the tribes. During the Revolutionary War, his interest in this objective led him to occasionally use specifically Christian language in his public statements. Later, as president, this usage seems to have lessened (replaced by references to the "great Spirit"), but Washington's war-time usage in this context is a notable (if unexplained) exception to his typical nondenominational approach.[26]

A few years into the war, for instance, Washington spoke to the Delaware Indian Chiefs, applauding their desire to learn "our arts and ways of life, and above all, the religion of Jesus Christ."[27] His next words promised public assistance for this specifically Christian goal: "Congress will do every thing they can to assist you in this wise intention," he reassured the chiefs.[28] Upon being introduced to Joseph Johnson, a "christianized" Indian, Washington wrote:

> I am very much pleased to find by the Strong recommendations you produce, that we have amongst our Brothers of the Six Nations a person who can explain to them, the Sense of their Brothers, on the dispute between us and the Ministers of Great Britain . . . .
>
> . . . .
>
> . . . [W]e recommend you to them, and hope by your Spreading the truths of the Holy Gospel amongst them, it will Contribute to keep the Chain so bright, that, the malicious insinuations, or practices of our Enemies will never be able to break this Union, so much for the benefit of our Brothers of the Six Nations and of us.[29]

Early in the Revolution, General Washington wrote to the Continental Congress on behalf of Samuel Kirkland, a missionary to the Oneida Indians.[30] Kirkland had persuaded the Oneidas to remain neutral between Britain and America.[31] "I cannot but intimate my Sense of the Importance of his Station," Washington observed to the president of Congress, "& the great Advantages which have & may result to the United Colonies from his Situation being made respectable."[32] Congress later approved funds to support Kirkland's continued missionary and peacekeeping efforts among the Oneidas.[33] Washington continued to support missionary efforts following the war. His endorsement of the Countess of Huntingdon's plan for a private-public venture to facilitate the work of missionaries among the Indians was discussed in chapter four.

Washington's interest in government-sponsored religious aid to the Indians continued after he became president. Indeed, after only a few months in office, the Washington administration issued written instructions to commissioners assigned to negotiate a peace with the southern Indians. The president asked the American representatives to "endeavor to obtain a stipulation for certain missionaries, to reside in the nation . . . . The object of this establishment would be the happiness of the Indians, teaching them the great duties of religion and morality, and to inculcate a friendship and attachment to the United States."[34] But Washington qualified his statement, slightly. The missionaries would be appointed only if the "General Government should think proper to adopt the measure."[35] Washington's deference to Congress was typical. In January 1790, for instance, Washington received a request for a "small Salary to an Indian Preacher."[36] Washington expressed support for the idea, but referred the request to Congress, noting that it required the "operation of legislative power rather than any agency of mine at present."[37]

In Washington's view, then, public funding of missionaries could be constitutionally permissible, but it was ultimately a policy matter for Congress to decide. Later, he advocated the congressional endorsement of his religion-friendly policy toward the Indians, declaring in his October 25, 1791, address to Congress that a "System corrisponding with the mild principles of religion and philanthropy towards an unenlightened race of men," would be "as honorable to the national character as conformable to the dictates of sound policy."[38] The First Amendment was ratified several weeks after this presidential address, on December 15, 1791.

The tenor of Washington's statements and actions did not change following ratification of the First Amendment. To the contrary, he remained favorably inclined toward such policies, as exhibited by his response to a March 1792 letter from the bishop of Baltimore, John Carroll. The bishop had requested a "small allowance for the necessary subsistance of clergymen employed in disseminating the principles of Christianity amongst the natives of the Western Territory; and to make them a grant [of land]."³⁹ Washington expressed general support for Carroll's "pious & benevolent wishes to effect this desireable end upon the mild principles of Religion & Philanthropy."⁴⁰ Unfortunately, the president noted, Carroll's proposal could not be implemented—but not because of the First Amendment or any other legal impediment. There was, instead, a logistical problem: "The war now existing between the United States and some tribes of the Western Indians," he concluded, "prevents, for the present, any intercourse of this nature with them."⁴¹ With regard to other Indian tribes in the east, however, Washington suggested that the bishop request assistance from the government in Massachusetts, as "that State has always considered them as under its immediate care & protection."⁴² Washington's letter concluded with a statement showing his appreciation for the public purpose of such funding: "[T]he most effectual means of securing the permanent attachment of our savage neighbors is to convince them that we are just."⁴³

Not long thereafter, Washington found himself relying upon religious assistance in a slightly different context. In 1793, peace talks were scheduled between the United States and the hostile Indians in the Northwest Territory. The Indians requested that representatives from the Quakers be allowed to attend the talks.⁴⁴ Washington's secretary of war, Henry Knox, conveyed the request to the president, suggesting that one of the Moravian missionaries living among the Indians might be helpful as well. "The influence he will have with the said Tribes," Knox wrote, "may be expected to be very considerable."⁴⁵ The journal kept by Washington's office shows that the president approved the idea, in principle, and he thought the Quakers' expenses should be "borne by the public as their attendg. is for the public good & by the desire of the Indians."[46] Washington then sought advice from his cabinet. "[Y]ou will consider how far," his circular to the cabinet stated, "they ought to be recognized in the Instructions to the Commissioners—and how proper it may be for them to participate therein or to be made acquainted therewith."[47] No written record of Washington's subsequent deliberations with his cabinet on this issue, if there were any, has been identified, but the Quakers and the Moravian were authorized to attend the treaty negotiations as part of the American delegation.[48] At a minimum, this episode indicates that Washington found it permissible for individuals not affiliated with the government, including representatives from religious organizations, to attend negotiations as part of an official American delegation.

The Washington administration continued to negotiate treaties with its Indian neighbors, and in January 1795, the president sent the Senate a treaty with the Oneida Indians.[49] By the terms of this treaty, the United States was to pay $1,000 for "building a convenient church at Oneida, in the place of the one which was there burnt by the enemy, in the late war."[50] Arguably, the purpose of this provision was secular: the United States was making restitution for losses suffered by an ally in wartime.[51] On the other hand, some modern-day Americans have argued that analogous purposes, such as government restoration of a religious building damaged by an earthquake, violates the principles of church and state put in place by the Founders. The treaty with the Oneida Indians indicates that the first president of the United States would not agree with constitutional interpretations that create such a stark separation between church and state.[52]

During his last year in office, Washington signed legislation that facilitated grants of land to certain missionaries living

among the Indians. The legislation built upon actions taken by
the Continental Congress, before either the Constitution or
the First Amendment existed.[53] These earlier enactments had
designated three towns in the territories "for the sole use of the
Christian Indians, who were formerly settled there, or the remains
of [the Moravians]" and had reserved ten thousand acres for the
"Moravian Brethern at Bethlehem in Pennsylvania, or a society
of the said Brethern for civilizing the Indians and promoting
Christianity, in trust."[54] Three tracts of land were ordered to be
conveyed "to the said United brethren or the society of the said
brethren for propagating the Gospel among the heathen."[55] Nearly
a decade later, after ratification of the Constitution and the First
Amendment, Congress passed an "Act Regulating the Grants
of Land Appropriated for Military Services, and for the Society
of the United Brethren, for Propagating the Gospel Among the
Heathen."[56] This act would ensure that the "society of United
Brethren for propagating the gospel among the heathen" would
receive their patents for the land, in trust, "without requiring any
fee therefor."[57]

Washington's signature on the bill reaffirmed sentiments that
he had previously expressed to the beneficiary of the land grants,
the Moravian Society for Propagating the Gospel. This society
wrote Washington a congratulatory letter shortly after his election
in 1789.[58] At that time, Washington applauded the society's missionary work, concluding that "it will be a desirable thing for the
protection of the Union to co-operate, as far as the circumstances
may conveniently admit, with the disinterested endeavours of your
society to civilize and Christianize the Savages of the Wilderness."[59] When the Fourth Congress gave Washington an opportunity, the president put his words into action by signing the bill
into law. The religion-friendly bills enacted during Washington's

administration would constitute the beginning of many decades of government-funded religious aid to the Indians.[60]

ADDITIONAL CORRESPONDENCE

In many respects, Washington's last years in office were more difficult than his first years. Internal dissension brewed as Americans disagreed on whether to remain neutral regarding conflicts in Europe. Issues such as the Whiskey Rebellion and disagreement over a treaty with Britain added fuel to the fire. Yet in the midst of this increasing partisanship and distrust, Washington remained a beloved figure, and he continued to receive supportive letters from churches, local governments, and other organizations. Importantly, the tenor of Washington's responses to his well-wishers remained the same as when he first took office in 1789. Adoption of the First Amendment did not discourage him from including religious themes in his official correspondence.

Much as they had at other points in his life, the president's letters often ruminated on America's providential blessings. These sentiments appeared not only in his private letters, but also in his official correspondence. "I am sure there never was a people," Washington remarked to one of his former military officers, "who had more reason to acknowledge a divine interposition in their affairs than those of the United States."[61] The president's letters to churches and local governments echoed with similar expressions of gratitude toward God. When the New Jerusalem Church of Baltimore sent Washington "testimonies of esteem and confidence," the president refused to take credit for the nation's blessings.[62] "But to the manifest interposition of an over-ruling Providence, and to the patriotic exertions of united America," Washington noted, "are to be ascribed those events which have given us a respectable rank among the nations of the Earth."[63] The president later reminded the inhabitants of Shepherds Town of "[t]hat Beneficent Providence, which, hitherto, has preserved us in Peace, and increased our prosperity," and he continued to make similar observations to legislative bodies.[64] When writing elected officials in Maryland, he noted his "gratitude to Heaven," for the "blessings of peace, liberty and prosperity."[65] His 1795 Address to Congress invited legislators to "join with me, in profound gratitude to the Author of all good, for the numerous, and extraordinary blessings we enjoy."[66]

The Providence in Washington's official correspondence was active in the present as well as the past, and the president continued to speak to his fellow countrymen of the need to "confid[e] in the protection of a just Providence."[67] As America sought to remain neutral in European conflicts, he urged the inhabitants of Richmond to remain "[t]rue to our duties and interests as Americans" and to "unite our fervent prayers to the great ruler of the Universe."[68] A few days later, he expressed similar sentiments to the inhabitants of New London. "Experienced as we have lately been in the calamities of war," Washington wrote, "it must be the prayer of every good Citizen that it may long be averted from our land, and that the blessings which a kind providence has bestowed upon us, may continue uninterrupted."[69] Interestingly, in both of these letters, as in his Thanksgiving Proclamation of 1795, Washington indicated that Americans had more than an *option* to gather together in prayer. Instead, he spoke of "our *duties* and interests as Americans" and indicated that the continuance of peace "*must* be the prayer of every good Citizen."

Washington's letters reflect confidence that dependence on divine aid will result in continued success for the nation. "With such aid and support, under direction of Divine Providence," he told the inhabitants of Morris County, New Jersey, "I trust the flourishing condition and inestimable blessings now enjoyed, will be long continued to our Country."[70] His letter to the inhabitants of James City County, Virginia, reflects similar optimism. "I place entire confidence," he wrote, "we may expect, under the protection of a kind providence, a continuation of those blessings which these States enjoy in a superior degree."[71] Not surprisingly, Washington could not omit his typical exhortations to morality. As was now normal for him, he combined his statements of "warmest gratitude to heaven" with encouragements to "[l]et the wise and the virtuous unite their efforts."[72] Divine benevolence, in Washington's view, was not an excuse for laziness or immorality. "[T]he good citizen will look beyond the applauses and reproaches of men," Washington wrote the citizens of Frederick County, Virginia, "and persevering in his duty, stand firm in conscious rectitude, and in the hope of approving Heaven."[73]

Washington saw no contradiction in making strong statements in favor of public religion even as he expressed support for freedom of conscience. "We have abundant reason to rejoice," the president observed to the New Jerusalem Church of Baltimore,

> that in this land the light of truth and reason have triumphed over the power of bigotry and superstition, and that every person may here worship God according to the dictates of his own heart. In this enlightened age and in this land of equal liberty, it is our boast, that a man's religious tenets will not forfeit the protection of the laws, nor deprive him of the right of attaining and holding the highest offices that are known in the United States.[74]

A later letter to a group of Episcopalians noted the importance of protecting these and other freedoms. "Government alone can be approved by Heaven," he wrote, "which promotes peace and secures protection to its Citizens in every thing that is dear and interesting to them."[75] Thus, he concluded, "it has been the great object of my administration to insure those invaluable ends."[76]

The modern-day concept of separation between church and state views official religion and freedom of religious conscience as mutually exclusive. Washington's post-First Amendment correspondence, however, reflects the opposite perspective: both are needed in a healthy, self-governing society. Indeed, the day before he left the presidency, Washington wrote a letter to the Philadelphia clergy, in which he approvingly described these two principles, residing together amicably. "Believing, as I do, that *Religion* and *Morality* are the essential pillars of Civil society," he wrote, "I view, with unspeakable pleasure, that harmony and brotherly love which characterizes the Clergy of different denominations."[77] Such an equilibrium, he concluded, "exhibit[s] to the world a new and interesting spectacle, at once the pride of our Country and the surest basis of universal Harmony."[78]

THE FAREWELL ADDRESS

Some Federalists hoped that Washington would agree to a third term, but Washington was eager to retire. By the spring of 1796, he was already preparing to leave. In May, he asked Alexander Hamilton to help him revise the farewell address that had been drafted with the help of James Madison four years earlier. Several drafts went back and forth between the two men before a final version was completed.[79] Washington's farewell was finally published in the *American Daily Advertiser* on September 19, 1796.[80]

Washington put a great deal of thought into his final address to the American people. Indeed, he was still editing it as it went to press, and he carefully reviewed the proof sheets when they were delivered by the *Advertiser*'s publisher on September 17.[81] The president had said goodbye to public life on many occasions, but this was virtually certain to be his last exit from the public scene. It was important to him to impart "some sentiments" that he had learned during his long life and career in public service.[82] These lessons, Washington wrote, "are the result of much reflection" and they "appear to me all important to the permanency of your felicity as a People."[83]

Certain aspects of the 1796 farewell echoed sentiments in the original 1792 draft. At that time, the president had asked Madison to ensure that the "Valadictory address from me to the public . . . invoke a continuation of the blessings of Providence upon [the country]."[84] The final version, completed nearly five years after ratification of the First Amendment, would retain its exhortations on behalf of morality and religion. The president who had entered office in 1789 with "fervent supplications to that Almighty Being who rules over the Universe" would leave office with a reminder to his fellow-citizens regarding the importance of such acts of public piety.[85]

Washington began his address by encouraging Americans to be unified, avoiding partisanship and petty rivalries. "The name of American, which belongs to you, in your national capacity, must always exalt the just pride of Patriotism, more than any appellation derived from local discriminations," he declared.[86] Differences of religious opinion, in Washington's address, pale in comparison to what unites the nation. "With slight shades of difference, you have the same Religeon, Manners, Habits & political Principles," he wrote, "You have in a common cause fought & triumphed together—The independence & liberty you possess are the work of joint councils, and joint efforts—of common dangers, sufferings and successes."[87] Washington's focus was on what Americans shared, not their political and religious differences. He hoped that others would do the same once he was gone.

Moreover, the acknowledged existence of some religious differences did not stop Washington from once again espousing the need for public reliance on divine assistance. He once again emphasized his position that official reliance on religion is more than merely *permissible* in American society—it is *"indispensable."*[88] Washington speaks best for himself:

> Of all the dispositions and habits which lead to political prosperity, Religion and morality are indispensable supports. In vain would that man claim the tribute of Patriotism, who should labour to subvert these great Pillars of human happiness, these firmest props of the duties of Men & citizens. The mere Politician, equally with the pious man ought to respect & to cherish them. A volume could not trace all their connections with private & public felicity.[89]

Washington's logic, as always, was straightforward. "[V]irtue or morality is a necessary spring of popular government," he concluded.[90] Because religion is a necessary prerequisite for morality, it is also essential for self-governance. Moreover, Washington wrote, Americans should "with caution indulge the supposition, that morality can be maintained without religion. . . . reason & experience both forbid us to expect that National morality can prevail in exclusion of religious principle."[91] Washington knew that religion, morality, and the health of a nation are inevitably entwined, and he sought to convey the importance of these principles to his fellow-citizens. "Can it be," he rhetorically asked later in his address, "that Providence has not connected the permanent felicity of a Nation with its virtue?"[92]

Washington's farewell address was long, filling more than a page of the *Advertiser*.[93] But Washington had spent many years developing his views on various matters of public policy, whether on the battlefield, as a state legislator, or as president. It was important to him to pass on these valuable lessons before he departed the public stage forever. The important role of religion in civic life would not be left unspoken before his departure.

THROUGHOUT HIS PRESIDENCY, Washington knew that his actions would set precedents for future presidents, and he worked diligently to adhere to the Constitution. Indeed, his first veto was issued for one simple reason: he believed the bill to be unconstitutional.[94] On another occasion, Washington refused to submit to a request made by the House of Representatives because he believed that the House was intruding into Senate prerogatives.[95] Given the president's conscientious approach to his presidency, his actions during this time make a significant statement about his understanding of the Constitution and the First Amendment.

Freedom of religious conscience remained important to Washington during the final years of his presidency. In 1795, he wrote an acquaintance: "For in politics, as in religion my tenets are few and simple: the leading one of which, and indeed that which embraces most others, is to be honest and just ourselves, and to exact it from others; medling as little as possible in their affairs where our own are not involved."[96] On the other hand, Washington recognized the importance of morality, and thus religion, in a self-governing society. Religious freedom could not entail a total separation of religious and governmental matters. To the contrary, religion and government must support each other.

CONCLUSION

ɚ

Public Homage

I NSTEAD OF GOING TO COLLEGE, Washington went to war,"
one of his biographers, Joseph Ellis, has written.[1] And it is,
indeed, fair to view Washingon's early military experience as
his education in life lessons, including those that would shape his
views about the relationship between church and state.

Washington was only twenty years old when he received his
first military appointment, and he was twenty-three when he
was appointed commander of the Virginia Regiment. A little
over three years later, he retired from the Regiment at the age of
twenty-six. During this first stint of military service, Washington
was nearly killed several times.[2] He defended the frontier against
Indian raiding parties, and he developed a method for handling
insubordinate soldiers. He learned to unify diverse groups of men
behind a common cause, and he coped with personal, political,
and religious controversies among his troops. By the age of thirty,
Washington had not only borne more responsibility than most,
but he had also witnessed a great deal of tragedy on the battlefield.

These experiences would shape him. He could not then foresee that these early years would lay the groundwork for many more years of public service, first at the head of an American army, then at the head of an American nation. Among the many lessons he learned, however, was that religion had an important place in public affairs, and that it could and should be accommodated and nurtured by government.

During his years with the Virginia Regiment, Washington was confronted with pervasive problems of insubordination, desertion, and failed recruitment. He was mortified when newspaper allegations emerged regarding rampant immorality among his troops. Colonel Washington was young and inexperienced. He was learning on the job, but he eventually settled upon a few tactics for dealing with these and other issues. His approach would later be honed with age and experience, but his basic convictions were established during these Virginia years. In regards to matters of church and state, three general principles ruled his decision-making.

First, government entities under Washington's command—whether armies or, later, a national government—were religion-friendly. The logic that develops in Washington's writings over the years is straightforward: religion is a necessary prerequisite to morality, and morality is a necessary prerequisite for discipline in an army and for self-government in a nation. Logically, then, religion is necessary for orderly armies and healthy, self-governing societies. Government thus serves the greater good when it fosters a reliance on religion among the people. Washington would therefore take such actions as ordering his troops to attend divine service or declaring days of public thanksgiving. His goal was to promote religion, officially, in a way that would maximize the public good.

Second, Washington recognized nevertheless that religious controversies among the people threatened to undermine any public benefit obtained from such religious activity. "Religious controversies," he would write during his presidency, "are always productive of more acrimony and irreconcilable hatreds than those which spring from any other cause."[3] His public writings reveal his efforts to avoid these controversies. Moreover, his letters, military orders, and speeches contain many religious references, but almost all of these are nondenominational. Virtually any adherent to a monotheistic religion could agree with the phrases that he chose to use, including "Divine Providence," the "great Author of the Universe," and the "great Disposer of events," among others.

Last, Washington's religion-friendly approach was balanced by a firm belief in freedom of individual religious conscience. He regularly sought to accommodate those with differing religious views, if such an accommodation could be made without compromising the public good. During both the French and Indian War and the Revolution, he worked with the Quakers who, for religious reasons, refused to fight. He was also instrumental in ending North American celebrations of the anti-Catholic Pope's Day, and he supported a ban on religious tests for federal office when the Constitution was drafted. "The liberty enjoyed by the People of these States, of worshipping Almighty God agreable to their Consciences," he wrote the Quakers in 1789, "is not only among the choicest of their *Blessings*, but also of their *Rights*."[4] The government has only one requirement, he later told the Hebrew Congregation in Newport, Rhode Island, "that they who live under its protection should demean themselves as good citizens, in giving it on all occasions their effectual support."[5] The government could not reasonably demand more from citizens once these requirements of good citizenship were met.

The approach that Washington developed over the years is strikingly different from the concept of separation that would later be advocated by Jefferson in his letter to the Danbury Baptists. The nation's first president did not seek a separation between church and state. Instead, Washington proactively supported general, official expressions of religion. His writings reflect a view that such official support for religion is not only necessary for the health of society, but can also be implemented without treading on religious freedom or violating the Constitution. His approach toward matters of church and state was a constant balancing act. While he endorsed official support of religion because of its healthy effects, he knew that religious controversy must be avoided and individual religious freedom must be respected. In Washington's mind, the perfect approach was found when these factors were harmonized in such a way that the public good was maximized. His approach was thus pragmatic, not doctrinaire.

Indeed, Washington was an intensely practical man. He almost certainly would not expect modern-day American leaders to make policy decisions identical to the ones that he made. He would have been the first to recognize that the balance between officially fostered religion and individual religious liberty may vary as public needs change. In his own lifetime, he changed his stance regarding the desirability of using Virginia state taxes to pay church ministers. Although he was not opposed to this kind of activity by a state, at least in principle, he feared that enactment of the tax would "rankle, & perhaps convulse the State."[6] His policy stance thus changed as the assessment's ability to serve his fellow Virginians diminished. Notably, this episode seems to have marked the last time that Washington came close to supporting establishment of an official government religion or denomination. Potentially, he still found such activities to be permissible (at least at the state, as opposed to the federal, level), but he also seems to have come to the conclusion that the public benefits of such a religious establishment were diminished in the new nation. Or perhaps the man who had once served comfortably in an establishment-era House of Burgesses had learned to place greater weight on religious freedom following his years leading the religiously diverse Continental Army.

We cannot know, with certainty, what position Washington would take on the issues of our time. Would he advocate prayer in public schools? Would he side with those who want to use public school vouchers to send their own children to private, religious schools? Washington is not here to tell us what he would do, but he left clues as to his positions in his writings.

First, Washington's basic concern was always to abide by the requirements of the Constitution. The constitutional guarantee of religious liberty must be respected, as it is one of Americans' fundamental rights. "The establishment of Civil and Religious Liberty," he told the New York Reformed German Congregation following the Revolution, "was the Motive which induced me to the Field."[7] While Washington never laid out a specific legal definition of religious liberty, his beliefs as expressed in his writings reveal that he did not find such liberty to be at odds with governmental accommodation of (or even promotion of) religion. His writings seem to assume that the religion clauses of the First Amendment mean what they say—and only what they say: "Congress shall make no law respecting an establishment of religion, or prohibiting the free exercise thereof."

With respect to government actions that neither established a national religion nor prohibited the exercise of religion, Washington would turn to an evaluation of the governmental action as a matter of policy. He would consider and balance several factors against one another to determine the wisdom of such action. For instance, he would consider the harm to individuals and the amount of religious discord that would be created by a particular policy decision. He would seek to avoid discord if possible, knowing that such divisiveness can be a destructive force in society. But Washington would also give weight to the real, communal benefits that are achieved when government fosters religion. He would make public policy decisions based on how he saw these factors balancing against each other, and he would ultimately defer to the decisions made by elected legislators.

Washington's approach to church-state relations differs from Jefferson's "wall of separation" and the line of modern-day legal decisions that it has spawned. Washington's perspective on the First Amendment and the Constitution would permit a much more religion-friendly government, even as it emphasized the importance of religious freedom. His imprimatur cannot be seriously questioned—unless one believes that the father of the country, who presided over the Constitutional Convention and served as president during passage of the First Amendment, misunderstood and indeed violated the Constitution.

Washington viewed America as unique. Its citizens may enjoy the benefits of public religion, while individuals are left free to hold their own religious beliefs. Both of these characteristics are necessary and healthy. As he told the Philadelphia clergy in 1797, "*Religion* and *Morality* are the essential pillars of Civil society."[8] When Americans of differing religious faiths uphold this principle, even as they reside together, they are "exhibiting to the world a new and interesting spectacle, at once the pride of our Country and the surest basis of universal Harmony."[9]

Whence Jefferson's Wall?

I contemplate with sovereign reverence that act of
the whole American people which declared that their
legislature should "make no law respecting an establishment
of religion, or prohibiting the free exercise thereof," thus
building a wall of separation between Church & State.

Thomas Jefferson, Letter to the Danbury Baptists
January 1, 1802[1]

THE YEAR WAS 1801. The nation's new capital, Washington,
D.C., had just witnessed its first presidential oath of office.
By this oath, Thomas Jefferson became the third president
of the United States.[2] For the first time in American history, power
had peacefully transferred from one political party, the Federalist
Party, to a second political party, the Democratic-Republicans.[3]
The outgoing Federalist Party president, John Adams, was on his
way home to Massachusetts.[4]

The 1800 presidential campaign between Jefferson and Adams
had been a messy one. Jefferson and Adams had once been good
friends, but their relationship had fallen on hard times.[5] First,

their friendship had endured a rocky 1796 election that resulted in an Adams presidency and a Jefferson vice presidency, despite the fact that the two men were from different political parties.[6] Following that election, Jefferson was largely excluded from the operations of the Adams administration.[7] Neither man seemed to trust the other. The two would be friends again, later, but that renewed friendship was many years in the future.[8] In the meantime, political mudslinging was the *modus operandi*.

The 1800 election must have been remarkably intense for a country still new to such partisan rancor. Jefferson supporters blasted the Adams administration for such policies as the Alien and Sedition Acts, which outlawed certain forms of speech against the administration.[9] Adams supporters, in return, blasted Jefferson for his alleged hostility to religion. Federalist ministers in the Northeast accused Jefferson of being a deist—or even an atheist.[10] The *Gazette of the United States* repeatedly asked its readers: "Shall I continue in allegiance to GOD—AND A RELIGIOUS PRESIDENT; or impiously declare for JEFFERSON—AND NO GOD!!!"[11] The allegations were denied fervently by Jefferson supporters.[12]

In the end, the charges of atheism against Jefferson were insufficient to push Adams to victory. Jefferson was elected president, replacing his former friend. Despite his victory, the 1800 election left Jefferson with a distaste for the Federalist clergy from New England. He would have a hard time forgetting the manner in which these men had used their pulpits to make political statements against him during the presidential campaign.[13] If given the opportunity, he would certainly take time to make a political, anti-clerical statement of his own.

Jefferson's opponents in the 1800 campaign were wrong to label him an "atheist." He was not an atheist.[14] They were correct in one regard, however: Jefferson was arguably less devout (and certainly less orthodox) than many of his peers.[15] Jefferson's more secular viewpoint was destined to influence the policies that he would promote during his administration.

SOWING USEFUL TRUTHS AND PRINCIPLES

Jefferson's inauguration on March 4, 1801, was relatively informal compared to those of his predecessors. He wore a plain suit, as Washington and Adams had, but he refused to follow their example further by powdering his hair or strapping a sword to his waist. He also declined to take a carriage, instead walking from his boarding house to the Capitol.[16] Jefferson believed that such pomp and ceremony were incompatible with limited government, so he sought to avoid it.[17]

While Jefferson personally preferred simplicity, he could not stop his supporters from their festivities and rejoicing. As he took his oath of office, towns and cities across the nation hosted parades and fired cannons in celebration.[18] One creative town decided to create a mammoth cheese as a tribute to their first Democratic-Republican president. Cheshire, Massachusetts, spent large portions of the next year creating the cheese, and they finally delivered it to Jefferson on New Years Day 1802.[19] Other local groups, congregations, and governments took a simpler approach, merely sending letters of congratulations to the new president. One of these, from the Danbury Baptist Association, landed on Jefferson's desk on December 30, 1801.[20]

These Danbury Baptists were very much in the religious minority early in the nineteenth century. They, along with other so-called "religious dissenters," such as Jews, Quakers, and Catholics, had struggled long and hard to overcome unequal treatment at the hands of their local governments. The Danbury Baptists felt that their freedoms had improved since the American Revolution, yet they were still faced with a powerful, state-established religion in their home state of Connecticut: Congregationalism. Indeed, the Congregationalists were so closely affiliated with the Federalists that the two were collectively known in that state as the "Standing Order."[21] The Danbury Baptists were glad to see the Standing Order defeated and Jefferson victorious.[22]

Importantly, the Danbury Baptists did not believe those who had charged Jefferson with hostility toward religion in the 1800 election; they instead saw him as a champion of religious liberty who had been unfairly persecuted for his stance against the establishment.[23] They wrote their letter to Jefferson, knowing that the "national government cannot destroy the Laws of each State," but hoping that Jefferson's example would "shine & prevail through all these States and all the world till Hierarchy and tyranny be destroyed from the Earth."[24]

As Daniel Dreisbach has explained, Jefferson welcomed the opportunity presented by the Danbury Baptists' correspondence, and he put considerable thought into his response.[25] Jefferson probably saw the letter as presenting him with a two-fold opportunity. First, he could strike back at the Congregationalist ministers who had attacked him so ferociously during the 1800 campaign.[26] These ministers benefited from government money. To the degree that he could undermine their connections to their respective states, he would hurt them. This reasoning was political, not constitutional.[27]

Second, Jefferson's views on religious policies differed from those of his contemporaries. For instance, he had been criticized for his failure to issue thanksgiving proclamations, as Washington and Adams had.[28] Jefferson thus saw the letter not only as an opportunity to explain himself, but also to promote his views. He told his attorney general that responding to the letter would provide an occasion for "sowing useful truths & principles among the people, which might germinate and become rooted among their political tenets."[29] Even this reasoning was self-evidently rooted more in Jefferson's political opinions than in the text or history of the written Constitution. As Dreisbach has observed: "A plausible reading of this passage is that, although Jefferson believed that his separationist construction of the First Amendment revealed 'useful truths & principles,' he implicitly conceded that these ideas were not yet political tenets accepted by the people."[30] Thus, Jefferson's response to the Danbury Baptists was a vehicle to promote his own religious *policy* views, much as he might have sought to advance his own economic policy or his own foreign policy.

When Jefferson responded to the Danbury Baptists, however, he chose to anchor his statement regarding religious liberty to the words of the First Amendment. In the letter, completed on January 1, 1802, Jefferson declared: "I contemplate with sovereign reverence that act of the whole American people which declared that *their* legislature should 'make no law respecting an establishment of religion, or prohibiting the free exercise thereof,' *thus building a wall of separation between Church & State.*"[31] With a few strokes of the pen, Jefferson thus became the first American to authoritatively suggest that the First Amendment to the Constitution requires separation between religious and civil entities.[32]

Interestingly, the Danbury Baptists, despite their minority status, seemed unhappy with Jefferson's response, as Professor Philip Hamburger has persuasively discussed.[33] Normally, a letter from the president of the United States would be something to publicize. One would expect the missive to have been circulated—proudly—among other Baptist congregations or reprinted in a local newspaper. The Danbury Baptists failed to publicize their receipt of the letter, however, suggesting their disapproval of its contents.[34] The objectionable terminology seems to have been Jefferson's strong language about "separation between Church & State."[35] As a religious minority, the Danbury Baptists sought a government that respected freedom of conscience, of course, but they did not want a government that was *opposed* to religion. To the contrary, as devout Baptists, they believed the positive influence of God on the civic aspects of their lives was as important as his influence on their personal concerns.[36]

For his part, Jefferson may have regretted sending his letter—or, at a minimum, he seems to have realized that the missive might have unfavorable political repercussions. Two days after he sent the letter, he made a point of attending church services in the U.S. Capitol, a habit that he maintained throughout his presidency.[37] More importantly, Jefferson apparently never again directly advocated—at least publicly—the concept of separation of church and state.[38] Indeed, during the remainder of his time in office, Jefferson took the opportunity to endorse the official use of religion in many ways, and he used religious terminology in many of his public speeches.[39]

Jefferson's letter to the Danbury Baptists, when examined in political and historical context, shows merely that Jefferson espoused separation between church and state as a matter of public policy. Nor did he always practice the separation that he preached. Some scholars take this observation a step further and argue that, even to the degree that Jefferson advocated separation, he sought this policy only at the federal level, not at the state level.[40] Regardless, Jefferson was ultimately more successful in advancing his public policy views than he could ever have imagined. Jefferson did not live to see the full impact of his "wall of separation." But, many years later, the seeds that he sowed did finally germinate and bloom.

THE JEFFERSIONIAN VIEW TAKES ROOT

Today, Jefferson's "separation between Church & State" terminology has become rooted in the vocabulary of many Americans.[41] Most people don't realize that this separationism has political rather than constitutional origins, as described above. To the contrary, they may go so far as to think that Jefferson's phrase is—and always has been—a part of the constitutional text.

In reality, the phrase did not come to have constitutional significance until more than seventy-five years after Jefferson wrote his letter to the Danbury Baptists. The Supreme Court did not refer to the phrase—at all—until the 1879 case of *Reynolds v. United States.*[42] Even then, the reference to Jefferson's letter was simply one of several bases for the Court's decision. The Court took nearly seventy *more* years to mention the phrase in any sort of meaningful way again.[43] This second mention in 1947, however, solidified separationism in modern constitutional jurisprudence. Since that time, the Court has relied heavily upon Jefferson's phrase in deciding religion cases that come before it.[44]

The Supreme Court first embraced Jefferson's letter to the Danbury Baptists in an 1879 case concerning a Mormon man, George Reynolds, who was convicted of the crime of bigamy.[45] Reynolds argued that his conviction was unconstitutional, because his religious beliefs required him to engage in such behavior.[46] Ultimately, the Court decided that the punishment imposed on Reynolds was constitutional, relying in part upon Jefferson's separation terminology.[47] Writing for the Court, Chief Justice Morrison Waite brushed off the fact that Jefferson was not involved in writing the Constitution, and he skirted the fact that Jefferson was not a member of the First Congress, which drafted the First Amendment.[48] Jefferson's views hold great weight, the chief justice determined, because Jefferson was an "acknowledged leader" of those who advocated for religious freedom in early America.[49] Without further justification, Waite concluded that Jefferson's separationist terminology "may be accepted almost as an authoritative declaration of the scope and effect" of the First Amendment.[50] He did so without so much as acknowledging the political history behind Jefferson's letter to the Danbury Baptists.[51]

After *Reynolds*, the Court more or less ignored the separationist doctrine for several decades, but a 1947 case, *Everson v. Board of Education*, brought the idea back to the forefront of American jurisprudence.[52] The issue before the *Everson* Court was whether a public school district could provide for pupils' transportation not only to public, but also to parochial, schools. The Court narrowly decided that the district could fund transportation to both types of schools under the Constitution.[53] Despite this apparently religion-friendly outcome, the Court used the opportunity to reaffirm Jefferson's statement as the ultimate test of what is or is not permissible under the First Amendment: "In the words of Jefferson," the Court held, "the clause against establishment of religion by law was intended to erect 'a wall of separation between church and State.'"[54] Indeed, the Court did not stop with a mere regurgitation of Jefferson's words. It went on to conclude with an even stronger statement: "The First Amendment has erected a wall between church and state. That wall must be kept high and impregnable. We could not approve the slightest breach."[55]

It was thus more than 150 years after the First Amendment was ratified that a majority of justices on the Supreme Court plucked

Jefferson's phrase out of virtual obscurity and raised it to the level of constitutional truth.[56] By judicial fiat, Jefferson's letter to the Danbury Baptists finally achieved its purpose—"sowing useful truths & principles among the people, which might germinate and become rooted among their political tenets."[57]

The Court soon showed the country how stubbornly it intended to cling to its new metaphor. In 1947, the Supreme Court heard the case of Vashti McCollum, who had sued the Board of Education responsible for her child's public school.[58] McCollum claimed that the school should not be able to invite religious teachers to teach classes during regular school hours, even though the religious classes were purely voluntary and were financed by a nonpublic religious council.[59] In a rather succinct opinion, the Court cited Jefferson's wall multiple times and sided with Ms. McCollum.[60] Remember, Jefferson's wall was virtually unheard of in constitutional jurisprudence until merely one year before, but now it was cited as nearly the sole basis for overturning a public school program as unconstitutional.[61]

McCollum v. Board of Education was just the first of a string of Court decisions revealing that Jefferson's attempts to "sow[ ] useful truths" had succeeded beyond his wildest dreams. Within a matter of months, Jefferson's once-obscure wall had become firmly entrenched in the law of the land as pronounced by the Supreme Court. It was thus only a matter of time before most Americans would come to believe that separationism is the appropriate standard by which to judge church-state relations in America.

THE WALL VS. PUBLIC HOMAGE[62]

For the most part, both sides of modern church-state disputes have accepted the "Jeffersonian" model of religious liberty, perhaps because they are driven by the practical need to navigate Supreme Court jurisprudence. History, however, demands a rethinking of this premise. Even assuming Jefferson's view to be a legitimate reflection of what some members of the founding generation desired for American church-state relations, his is not the only such view that should be considered. Washington's view should be accorded respect as well.

Comparisons of Washingtonian and Jeffersonian views are almost as old as the country. As early as 1796, the contrast between the two men served as campaign fodder for Adams' supporters. America's third presidential election was intense because the race was the first in which Washington was not a candidate. During this time, at least one Federalist, William Loughton Smith, wrote a pamphlet comparing Washington's views on public religion with those of Jefferson.[63] Perhaps unsurprisingly, Smith's assessment was critical of the Democratic-Republican candidate. Jefferson's bill for establishing religious freedom in Virginia had produced a "total disregard to *public worship*, an absolute *indifference to all religion whatever*," Smith alleged.[64] "Good God!," he speculated, "is this the man the *patriots* have cast their eyes on as successor to the *virtuous Washington*, who, in his farewell address, so warmly and affectionately recommends to his fellow-citizens, the *cultivation of religion*"?[65]

The comparison between the two men may have been unfair, driven primarily by the intensity of the political season. Nevertheless, the premise of the pamphlet contradicts modern deference to Jefferson's writings over Washington's. Instead, the pamphleteer implicitly proceeds from the opposite premise: *Washington* is the standard by which all future presidents should be measured—even when it comes to matters of church and state. Jefferson, in Smith's view, fell far short of the standard set by Washington.

Jefferson himself respected Washington's statements regarding American government, perhaps to a greater degree than many modern Americans realize. Indeed, in 1825, Jefferson authored a resolution that was subsequently adopted by the Board of Visitors of the University of Virginia. This resolution named Washington's Farewell Address as one of the "best guides" for understanding the "distinctive principles of the government of our State, and of that of the United States."[66] In this farewell address, it will be remembered, the nation's first president declared: "Of all the dispositions and habits which lead to political prosperity, Religion and morality are indispensable supports. . . . The mere Politician, equally with the pious man ought to respect & to cherish them."[67] If Jefferson thought that the religious principles in Washington's address were problematic, he did not take this opportunity to say so. To the contrary, his resolution included Washington's Farewell Address on a reading list for the University of Virginia law school.

Washington was a public figure for most of his adult life. Not only did he serve in a military capacity, but he also served as an elected official in the state and federal governments. His many years of public service earned him the trust and respect of the founding generation, and he was easily the most admired man of his age. In all likelihood, early Americans would be surprised to learn that the roles of the two men have been reversed in modern American society, allowing Washington's perspective to take a back seat to Jefferson's views. Such a reversal does not do justice to the first president. Washington's opinions deserve at least as much attention as those of Jefferson.

PART TWO

*Washington in
His Own Words*

ONE

๛

Commander of the
Virginia Regiment

1755–1758

Orders, August 21, 1756[1]

All the Soldiers to parade to-morrow morning at the long-roll—
They are to be marched by the Sergeants of their respective companies
to the Fort, to attend Divine Service. The officers are desired to see
that their men are clean, and dressed in the best and most Soldier-like
manner they can, before they are marched from the parade.

Orders, September 18, 1756

The men to parade to-morrow morning at beating the long roll,
with their arms and ammunition clean and in good order, and to be
marched by the Sergeants of the respective companies to the Fort, there
to remain until prayers are over.

To Governor Robert Dinwiddie, September 23, 1756

The want of a Chaplain does, I humbly conceive, reflect dishonor upon
the Regiment, as all other Officers are allowed. The Gentlemen of

the Corps are sensible of this, and did propose to support one at their private expence—But I think it would have a more graceful appearance were *he appointed* as others are.

Orders, September 25, 1756

The men are to parade at beating the long roll to-morrow morning at 10 o'clock; and be marched as usual to the Fort, to attend Divine Service. The Officers to be present at calling the roll, and see that the men do appear in the most decent manner they can.

Orders, October 2, 1756

The men to parade to-morrow morning as usual, for Divine Service.

Orders, October 9, 1756

The men to parade at 10 o'clock to-morrow morning, to attend Divine Service.

Orders, October 30, 1756

The men to parade at 12 o'clock to-morrow, on beating the Long Roll, to attend prayers.

Orders, November 6, 1756

The men to parade to-morrow at 12 o'clock, at long-roll beating, to attend prayers.

To Governor Robert Dinwiddie, November 9, 1756

As touching a Chaplain—If the Government will grant a subsistance we can readily get a person of merit to accept of the place, without giving the Commissary any trouble on that point: as it is highly necessary we shou'd be reformed from those crimes and enormities we are so universally accused of.

To Speaker John Robinson, November 9, 1756

A Chaplain for the Regiment ought to be provided; that we may at least have the show, if we are said to want the substance of Godliness! As Fort Loudon must be supported—I would represent the prejudice we suffer by the number of Tippling-houses kept in this Town; by which our men are debauched, and rendered unfit for duty, while their pay lasts: neither do the Court take any notice of them, tho' often complained of.

Orders, November 13, 1756

The Soldiers to parade to-morrow at 11 o'clock, to hear prayers: and this to be a standing order for the future.

To Governor Robert Dinwiddie, November 24, 1756

When I spoke of a Chaplain, it was in answer to yours: I had no person in view, tho' many have offered and only said, if the country would provide a Subsistance, we cou'd procure a Chaplain: without thinking there was offence in the expression—Because I was told, the commissary had endeavoured, but cou'd get no one to accept of it.

To Governor Robert Dinwiddie, April 29, 1757

It is a hardship upon the Regiment, I think, to be denied a Chaplain.

To Governor Robert Dinwiddie, June 12, 1757

We shou'd also be glad if our Chaplain was appointed, and that a Gentleman of sober, serious and religious deportment were chosen for this important Trust! Otherwise, we shou'd be better without.

To Acting Governor John Blair, April 17, 1758

The last Assembly in their *Supply Bill*, provided for a Chaplain to our Regiment; for whom I had often very unsuccessfully applied to Governor Dinwiddie. I now flatter myself, that your Honor will be pleased to appoint a sober, serious man for this Duty. Common decency, Sir, in a camp calls for the services of a Divine; and which ought not to be dispensed with, altho' the *world* should be so uncharitable as to think us void of Religion, & incapable of good Instructions.

✎

Commander-in-Chief
of the Continental Army
1775–1783

General Orders, July 4, 1775[1]

The General most earnestly requires, and expects, a due observance of those articles of war, established for the Government of the army, which forbid profane cursing, swearing & drunkeness; And in like manner requires & expects, of all Officers, and Soldiers, not engaged on actual duty, a punctual attendance on divine service, to implore the blessings of heaven upon the means used for our safety and defence.

General Orders, July 16, 1775

The Continental Congress having earnestly recommended, that "Thursday next the 20th Instant, be observed by the Inhabitants of all the english Colonies upon this Continent; as a Day of public Humiliation, Fasting and Prayer; that they may with united Hearts & Voice, unfeignedly confess their Sins before God, and supplicate the all wise and merciful disposer of events, to avert the Desolation and Calamities of an unnatural war:" The General orders, that Day to be religiously observed by the Forces under his Command, exactly in manner directed by the proclamation of the Continental Congress: It is therefore strictly enjoin'd on all Officers and Soldiers, (not upon duty) to attend Divine

Service, at the accustomed places of worship, as well in the Lines, as the Encampments and Quarters; and it is expected, that all those who go to worship, do take their Arms, Ammunition and Accoutrements, & are prepared for immediate Action if called upon. If in the Judgment of the Officers, the Works should appear to be in such forwardness as the utmost security of the Camp requires, they will command their men to abstain from all Labour upon that solemn day.

General Orders, August 5, 1775

The Church to be cleared to morrow, and the Rev'd Mr Doyles will perform Divine Service therein at ten OClock.

To Colonel Benedict Arnold, September 14, 1775

Sir,

You are intrusted with a Command of the utmost Consequence to the Interest & Liberties of America: Upon your Conduct & Courage & that of the Officers and Soldiers detached on this Expedition, not only the Success of the present Enterprize & your own Honour, but the Safety and Welfare of the Whole Continent may depend. I charge you therefore and the Officers & Soldiers under your Command as you value your own Safety and Honour, & the Favour and Esteem of your Country that you consider yourselves as marching not through an Enemies Country, but that of our Friends and Brethren, for such the Inhabitants of Canada & the Indian Nations have approved themselves in this unhappy Contest between Great Britain & America.

That you check by every Motive of Duty, and Fear of Punishment every Attempt to Plunder or insult any of the Inhabitants of Canada. Should any American Soldier be so base and infamous as to injure any Canadian or Indian in his Person or Property, I do most earnestly enjoin you to bring him to such severe & exemplary Punishment as the Enormity of the Crime may require. Should it extend to Death itself, it will not be disproportionate to its Guilt at such a Time and in such a

Cause. But I hope and trust that the brave Men who have voluntarily engaged in this Expedition will be govern'd by different Views that Order, Discipline, & Regularity of Behaviour will be as conspicuous as their Courage & Valour. I also give it in Charge to you to avoid all Disrespect or Contempt of the Religion of the Country and its Ceremonies—Prudence, Policy and a true Christian Spirit will lead us to look with Compassion upon their Errors without insulting them—While we are Contending for our own Liberty, we should be very cautious of violating the Rights of Conscience in others; ever considering that God alone is the Judge of the Hearts of Men and to him only in this Case they are answerable.

Upon the whole, Sir, I beg you to inculcate upon the Officers, the Necessity of preserving the Strictest Order during their March thro' Canada to represent to them the Shame & Disgrace and Ruin to themselves & Country if they should by their Conduct turn the Hearts of our Brethren in Canada against us. And on the other Hand the Honour and Rewards which await them, if by their Prudence, and good Behaviour they conciliate the Affections of the Canadians & Indians to the great Interests of America, & convert those favourable Dispositions they have shewn into a lasting Union and Affection.

Thus wishing you and the Officers and Soldiers under your Command all Honour, Safety and Success I remain Sir Your most Obedt Humble Servt

Instructions to Colonel Benedict Arnold, September 14, 1775

14. As the Contempt of the Religion of a Country by ridiculing any of its Ceremonies or affronting its Ministers or Votaries has ever been deeply resented—You are to be particularly careful to restrain every Officer & Soldier from such Imprudence & Folly & to punish every Instance of it—On the other Hand as far as lays in your Power you are to protect & support the free Exercise of the Religion of the Country & the undisturbed Enjoyment of the Rights of Conscience in religious Matters with your utmost Influence & Authority.

General Orders, September 17, 1775

The Revd Mr John Murray is appointed Chaplain to the Rhode-Island Regiments and is to be respected as such.

To John Hancock, President of Congress, September 30, 1775

Sir

The Revd Mr Kirtland the Bearer of this having been introduced to the Honle Congress can need no particular Recommendation from me: But as he now wishes to have the Affairs of his Mission & publick Employ put upon some suitable Footing, I cannot but intimate my Sense of the Importance of his Station, & the great Advantages which have & may result to the United Colonies from his Situation being made respectable.

All Accounts agree that much of the favourable Disposition shewn by the Indians may be ascribed to his Labour & Influence. He has accompanied a Chief of the Oneidas to this Camp, which I have endeavoured to make agreeable to him both by Civility & some small Presents. Mr. Kirkland being also in some Necessity for Money to bear his travelling Charges & other Expences I have supplied him with £32 lawful Money—I cannot but congratulate the Honourable Congress on the happy Temper of the Canadians & Indians our Accounts of which are now fully confirmed by some intercepted Letters from Officers in Canada to General Gage and others in Boston, which were found on Board the Vessel lately taken going into Boston with a Donation of Cattle & other fresh Provisions for the Ministerial Army. I have the Honour to be with great Respect & Regard Sir Your most Obedient Hbble Servt

General Orders, November 5, 1775

As the Commander in Chief has been apprized of a design form'd, for the observance of that ridiculous and childish Custom of burning the Effigy of the pope—He cannot help expressing his surprise that there should be Officers and Soldiers, in this army so void of common sense, as not to see the impropriety of such a step at this Juncture; at a Time when we are solliciting, and have really obtain'd, the friendship & alliance of the people of Canada, whom we ought to consider as Brethren embarked in the same Cause. The defence of the general Liberty of America: At such a juncture, and in such Circumstances, to be insulting their Religion, is so monstrous, as not to be suffered, or excused; indeed instead of offering the most remote insult, it is our duty to address public thanks to these our Brethren, as to them we are so much indebted for every late happy Success over the common Enemy in Canada.

General Orders, November 14, 1775

This moment a confirmation is arrived, of the glorious Success of the Continental Arms, in the Reduction, and Surrender, of the Fortress of St Johns; the Garrisons of that place and Chamblee being made Prisoners of war—The Commander in Chief is confident, the Army under his immediate direction, will shew their Gratitude to providence, for thus favouring the Cause of Freedom and America; and by their thankfulness to God, their zeal and perseverance in this righteous Cause, continue to deserve his future blessings.

General Orders, November 18, 1775

The Honorable the Legislature of this Colony having thought fit to set apart Thursday the 23rd of November Instant, as a day of public thanksgiving "to offer up our praises, and prayers, to Almighty God, the Source and Benevolent Bestower of all good; That he would be pleased graciously to continue, to smile upon our Endeavours, to restore peace, preserve our Rights, and Privileges, to the latest posterity; prosper the American Arms, preserve and strengthen the Harmony of the United Colonies, and avert the Calamities of a civil war." The General therefore commands, that day to be observed with all the Solemnity directed by the Legislative Proclamation, and all Officers, Soldiers & others, are hereby directed, with the most unfeigned Devotion, to obey the same.

General Orders, November 28, 1775

An Express last Night from General Montgomery, brings the joyful tidings of the Surrender of the City of Montreal, to the Continental Arms—The General hopes such frequent Favors from divine providence will animate every American to continue, to exert his utmost, in the defence of the Liberties of his Country, as it would now be the basest ingratitude to the Almighty, and to their Country, to shew any the least backwardness in the public cause.

General Orders, December 10, 1775

The General has great pleasure in thanking Colonel Bridge and the Officers of the 27th Regt (who from a peculiarity of circumstances, or want of vacancies, have no appointment in the new-established Army) for their polite address to him; he considers the assurances which they have given, of their determination to continue in service (if required) until the new Regiments are compleated, in a very favourable light; especially, as it is accompanied with further assurances, that the men of the 27th Regt, are consenting thereto; such a Conduct, at this important Crisis, cannot fail of giving pleasure to every well-wisher to his Country, and next to engaging for another Year, is the highest proof they can give, of their Attachment to the noble cause of Liberty, at the same time that it reflects honor upon themselves, it may under providence give Posterity reason to bless them, as the happy Instruments of their delivery from those Chains which were actually forging for them.

To Governor Jonathan Trumbull, Sr., December 15, 1775

Having heard that it is doubtful whether the Reverend Mr Leonard from your Colony, from the circumstances of his affairs, will have it in his power to continue here as a Chaplain, I cannot but express some concern, as I think his departure will be a loss—His general conduct has been exemplary and praiseworthy—In discharging the duties of his office, active and industrious—He has discovered himself a warm and steady friend to his Country, and taken great pains to animate the

Soldiery and impress them with a knowledge of the important Rights we are contending for—Upon the late desertion of the Troops he delivered a sensible and judicious discourse, holding forth the necessity of courage and bravery, and at the same time of perfect obedience and subordination to those in Command.

In justice to the merits of this Gentleman, I thought it only right to give you this testimonial of my opinion of him, and to mention him as worthy of your esteem and that of the public. I am Sir with great Regard Your most obedient Servant

To John Hancock, President of Congress, December 31, 1775

I have Long had it on my mind to mention to Congress, that frequent applications had been made to me, respecting the Chaplains pay—which is too Small to encourage men of Abilities—Some of them who have Left their flocks, are obliged to pay the parson acting for them, more than they receive—I need not point out the great utility of Gentlemen whose Lives & Conversation are unexceptionable, being employed for that Service, in this Army, there are two ways of makeing it worth the attention of Such—one is, an advancement of their pay, the other, that one Chaplain be appointed to two Regiments, this Last I think may be done without inconvenience I beg Leave to reccommend this matter to Congress whose Sentiments hereon, I Shall impatiently expect.

General Orders, January 1, 1776

This day giving commencement to the new-army, which, in every point of View is entirely Continental; The General flatters himself, that a laudable Spirit of emulation, will now take place, and pervade the whole of it; without such a Spirit, few Officers have ever arrived to any degree of Reputation, nor did any Army ever become formidable: His Excellency hopes that the Importance of the great Cause we are engaged in, will be deeply impressed upon every Man's mind, and wishes it to be considered, that an Army without Order, Regularity & Discipline, is no better than a Commission'd Mob; Let us therefore, when every thing dear and valuable to Freemen is at stake; when our unnatural Parent is threat'ning of us with destruction from every quarter, endeavour by all the Skill and Discipline in our power, to acquire that knowledge, and conduct, which is necessary in War—Our Men are brave and good; Men who with pleasure it is observed, are addicted to fewer Vices than are commonly found in Armies; but it is Subordination & Discipline (the Life and Soul of an Army) which next under providence, is to make us formidable to our enemies, honorable in ourselves, and respected in the world; and herein is to be shewn the Goodness of the Officer.

General Orders, February 26, 1776

All Officers, non-commissioned Officers and Soldiers are positively forbid playing at Cards, and other Games of Chance; At this time of public distress, men may find enough to do in the service of their God, and their Country, without abandoning themselves to vice and immorality.

General Orders, February 27, 1776

Next to the favour of divine providence, nothing is more essentially necessary to give this Army the victory of all its enemies, than Exactness of discipline, Alertness when on duty, and Cleanliness in their arms and persons; unless the Arms are kept clean, and in good firing Order, it is impossible to vanquish the enemy; and Cleanliness of the person gives health, and soldier-like appearance.

General Orders, March 6, 1776

Thursday the seventh Instant, being set apart by the Honorable the Legislature of this province, as a day of fasting, prayer, and humiliation, "to implore the Lord, and Giver of all victory, to pardon our manifold sins and wickedness's, and that it would please him to bless the Continental Arms, with his divine favour and protection"—All Officers, and Soldiers, are strictly enjoined to pay all due reverance, and attention on that day, to the sacred duties due to the Lord of hosts, for his mercies already received, and for those blessings, which our Holiness and Uprightness of life can alone encourage us to hope through his mercy to obtain.

Address to the Massachusetts General Court, April 1, 1776

Gentn

I return you my most sincere, & hearty thanks for your polite address; and feel myself called upon by every principle of Gratitude, to acknowledge the honor you have done me in this Testimonial of your approbation of my appointment to the exalted station I now fill; & what is more pleasing, of my conduct in discharging Its important duties.

When the Councils of the British Nation had formed a plan for enslaving America, and depriving her sons of their most sacred & invaluable privileges, against the clearest remonstrances of the constitution—of Justice—and of Truth; and to execute their schemes, had appealed to the sword, I esteemed It my duty to take a part in the contest, and more especially, when called thereto by the unsollicited Suffrages of the Representatives of a free people; wishing for no other reward than that arising from a conscientious discharge of the important trust, & that my services might contribute to the establishment of Freedom & peace, upon a permanent foundation; and merit the applause of my Countrymen & every virtuous Citizen.

Your professions of my attention to the civil constitution of this Colony, whilst acting in the line of my department, also demand my gratefull thanks—A regard to every provincial institution, where not incompatible with the common Interest, I hold a principle of duty, & of policy, and shall ever form a part of my conduct—had I not learned this before, the happy experience of the advantages resulting from a friendly intercourse with your Honorable body—their ready, and willing concurrence to aid and to counsel, when ever called upon in cases of difficulty and emergency, would have taught me the usefull lesson.

That the metropolis of your Colony, is now relieved from the cruel and oppressive invasion of those who were sent to erect the Standard of lawless domination, & to trample on the rights of humanity, and is again open & free for Its rightfull possessors, must give pleasure to every virtuous and Sympathetic heart—and being effected without the blood of our Soldiers, and fellow Citizens, must be ascribed to the Interposition of that providence, which has manifestly appeared in our behalf thro the whole of this important struggle, as well as to the measures pursued for bringing about the happy event.

May that being who is powerfull to save, and in whose hands is the fate of Nations, look down with an eye of tender pity & compassion upon the whole of the United Colonies—May he continue to smile upon their Councils and Arms, & crown them with success, whilst employed in the cause of virtue & of mankind—May this distressed Colony & Its Capitol, and every part of this wide, extended Continent, thro his divine favor, be restored to more than their former lustre and once happy state, and have peace, liberty & safety secured upon a solid, permanent, and lasting foundation.

To John Adams, Member of the Continental Congress, April 15, 1776

Dear Sir

This Morning your polite Letter of the 1st Instt, was delivered to me by Mr Dana. I am much obliged to you for your introduction of that Gentleman and you may rely on my shewing him every Civility in my power. I have ever thought, and am still of opinion that no terms of accomodation will be offer'd by the British Ministry, but such as cannot be accepted by America. We have nothing my Dear Sir to depend upon, but the protection of a kind Providence and Unanimity among ourselves.

I am impressed with the deepest Gratitude for the high honor intended me by the Congress. Whatever Device may be determined upon by the respectable Committee they have chosen for that purpose will be highly agreeable to me. I have the honor to be, most respectfully Sir Your obedient & affectionate humble Servant

General Orders, May 15, 1776

The Continental Congress having ordered, Friday the 17th Instant to be observed as a day of "fasting, humiliation and prayer, humbly to supplicate the mercy of Almighty God, that it would please him to pardon all our manifold sins and transgressions, and to prosper the Arms of the United Colonies, and finally, establish the peace and freedom of America, upon a solid and lasting foundation"—The General commands all officers, and soldiers, to pay strict obedience to the Orders of the Continental Congress, and by their unfeigned, and pious observance of their religious duties, incline the Lord, and Giver of Victory, to prosper our arms.

General Orders, May 16, 1776

As the Troops are to be exempt from all duties of fatigue to mor-row, the regiments are to parade on their regimental parades, and to be marched from thence a little before Ten, to hear divine service from their respective chaplains.

To John Hancock, President of Congress, June 28, 1776

I would also beg leave to mention to Congress the necessity there is of some New regulations being entered into, respecting the Chap-lains of this Army. they will remember that applications were made to increase their pay which was conceived too low for their support, & that It was proposed, If It could not be done for the whole, that the number should be lessened, and one be appointed to Two Regiments with an additional allowance. This latter expedient was adopted and while the Army continued altogether at one encampment answered well, or at least did not produce many Inconveniences; But the Army now being differently circumstanced from what It then was, part here, part at Boston and a third part detached to Canada, has Induced much confusion and disorder in this Instance; nor do I know how It is possible to remedy the evil but by affixing one to each Regiment with Salaries competent to their support. no shifting, no change from one Regiment to another can answer the purpose, and in many cases It could never be done, Tho the Regiments should consent; as where detachments are composed of unequal numbers or ordered from different posts. many more Inconveniences might be pointed out, but these It is presumed will sufficiently shew the defect of the present establishment, and the propriety of an alteration—what that alteration shall be, Congress will please to determine.

General Orders, July 2, 1776

The time is now near at hand which must probably determine, whether Americans are to be, Freemen, or Slaves; whether they are to have any property they can call their own; whether their Houses, and Farms, are to be pillaged and destroyed, and they consigned to a State of Wretchedness from which no human efforts will probably deliver them. The fate of unborn Millions will now depend, under God, on the Courage and Conduct of this army—Our cruel and unrelenting Enemy leaves us no choice but a brave resistance, or the most abject submission; this is all we can expect—We have therefore to resolve to conquer or die: Our own Country's Honor, all call upon us for a vigorous and manly exertion, and if we now shamefully fail, we shall become infamous to the whole world—Let us therefore rely upon the goodness of the Cause, and the aid of the supreme Being, in whose hands Victory is, to animate and encourage us to great and noble Actions—The Eyes of all our Countrymen are now upon us, and we shall have their blessings, and praises, if happily we are the instruments of saving them from the Tyranny meditated against them. Let us therefore animate and encourage each other, and shew the whole world, that a Freeman contending for Liberty on his own ground is superior to any slavish mercenary on earth.

General Orders, July 9, 1776

The Honorable Continental Congress having been pleased to allow a Chaplain to each Regiment, with the pay of Thirty-three Dollars and one third [per] month—The Colonels or commanding officers of each regiment are directed to procure Chaplains accordingly; persons of good Characters and exemplary lives—To see that all inferior officers and soldiers pay them a suitable respect and attend carefully upon religious exercises: The blessing and protection of Heaven are at all times necessary but especially so in times of public distress and danger—The General hopes and trusts, that every officer, and man, will endeavour so to live, and act, as becomes a Christian Soldier defending the dearest Rights and Liberties of his country.

General Orders, July 21, 1776

This glorious Example of our Troops, under the like Circumstances with us, The General hopes will animate every officer, and soldier, to imitate, and even out do them, when the enemy shall make the same attempt on us: With such a bright example before us, of what can be done by brave and spirited men, fighting in defence of their Country, we shall be loaded with a double share of Shame, and Infamy, if we do not acquit ourselves with Courage, or a determined Resolution to conquer or die: With this hope and confidence, and that this Army will have its equal share of Honour, and Success; the General most earnestly exhorts every officer, and soldier, to pay the utmost attention to his Arms, and Health; to have the former in the best order for Action, and by Cleanliness and Care, to preserve the latter; to be exact in their discipline, obedient to their Superiors and vigilant on duty: With such preparation, and a suitable Spirit, there can be no doubt, but by the blessing of Heaven, we shall repel our cruel Invaders; preserve our Country, and gain the greatest Honor.

General Orders, August 3, 1776

That the Troops may have an opportunity of attending public worship, as well as take some rest after the great fatigue they have gone through; The General in future excuses them from fatigue duty on Sundays (except at the Ship Yards, or special occasions) until further orders. The General is sorry to be informed that the foolish, and wicked practice, of profane cursing and swearing (a Vice heretofore little known in an American Army) is growing into fashion; he hopes the officers will, by example, as well as influence, endeavour to check it, and that both they, and the men will reflect, that we can have little hopes of the blessing of Heaven on our Arms, if we insult it by our impiety, and folly;

added to this, it is a vice so mean and low, without any temptation, that every man of sense, and character, detests and despises it.

To the Pennsylvania Associators, August 8, 1776

Gentlemen

I had fully resolved to have paid you a visit in New Jersey if the movements of the Enemy and some late intelligence indicating an early attack had not induced me to suspend it. Allow me therefore to address you in this Mode as fellow Citizens & fellow Soldiers, engaged in the same glorious Cause. to represent to you that the Fate of our Country depends in all human probability on the Exertion of a few Weeks. That it is of the utmost importance to keep up a respectable Force for that time, & there can be no doubt that Success will crown our Efforts, if we firmly and resolutely determine to conquer or to die. I have placed so much confidence in the spirit & Zeal of the associated Troops of Pennsylvania that I cannot persuade myself an impatience to return Home or a less honorable Motive will defeat my well grounded expectation, that they will do their Country essential Service at this critical time, when the Powers of Despotism are all combined against it, and ready to strike their most decisive Stroke.

If I could allow myself to doubt your Spirit & Perseverance I should represent the ruinous Consequences of your leaving the Service, by setting before you the discouragement it would give the Army, the confusion and Shame of our Friends, and the still more galling triumph of our Enemies—But as I have no such doubts I shall only thank you for the Spirit & Ardor you have shewn in so readily marching to meet the Enemy and am most confident you will crown it by a glorious Perseverance.

The Honor & Safety of our bleeding Country & and every other motive that can influence the brave and heroick Patriot call loudly upon us to acquit ourselves with Spirit. In short, we must now determine to be enslaved or free—If we make Freedom our Choice we must obtain it by the Blessing of Heaven on our united & vigorous Efforts.

I salute you Gentlemen most Affectionately and beg leave to remind you, that Liberty, Honor, & Safety are all at Stake—and I trust

Providence will smile on our Efforts, and establish us once more the Inhabitants of a free & happy Country. I am Gentn Your most hble Servt

General Orders, August 9, 1776

The General exhorts every man, both officer and soldier, to be prepared for action, to have his arms in the best order, not to wander from his encampment or quarters; to remember what their Country expects of them, what a few brave men have lately done in South Carolina, against a powerful Fleet & Army; to acquit themselves like men and with the blessing of heaven on so just a Cause we cannot doubt of success.

General Orders, August 12, 1776
AFTER ORDERS

The Brigadier Generals, James Clinton, Scott and Fellows, are to be under the immediate Command of Major General Putnam. The Brigadiers Mifflin and George Clinton's Brigades, to be commanded by Major General Heath. Brigadiers, Parsons & Wadworth's Brigades to be under the Command of Major General Spencer. Brigadiers Nixon and Heards Brigade to be commanded by Major General Greene—'till General James Clinton can join his Brigade at this place Col. Read is to command it. Under this disposition, formed as well as times will allow, the united efforts of the officers, of every Rank, and the Soldiers, with the smiles of providence; The General hopes to render a favourable account to his Country, and Posterity of the enemy, whenever they chuse to make the appeal to the great Arbitor of the universe.

General Orders, August 13, 1776

The Enemy's whole reinforcement is now arrived, so that an Attack must, and will soon be made; The General therefore again repeats his earnest request, that every officer, and soldier, will have his Arms and Ammunition in good Order; keep within their quarters and encampment, as much as possible; be ready for action at a moments call; and when called to it, remember that Liberty, Property, Life and Honor, are all at stake; that upon their Courage and Conduct, rest the hopes of their bleeding and insulted Country; that their Wives, Children and Parents, expect Safety from them only, and that we have every reason to expect Heaven will crown with Success, so just a cause. The enemy will endeavour to intimidate by shew and appearance, but remember how they have been repulsed, on various occasions, by a few brave Americans; Their Cause is bad; their men are conscious of it, and if opposed with firmness, and coolness, at their first onsett, with our advantage of Works, and Knowledge of the Ground; Victory is most assuredly ours.

General Orders, August 14, 1776

The General flatters himself, that every man's mind and arms are now prepared for the glorious Contest, upon which so much depends: The time is too precious, nor does the General think it necessary to spend it in exhorting his brave Countrymen and fellow Soldiers to behave like men, fighting for every thing that can be dear to Freemen—We must resolve to conquer, or die; with this resolution and the blessing of Heaven, Victory and Success certainly will attend us: There will then be a glorious Issue to this Campaign, and the General will reward, his brave Fellow Soldiers! with every Indulgence in his power.

Proclamation for the Evacuation of New York, August 17, 1776

By his Excellency, GEORGE WASHINGTON, Esquire, General, and Commander in Chief of the Army of the United States of North-America.

Whereas, a Bombardment and Attack upon the City of New-York, by our cruel, and inveterate Enemy, may be hourly expected: And as there are great Numbers of Women, Children, and infirm Persons, yet remaining in the City, whose Continuance will rather be prejudicial than advantageous to the Army, and their Persons exposed to great Danger and Hazard: I Do therefore recommend it to all such Persons, as they value their own Safety and Preservation, to remove with all Expedition, out of the said Town, at this critical Period,—trusting, that with the

Blessing of Heaven, upon the American Arms, they may soon return to it in perfect Security. And I do enjoin and require, all the Officers and Soldiers in the Army, under my Command, to forward and assist such Persons in their Compliance with this Recommendation. GIVEN, under my Hand, at Head-Quarters, New-York, August 17, 1776.

General Orders, August 23, 1776

The Enemy have now landed on Long Island, and the hour is fast approaching, on which the Honor and Success of this army, and the safety of our bleeding Country depend. Remember officers and Soldiers, that you are Freemen, fighting for the blessings of Liberty—that slavery will be your portion, and that of your posterity, if you do not acquit yourselves like men: Remember how your Courage and Spirit have been dispised, and traduced by your cruel invaders; though they have found by dear experience at Boston, Charlestown and other places, what a few brave men contending in their own land, and in the best of causes can do, against base hirelings and mercenaries—Be cool, but determined; do not fire at a distance, but wait for orders from your officers—It is the General's express orders that if any man attempt to skulk, lay down, or retreat without Orders he be instantly shot down as an example, he hopes no such Scoundrel will be found in this army; but on the contrary, every one for himself resolving to conquer, or die, and trusting to the smiles of heaven upon so just a cause, will behave with Bravery and Resolution: Those who are distinguished for their Gallantry, and good Conduct, may depend upon being honorably noticed, and suitably rewarded: And if this Army will but emulate, and imitate their brave Countrymen, in other parts of America, he has no doubt they will, by a glorious Victory, save their Country, and acquire to themselves immortal Honor.

General Orders, September 3, 1776

The General hopes the justice of the great cause in which they are engaged, the necessity and importance of defending this Country, preserving its Liberties, and warding off the destruction meditated against it, will inspire every man with Firmness and Resolution, in time of action, which is now approaching—Ever remembring that upon the blessing of Heaven, and the bravery of the men, our Country only can be saved.

General Orders, February 4, 1777

The Honorable The Governor and Assembly of New-Jersey, having directed Thursday the 6th day of this Month, to be observed as a Day of Fasting, Humiliation and Prayer, by the Inhabitants of the State—The General desires the same may be observed by the Army.

General Orders, April 12, 1777

All the troops in Morristown, except the Guards, are to attend divine worship to morrow morning at the second Bell; the officers commanding Corps, are to take especial care, that their men appear clean, and decent, and that they are to march in proper order to the place of worship.

General Orders, April 19, 1777

All the troops in town (not on duty) to attend divine service to morrow, agreeable to the orders of the 12th Instant.

To Brigadier General Samuel Holden Parsons, April 23-25, 1777

Dr Sir

I this morning received your favor of the 15th Instant. One of the Detachments you mention, I presume was that under Lieutt Colo. Butler, who arrived here the latter end of last Week. The Other has probably stopped at Pecks Kill agreable to directions lately transmitted General McDougal, till further Orders. This I was induced to direct, 'till the designs of the Enemy became unfolded and so apparent, that they cannot be misunderstood. You will not remit your exertions in forwarding the Men, as fast, as circumstances will admit. No time is to be lost; the exigency of our Affairs having been never more pressing, nor requiring more strenuous efforts than at present. The lanquor & Supineness that have taken place, but too generally, of late, are truly mortifying, and are difficult to be accounted for. All agree our claims are righteous and must be supported; Yet all, or at least, too great a part among us, withhold the means, as if providence, who has already done much for us, would continue his gracious interposition & work Miracles for our deliverance without troubling ourselves about the matter.

General Orders, May 17, 1777

All the troops in, and about Morristown, (those on duty excepted) are to attend divine service, to morrow morning.

To Colonel George Baylor, May 23, 1777

Dear Sir

By this day's post, I received your favor of the 13th Instant. I am sorry to find you have to combat so many difficulties in raising your Regiment; These However, I flatter myself, in a little time will all be surmounted by your persevering activity.

A Chaplain is part of the Establishment of a Corps of Cavalry, and I see no Objection to your having One, Unless you suppose yours will be too virtuous and Moral to require instruction. Let him be a Man of Character & good conversation, and who will influence the manners of the Corps both by precept & example. A paymaster is indispensably necessary, and as his duty will be to make up All Abstracts and receive & pay all Money due to the Corps, & also to keep & settle all transactions respecting It, he must be a person of good character and well versed in Accounts; His pay will be fifty Dollars [per] Month, and I hope you will make choice of One who will answer the description I have given. I am Dr Baylor your Affecte Hbl. servant

General Orders, May 24, 1777

All the troops in, and near Morristown, (except on duty) to attend divine service, to morrow morning.

Circular Instructions to the Brigade Commanders, May 26, 1777

Let Vice & Immorality of every kind be discouraged as much as possible in your Brigade & as a Chaplain is allowed to each Regiment see that the Men regularly attend divine Worship—Gaming of every kind is expressly forbid as the foundation of evil & the cause of many Gallant & Brave Officers Ruin. Games of exercise for amusement may not only be permitted but encouraged.

These Instructions you will consider as Obligatory unless they should Interfere with General Orders. Which you must always endeavor to have executed in your Brigade with Punctuality.

To John Hancock, President of Congress, May 29, 1777

I shall pay the strictest attention to the Resolutions transmitted me; However I am not without apprehensions, that the Regulation lately adopted, respecting Chaplains, will not answer. I recollect when One was assigned, in the course of last year, to Two Regiments, the prevailing Opinion was, and that founded on a variety of reasons, that it would not do, and the old mode of appointment was introduced again.

General Orders, May 31, 1777

It is much to be lamented, that the foolish and scandalous practice of *profane Swearing* is exceedingly prevalent in the American Army—Officers of every rank are bound to discourage it, first by their example, and then by punishing offenders—As a mean to abolish this, and every other species of immorality—Brigadiers are enjoined, to take effectual care, to have divine service duly performed in their respective brigades.

To John Hancock, President of Congress, June 8, 1777

I shall order a return to be made of the Chaplains in service, which shall be transmitted, as soon as it is obtained. At present as the Regiments are greatly dispersed, part in one place & part in Another, and accurate States of them have not been made, it will not be in my power to forward it immediately. I shall here take Occasion to mention, that

I communicated the Resolution appointing a Brigade Chaplain in the place of all Others, to the several Brigadiers: They are all of opinion, that it will be impossible for 'em to discharge the duty—that many inconveniences & much dissatisfaction will be the result, and that no Establishment appears so good in this instance as the Old One. Among many other weighty objections to the measure, It has been suggested, that it has a tendency to introduce religious disputes into the Army, which above all things should be avoided, and in many instances would compell men to a mode of Worship, which they do not profess. The Old Establishment gives every Regiment an Opportunity of having a Chaplain of their own religious Sentiments—is founded on a plan of a more generous toleration—and the choice of Chaplains to officiate, has been generally in the Regiments. Supposing One Chaplain could do the duties of a Brigade (Which supposition However is inadmissible, when we view things in practice), that being composed of Four or five—perhaps in some instances Six Regiments, there might be so many different modes of Worship. I have mentioned the Opinion of the Officers and these hints to Congress upon this subject, from a principle of duty, and because, I am well assured, it is most foreign to their wishes or intention to excite by any act, the smallest uneasiness & jealousy among the Troops.

General Orders, June 28, 1777

All Chaplains are to perform divine service to morrow, and on every succeeding Sunday, with their respective brigades and regiments, where the situation will possibly admit of it: And the commanding officers of corps are to see that they attend; themselves, with officers of all ranks, setting the example. The Commander in Chief expects an exact compliance with this order, and that it be observed in future as an invariable rule of practice—And every neglect will be considered not only a breach of orders, but a disregard to decency, virtue and religion.

General Orders, July 5, 1777

Divine service to be performed to morrow, in all the regiments which have chaplains.

General Orders, September 13, 1777

The General, with peculiar satisfaction, thanks those gallant officers and soldiers, who, on the 11th instant, bravely fought in their country and its cause—If there are any whose conduct reflects dishonour upon soldiership, and their names are not pointed out to him, he must, for the present, leave them to reflect, how much they have injured their country—how unfaithful they have proved to their fellow-soldiers; but with this exhortation, that they embrace the first opportunity which may offer, to do justice to both, and to the profession of a soldier. Altho' the event of that day, from some unfortunate circumstances, was not so favorable as could be wished, the General has the satisfaction of assuring the troops, that from every account he has been able to obtain, the enemy's loss greatly exceeded ours; and he has full confidence that in another Appeal to Heaven (with the blessing of providence, which it becomes every officer and soldier humbly to supplicate) we shall prove successful.

General Orders, September 27, 1777

As the troops will rest to day, divine service is to be performed in all the corps which have chaplains.

General Orders, October 5, 1777

The Commander in Chief returns his thanks, to the Generals and other officers and men concerned in yesterday's attack, on the enemy's left wing, for the spirit and bravery they manifested in driving the enemy from field to field—And altho' an unfortunate fog, joined with the smoke, prevented the different brigades seeing and supporting each other, or sometimes even distinguishing their fire from the enemy's—and from some other causes, which as yet cannot be well accounted for, they finally retreated—they nevertheless see that the enemy are not proof against a vigorous attack, and may be put to flight when boldly pushed—This they will remember, and assure themselves that on the next occasion, by a proper exertion of the powers which God has given them, and inspired by the cause of freedom in which they are engaged, they will be victorious—The Commander in Chief not seeing the engagement with the enemy's right wing, desires the General officers who commanded there, to thank those officers and men who behaved with becoming bravery; and such in either wing who behaved otherwise are to be reported.

General Orders, October 7, 1777

The situation of the army, frequently not admitting, of the regular performance of divine service, on Sundays, the chaplains of the army are forthwith to meet together, and agree on some method of performing it, at other times, which method they will make known to the Commander in Chief.

General Orders, October 15, 1777

The General congratulates the troops upon this signal victory, the third capital advantage, which under divine providence, we have gained in that quarter; and hopes it will prove a powerful stimulus to the army under his immediate command; at least to equal their northern brethren in brave and intrepid exertions when called thereto—The General wishes them to consider that this is the Grand American Army; and that of course great things are expected from it—'Tis the army of whose superior prowess some have boasted—What shame then and dishonour will attend us, if we suffer ourselves in every instance to be outdone? We have a force sufficient, by the favor of Heaven, to crush our foes; and nothing is wanting but a spirited, persevering exertion of it, to which, besides the motives before mentioned, duty and the love of our Country irresistably impel us. The effect of such powerful motives, no man, who possesses the spirit of a soldier can withstand, and spurred on by them, the General assures himself, that on the next occasion his troops will be completely successful.

General Orders, October 18, 1777

The General has his happiness completed relative to the successes of our northern Army. On the 14th instant, General Burgoyne, and his whole Army, surrendered themselves prisoners of war—Let every face brighten, and every heart expand with grateful Joy and praise to the supreme disposer of all events, who has granted us this signal success—The Chaplains of the army are to prepare short discourses, suited to the joyful occasion to deliver to their several corps and brigades at 5 O'clock this afternoon—immediately after which, *Thirteen* pieces of cannon are to be discharged at the park of artillery, to be followed by a *feu-de-joy* with blank cartridges, or powder, by every brigade and corps of the army, beginning on the right of the front line, and running on to the left of it, and then instantly beginning on the left of the 2nd line, and running to the right of it where it is to end—The Major General of the day will superintend and regulate the *feu-de-joy*.

General Orders, November 30, 1777

On the 25th of November instant, the Honorable Continental Congress passed the following resolve—vizt.

"Resolved. That General Washington be directed to publish in General orders, that Congress will speedily take into consideration the merits of such officers as have distinguished themselves by their intrepidity and their attention to the health and discipline of their men; and adopt such regulations as shall tend to introduce order and good discipline into the army, and to render the situation of the officers and soldiery, with respect to cloathing and other necessaries, more eligible than it has hitherto been.

"Forasmuch as it is the indispensible duty of all men, to adore the superintending providence of Almighty God; to acknowledge with gratitude their obligations to him for benefits received, and to implore such further blessings as they stand in need of: and it having pleased him, in his abundant mercy, not only to continue to us the innumerable bounties of his common providence, but also, to smile upon us in the prosecution of a just and necessary war, for the defence of our unalienable rights and liberties"—It is therefore recommended by Congress, that Thursday, the 18th day of December next be set apart for Solemn Thanksgiving and Praise, that at one time, and with one voice, the good people may express the grateful feelings of their hearts, and consecrate themselves to the service of their divine benefactor; and that, together with their sincere acknowledgements and offerings, they may join the penitent confession of their sins; and supplications for such further blessings as they stand in need of—The Chaplains will properly notice this recommendation, that the day of thanksgiving may be duly observed in the army, agreeably to the intentions of Congress.

General Orders, December 17, 1777

The Commander in Chief with the highest satisfaction expresses his thanks to the officers and soldiers for the fortitude and patience with which they have sustained the fatigues of the Campaign—Altho' in some instances we unfortunately failed, yet upon the whole Heaven hath smiled on our Arms and crowned them with signal success; and we may upon the best grounds conclude, that by a spirited continuance of the measures necessary for our defence we shall finally obtain the end of our Warfare—Independence—Liberty and Peace—These are blessings worth contending for at every hazard—But we hazard nothing. The power of America alone, duly exerted, would have nothing to dread from the force of Britain—Yet we stand not wholly upon our ground—France yields us every aid we ask, and there are reasons to believe the period is not very distant, when she will take a more active part, by declaring war against the British Crown. Every motive therefore, irresistably urges us—nay commands us, to a firm and manly perseverance in our opposition to our cruel oppressors—to slight difficulties—endure hardships, and contemn every danger . . . .

Tomorrow being the day set apart by the Honorable Congress for public Thanksgiving and Praise; and duty calling us devoutely to express our grateful acknowledgements to God for the manifold blessings he has granted us—The General directs that the army remain in it's present quarters, and that the Chaplains perform divine service with their several Corps and brigades—And earnestly exhorts, all officers and soldiers, whose absence is not indispensibly necessary, to attend with reverence the solemnities of the day.

To Israel Evans, Military Chaplain, March 13, 1778

Revd Sir

Your favor of the 17th Ulto inclosing the discourse which you delivered on the 18th of December—the day set apart for a general thanksgiving—to Genl Poors Brigade, never came to my hands till yesterday.

I have read this performance with equal attention & pleasure, and at the sametime that I admire, & feel the force of the reasoning which you have displayed through the whole, it is more especially incumbent upon me to thank you for the honorable, but partial mention you have made of my character; & to assure you, that it will ever be the first wish of my heart to aid your pious endeavours to inculcate a due sense of the dependance we ought to place in that allwise & powerful Being on whom alone our success depends; and moreover, to assure you, that with respect & regard I am Revd Sir, Yr Most Obedt Sert

General Orders, April 12, 1778

The Honorable Congress having thought proper to recommend to The United-States of America to set apart Wednesday the 22nd instant to be observed as a day of Fasting, Humiliation and Prayer, that at one time and with one voice the righteous dispensations of Providence may be acknowledged & His Goodness and Mercy towards us and our Arms supplicated and implored—The General directs that this day *also* shall be religiously observed in the Army, that no work be done thereon & that the Chaplains prepare discourses suitable to the Occasion.

General Orders, May 2, 1778

The Commander in Chief directs that divine Service be performed every sunday at 11 oClock in those Brigades to which there are Chaplains—those which have none to attend the places of worship nearest to them—It is expected that Officers of all Ranks will by their attendence set an Example to their men.

While we are zealously performing the duties of good Citizens and soldiers we certainly ought not to be inattentive to the higher duties of Religion—To the distinguished Character of Patriot, it should be our highest Glory to add the more distinguished Character of Christian—The signal Instances of providential Goodness which we have experienced and which have now almost crowned our labours with complete Success, demand from us in a peculiar manner the warmest returns of Gratitude & Piety to the Supreme Author of all Good.

General Orders, May 5, 1778
AFTER ORDERS

It having pleased the Almighty ruler of the Universe propitiously to defend the Cause of the United American-States and finally by raising us up a powerful Friend among the Princes of the Earth to establish our liberty and Independence upon lasting foundations, it becomes us to set apart a day for gratefully acknowledging the divine Goodness & celebrating the important Event which we owe to his benign Interposition.

The several Brigades are to be assembled for this Purpose at nine ôClock tomorrow morning when their Chaplains will communicate the Intelligence contain'd in the Postscript to the Pennsylvania Gazette of the 2nd instant and offer up a thanksgiving and deliver a discourse suitable to the Occasion—At half after ten ôClock a Cannon will be fired, which is to be a signal for the men to be under Arms—The Brigade Inspectors will then inspect their Dress and Arms, form the Battalions according to instructions given them and announce to the Commanding Officers of Brigades that the Battalions are formed: The Brigadiers or Commandants will then appoint the Field Officers to command the Battalions, after which each Battalion will be ordered to load & ground their Arms.

General Orders, June 30, 1778

The Men are to wash themselves this afternoon & appear as clean and decent as possible.

Seven ôClock this evening is appointed that We may publickly unite in thanksgivings to the supreme Disposer of human Events for the Victory which was obtained on sunday over the Flower of the British Troops.

General Orders, December 22, 1778[2]

The Honorable The Congress having been pleased by their Proc-lamation of the 21st. of November last to appoint Wednesday the 30th. instant as a day of Thanksgiving and Praise for the great and numer-ous Providential Mercies experienced by the People of These States in the course of the present War, the same is to be religiously observed throughout the Army in the manner therein directed, and the different Chaplains will prepare discourses suited to the Occasion.

General Orders, April 12, 1779

The Honorable the Congress having recommended it to the United States to set apart Thursday the 6th. day of May next to be observed as a day of fasting, humiliation and prayer, to acknowledge the gracious interpositions of *Providence*; to deprecate deserved punishment for our Sins and Ingratitude, to unitedly implore the Protection of Heaven; Success to our Arms and the Arms of our Ally: The Commander in Chief enjoins a religious observance of said day and directs the Chap-lains to prepare discourses proper for the occasion; strictly forbidding all recreations and unnecessary labor.

Speech to the Delaware Chiefs, May 12, 1779

Brothers: I am happy to see you here. I am glad the long Journey you have made, has done you no harm; and that you are in good health: I am glad also you left All our friends of the Delaware Nation well.

Brothers: I have read your paper. The things you have said are weighty things, and I have considered them well. The Delaware Nation have shown their good will to the United States. They have done wisely and I hope they will never repent. I rejoice in the new assurances you give of their friendship. The things you now offer to do to brighten the chain, prove your sincerity. I am sure Congress will run to meet you, and will do every thing in their power to make the friendship between the people of these States, and their Brethren of the Delaware nation, last forever.

Brothers: I am a Warrior. My words are few and plain; but I will make good what I say. 'Tis my business to destroy all the Enemies of these States and to protect their friends. You have seen how we have withstood the English for four years; and how their great Armies have dwindled away and come to very little; and how what remains of them in this part of our great Country, are glad to stay upon Two or three little Islands, where the Waters and their Ships hinder us from going to destroy them. The English, Brothers, are a boasting people. They talk of doing a great deal; but they do very little. They fly away on their Ships from one part of our Country to an other; but as soon as our Warriors get together they leave it and go to some other part. They took Boston and Philadelphia, two of our greatest Towns; but when they saw our Warriors in a great body ready to fall upon them, they were forced to leave them.

Brothers: We have till lately fought the English all alone. Now the Great King of France is become our Good Brother and Ally. He has taken up the Hatchet with us, and we have sworn never to bury it, till we have punished the English and made them sorry for All the wicked things they had in their Hearts to do against these States. And there are other Great Kings and Nations on the other side of the big Waters, who love us and wish us well, and will not suffer the English to hurt us.

Brothers: Listen well to what I tell you and let it sink deep into your Hearts. We love our friends, and will be faithful to them, as long as they will be faithful to us. We are sure our Good brothers the Delawares will always be so. But we have sworn to take vengeance on our Enemies, and on false friends. The other day, a handful of our young men destroyed the settlement of the Onondagas. They burnt down all their Houses, destroyed their grain and Horses and Cattle, took their Arms away, killed several of their Warriors and brought off many prisoners and obliged the rest to fly into the woods. This is but the beginning of the troubles which those Nations, who have taken up the Hatchet against us, will feel.

Brothers: I am sorry to hear that you have suffered for want of necessaries, or that any of our people have not dealt justly by you. But as you are going to Congress, which is the great Council of the Nation and hold all things in their hands, I shall say nothing about the supplies you ask. I hope you will receive satisfaction from them. I assure you, I will do every thing in my power to prevent your receiving any further injuries, and will give the strictest orders for this purpose. I will severely punish any that shall break them.

Brothers: I am glad you have brought three of the Children of your principal Chiefs to be educated with us. I am sure Congress will open the Arms of love to them, and will look upon them as their own Children, and will have them educated accordingly. This is a great mark of your confidence and of your desire to preserve the friendship between the Two Nations to the end of time, and to become One people with your Brethren of the United States. My ears hear with pleasure the other matters you mention. Congress will be glad to hear them too. You do well to wish to learn our arts and ways of life, and above all, the religion of Jesus Christ. These will make you a greater and happier people than you are. Congress will do every thing they can to assist you in this wise intention; and to tie the knot of friendship and union so fast, that nothing shall ever be able to loose it.

Brothers: There are some matters about which I do not open my Lips, because they belong to Congress, and not to us warriors; you are going to them, they will tell you all you wish to know.

Brothers: When you have seen all you want to see, I will then wish you a good Journey to Philadelphia. I hope you may find there every thing your hearts can wish, that when you return home you may be able to tell your Nation good things of us. And I pray God he may make your Nation wise and Strong, that they may always see their own true interest and have courage to walk in the right path; and that they never may be deceived by lies to do any thing against the people of these States, who are their Brothers and ought always to be one people with them.

To the Dutch Reformed Church at Raritan, June 2, 1779

Gentlemen: To meet the approbation of good men cannot but be agreeable. Your affectionate expressions make it still more so.

In quartering an army, and in supplying its wants, distress and inconvenience will often occur to the citizen. I feel myself happy in a consciousness that these have been strictly limited by necessity, and in your opinion of my attention to the rights of my fellow citizens.

I thank you gentlemen sincerely for the sense you entertain of the conduct of the army; and for the interest you take in my welfare. I trust the goodness of the cause and the exertions of the people under divine protection will give us that honourable peace for which we are contending. Suffer me Gentlemen to wish the reformed church at Raritan a long continuance of its present Minister and consistory and all the blessings which flow from piety and religion. I am, &c.

General Orders, July 29, 1779

Many and pointed orders have been issued against that unmeaning and abominable custom of *Swearing*, not withstanding which, with much regret the General observes that it prevails, *if possible*, more than ever; His feelings are continually wounded by the Oaths and Imprecations of the soldiers whenever he is in hearing of them.

The Name of That Being, from whose bountiful goodness we are permitted to exist and enjoy the comforts of life is incessantly imprecated and prophaned in a manner as wanton as it is shocking. For the sake therefore of religion, decency and order the General hopes and trusts that officers of every rank will use their influence and authority to check a vice, which is as unprofitable as it is wicked and shameful.

If officers would make it an invariable rule to reprimand, and if that does not do punish soldiers for offences of this kind it could not fail of having the desired effect.

To Major General Arthur St. Clair, April 2, 1780

Mr. Beatty shall have my instructions to interchange a certificate with Mr. Loring assenting to the proposal that chaplains belonging to either army, when taken are not to be considered as prisoners of war but immediately released.

General Orders, April 6, 1780

The Honorable the Congress having been pleased by their proclamation of the 11th. of last month to appoint wednesday the 22nd.

instant to be set apart and observed as a day of Fasting Humiliation and Prayer for certain special purposes therein mentioned, and recommended that there should be no labor or recreations on that day; The same is to be observed accordingly thro'out the Army and the different Chaplins will prepare discourses suited to the several objects enjoined by the said Proclamation.

To the Inhabitants of Providence, March 14, 1781

Gentn: I am happy in the oppertunity which your address affords me of testifying to you how deeply I am penetrated with those demonstrations of attachment which I have experienced from the Inhabitants of this Town. The confidence and affection of his fellow Citizens is the most valuable and agreeable reward a Citizen can receive. Next to the happiness of my Country, this is the most powerful inducement I can have to exert my self in its Service. Conscious of a sincere desire to promote that great object, however short of my wishes the success of my endeavours may fall I console myself with a perswasion that the goodness of my intentions in some measure justifies your approbation.

The determination you are pleased to express of making every effort for giving vigour to our military operations is consonant with the Spirit that has uniformly actuated this State. It is by this disposition alone we can hope, under the protection of Heaven, to secure the important blessings for which we contend.

With sincere gratitude for your sentiments and wishes towards me, I beg you to accept the assurances of that perfect esteem and regard with which I have the honor etc.

To Reverend Jacob Johnson, March 23, 1781

Sir: Your Memorial of the 24th of Feby addressed to me, was lodged at Head Quarters, while I was absent on a Journey to Rhode Island, from which place I have but lately arrived.

In answer to your request to be appointed Chaplain of the Garrison at Wyoming I have to observe; that there is no provision made by Congress for such an establishment; without which, I should not be at liberty to make any appointment of the kind, however necessary or expedient (in my opinion) or however I might be disposed to give every species of countenance and encouragement to the cultivation of Virtue, Morality and Religion. I am etc.

General Orders, April 27, 1781

Congress having been pleased to set apart and appoint Thursday the 3d. of May next for fasting humiliation and prayer, the General enjoins a strict obedience to it in the Army and calls upon the Chaplains thereof to prepare discourses suitable to the occasion.

All duties of Fatigue are to cease on that day.

General Orders, October 20, 1781
AFTER ORDERS

Divine Service is to be performed tomorrow in the several Brigades or Divisions.

The Commander in Chief earnestly recommends that the troops not on duty should universally attend with that seriousness of Deportment and gratitude of Heart which the recognition of such reiterated and astonishing interpositions of Providence demand of us.

To Thomas McKean, Member of the Continental Congress, November 15, 1781

Sir: I have the Honor to acknowledge the Receipt of your Favor. of the 31st. ulto. covering the Resolutions of Congress of 29th. and a Proclamation for a Day of public Prayer and Thanksgiving; And have to thank you Sir! most sincerely for the very polite and affectionate Manner in which these Inclosures have been conveyed. The Success of the Combined Arms against our Enemies at York and Gloucester, as it affects the Welfare and Independence of the United States, I viewed as a most fortunate Event. In performing my Part towards its Accomplishment, I consider myself to have done only my Duty and in the Execution of that I ever feel myself happy. And at the same Time, as it agurs well to our Cause, I take a particular Pleasure in acknowledging, that the interposing Hand of Heaven in the various Instances of our extensive Preparations for this Operation, has been most conspicuous and remarkable.

After the Receipt of your Favor I received Official Information, thro' the Secretary of Congress, of the new Choice of their President. While I congratulate you Sir on a Release from the Fatigues and Trouble of so arduous and important a Task: I beg you to accept my sincere Thanks for the Pleasure and Satisfaction which I have received in the Correspondence with which you have honored me, and the many Interesting Communications of Intelligence with which you have favored me. I am etc.

General Orders, April 22, 1782

The United States in Congress Assembled having been pleased by their Proclamation, dated the 19th March last, to appoint Thursday next the 25th. Instant to be set apart as a day of Fasting, humiliation and Prayr for certain special purposes therein Mentioned: the same is to be Observed accordingly throughout the Army, and the different Chaplains will prepare Discourses Suited to the Several Objects enjoin'd by the said Proclamation.

To the Reformed Dutch Church at Albany, June 28, 1782

Gentlemen: I am extremely happy in this opportunity of blending my public duty with my private satisfaction, by paying a due attention to the Frontiers and advanced Posts of this State, and at the same time visiting this antient and respectable City of Albany.

While I consider the approbation of the Wise and the Virtuous as the highest possible reward for my services, I beg you will be assured, Gentlemen, that I now experience the most sensible pleasure from the favorable sentiments you are pleased to express of my Conduct.

Your benevolent wishes and fervent prayers for my personal wellfare and felicity, demand all my gratitude. May the preservation of your civil and religious Liberties still be the care of an indulgent Providence; and may the rapid increase and universal extension of knowledge virtue and true Religion be the consequence of a speedy and honorable Peace. I am etc.

To the Magistrates and Military Officers of Schenectady, June 30, 1782

Gentlemen: I request you to accept my warmest thanks for your affectionate address.

In a cause so just and righteous as ours, we have every reason to hope the divine Providence will still continue to crown our Arms with success, and finally compel our Enemies to grant us that Peace upon equitable terms, which we so ardently desire.

May you, and the good People of this Town, in the mean time be protected from every insidious or open foe, and may the complicated blessings of Peace soon reward your arduous Struggles for the establishment of the freedom and Independence of our common country.

To the Reformed Dutch Church of Schenectady, June 30, 1782

Gentlemen: I sincerely thank you for your Congratulations on my arrival in this place.

Whilst I join in adoring that Supreme being to whom alone can be attrebuted the signal successes of our Arms I can not but express gratitude to you, for so distinguished a testemony of your regard

May the same providence that has hitherto in so remarkable a manner Envinced the Justice of our Cause, lead us to a speedy and honorable peace; and may its attendant Blessings soon restore this once flourishing Town to its former Prosperity.

To Benjamin Lincoln, Secretary at War, August 16, 1782

I shall have no objection to the exchange of the foreign Officers you mention in your favor of the 10th Inst. provided it does not contravene the spirit of the Resolution of Congress which directs Exchanges to be made according to priority of capture. Nor for my own part, shall I make any difficulty in acceeding to a late proposal of Sir Guy Carleton, for considering Chaplains, Surgeons, and Hospital Officers in future as not proper Subjects to be retained as prisoners of War, unless any of them should hold Commissions in the Line; indeed, I do not see that any very ill consequences would ensue from liberating those already in our possession. I submit therefore this matter to your discretion, and have the honor etc.

General Orders, November 14, 1782

Congress having been pleased to set a part Thursday the 28th. instant as a day of Solemn thanksgiving to god for all his Mercies, The General desires it may be most religiously observed by the army; and that the Chaplains will prepare discourses suitable to the occasion.

To the Reformed Protestant Dutch Church in Kingston, November 16, 1782

Gentlemen: I am happy in receiving this public mark of the esteem of the Minister, Elders and Deacons of the Reformed Protestant Dutch Church in Kingston.

Convinced that our Religious Liberties were as essential as our Civil, my endeavours have never been wanting to encourage and promote the one, while I have been contending for the other; and I am highly flattered by finding that my efforts have met the approbation of so respectable a body.

In return for your kind concern for my temporal and eternal happiness, permit me to assure you that my wishes are reciprocal; and that you may be enabled to hand down your Religion pure and undefiled to a Posterity worthy of their Ancesters is the fervent prayer of Gentn. Yrs. &c.

General Orders, February 15, 1783

The New building being so far finished as to admit the troops to attend public worship therein after tomorrow, it is directed that divine Service should be performed there every Sunday by the several Chaplains of the New Windsor Cantonment, in rotation and in order that the different brigades may have an oppertunity of attending at different hours in the same day (when ever the weather and other circumstances will permit which the Brigadiers and Commandants of brigades must determine) the General recommends that the Chaplains should in the first place consult the Commanding officers of their Brigades to know what hour will be most convenient and agreeable for attendance that they will then settle the duty among themselves and report the result to the Brigadiers and Commandants of Brigades who are desired to give notice in their orders and to afford every aid and assistance in their power for the promotion of that public Homage and adoration which are due to the supreme being, who has through his infinite goodness brought our public Calamities and dangers (in all humane probability) very near to a happy conclusion.

The General has been surprised to find in Winter Qrs. that the Chaplains have frequently been almost all absent, at the same time, under an idea their presence could not be of any utility at that season; he thinks it is proper, he should be allowed to judge of that matter himself, and therefore in future no furloughs will be granted to Chaplains except in consequence of permission from Head quarters, and any who may be now absent without such permission are to be ordered by the Commanding officers of their Brigades to join immediately, after which not more than one third of the whole number will be indulged with leave of absence at a time. They are requested to agree among themselves upon the time and length of their furloughs before any application shall be made to Head quarters on the subject.

The Commander in Chief also desires and expects the Chaplains in addition to their public functions will in turn constantly attend the Hospitals and visit the sick, and while they are thus publickly and privately engaged in performing the sacred duties of their office they may depend upon his utmost encouragement and support on all occasions, and that they will be considered in a very respectable point of light by the whole Army.

General Orders, March 22, 1783

In justice to the zeal and ability of the Chaplains, as well as to his own feelings, the Commander in chief thinks it a duty to declare the regularity and decorum with which divine service is now performed every sunday, will reflect great credit on the army in general, tend to improve the morals, and at the same time, to increase the happiness of the soldiery, and must afford the most pure and rational entertainment for every serious and well disposed mind.

No fatigue except on extra occasions, nor General review or inspections to be permitted on the Sabbath day.

General Orders, April 18, 1783

The Commander in Chief orders the Cessation of Hostilities between the United States of America and the King of Great Britain to be publickly proclaimed tomorrow at 12 o'clock at the Newbuilding, and that the Proclamation which will be communicated herewith, be read tomorrow evening at the head of every regiment and corps of the army. After which the Chaplains with the several Brigades will render thanks to almighty God for all his mercies, particularly for his over ruling the wrath of man to his own glory, and causing the rage of war to cease amongst the nations.

Although the proclamation before alluded to, extends only to the prohibition of hostilities and not to the annunciation of a general peace, yet it must afford the most rational and sincere satisfaction to every benevolent mind, as it puts a period to a long and doubtful contest, stops the effusion of human blood, opens the prospect to a more splendid scene, and like another morning star, promises the approach of a brighter day than hath hitherto illuminated the Western Hemisphere; on such a happy day, a day which is the harbinger of Peace, a day which compleats the eighth year of the war, it would be ingratitude not to rejoice! it would be insensibility not to participate in the general felicity.

The Commander in Chief far from endeavouring to stifle the feelings of Joy in his own bosom, offers his most cordial Congratulations on the occasion to all the Officers of every denomination, to all the Troops of the United States in General, and in particular to those gallant and persevering men who had resolved to defend the rights of their invaded country so long as the war should continue. For these are the men who ought to be considered as the pride and boast of the American Army;

And, who crowned with well earned laurels, may soon withdraw from the field of Glory, to the more tranquil walks of civil life.

While the General recollects the almost infinite variety of Scenes thro which we have passed, with a mixture of pleasure, astonishment, and gratitude; While he contemplates the prospects before us with rapture; he can not help wishing that all the brave men (of whatever condition they may be) who have shared in the toils and dangers of effecting this glorious revolution, of rescuing Millions from the hand of oppression, and of laying the foundation of a great Empire, might be impressed with a proper idea of the dignifyed part they have been called to act (under the Smiles of providence) on the stage of human affairs: for, happy, thrice happy shall they be pronounced hereafter, who have contributed any thing, who have performed the meanest office in erecting this steubendous *fabrick* of *Freedom* and *Empire* on the broad basis of Indipendency; who have assisted in protecting the rights of humane nature and establishing an Asylum for the poor and oppressed of all nations and religions. The glorius task for which we first fleu to Arms being thus accomplished, the liberties of our Country being fully acknowledged, and firmly secured by the smiles of heaven, on the purity of our cause, and the honest exertions of a feeble people (determined to be free) against a powerful Nation (disposed to oppress them) and the Character of those who have persevered, through every extremity of hardship; suffering and danger being immortalized by the illustrious appellation of the *patriot Army*: Nothing now remains but for the actors of this mighty Scene to preserve a perfect, unvarying, consistency of character through the very last act; to close the Drama with applause; and to retire from the Military Theatre with the same approbation of Angells and men which have crowned all their former vertuous Actions. For this purpose no disorder or licentiousness must be tolerated, every considerate and well disposed soldier must remember it will be absolutely necessary to wait with patience untill peace shall be declared or Congress shall be enabled to take proper measures for the security of the public stores &ca.; as soon as these Arrangements shall be made the General is confident there will be no delay in discharging with every mark of distinction and honor all the men enlisted for the war who will then have faithfully performed their engagements with the public. The General has already interested himself in their behalf; and he thinks he need not repeat the assurances of his disposition to be useful to them on the present, and every other proper occasion. In the mean time he is determined that no Military neglects or excesses shall go unpunished while he retains the command of the Army.

Circular to the States, June 8, 1783

Sir: The great object for which I had the honor to hold an appointment in the Service of my Country, being accomplished, I am now preparing to resign it into the hands of Congress, and to return to that domestic retirement, which, it is well known, I left with the greatest reluctance, a Retirement, for which I have never ceased to sigh through a long and painful absence, and in which (remote from the noise and trouble of the World) I meditate to pass the remainder of life in a state of undisturbed repose; But before I carry this resolution into effect, I think it a duty incumbent on me, to make this my last official communication, to congratulate you on the glorious events which Heaven has been pleased to produce in our favor, to offer my sentiments respecting some important subjects, which appear to me, to be intimately connected with the tranquility of the United States, to take my leave of your Excellency as a public Character, and to give my final blessing to that Country, in whose service I have spent the prime of my life, for whose sake I have consumed so many anxious days and watchfull nights, and whose happiness being extremely dear to me, will always constitute no inconsiderable part of my own.

Impressed with the liveliest sensibility on this pleasing occasion, I will claim the indulgence of dilating the more copiously on the subjects of our mutual felicitation. When we consider the magnitude of the prize we contended for, the doubtful nature of the contest, and the favorable manner in which it has terminated, we shall find the greatest possible reason for gratitude and rejoicing; this is a theme that will afford infinite delight to every benevolent and liberal mind, whether the event in contemplation, be considered as the source of present enjoyment or the parent of future happiness; and we shall have equal occasion to felicitate ourselves on the lot which Providence has assigned us, whether we view it in a natural, a political or moral point of light.

The Citizens of America, placed in the most enviable condition, as the sole Lords and Proprietors of a vast Tract of Continent, comprehending all the various soils and climates of the World, and abounding with all the necessaries and conveniencies of life, are now by the late satisfactory pacification, acknowledged to be possessed of absolute freedom and Independency; They are, from this period, to be considered as the Actors on a most conspicuous Theatre, which seems to be peculiarly designated by Providence for the display of human greatness and felicity; Here, they are not only surrounded with every thing which can contribute to the completion of private and domestic enjoyment, but Heaven has crowned all its other blessings, by giving a fairer oppertunity for political happiness, than any other Nation has ever been favored with. Nothing can illustrate these observations more forcibly, than a recollection of the happy conjuncture of times and circumstances, under which our Republic assumed its rank among the Nations; The foundation of our Empire was not laid in the gloomy age of Ignorance and Superstition, but at an Epocha when the rights of mankind were better understood and more clearly defined, than at any former period, the researches of the human mind, after social happiness, have been carried to a great extent, the Treasures of knowledge, acquired by the labours of Philosophers, Sages and Legislatures, through a long succession of years, are laid open for our use, and their collected wisdom may be happily applied in the Establishment of our forms of Government; the free cultivation of Letters, the unbounded extension of Commerce, the progressive refinement of Manners, the growing liberality of sentiment, and above all, the pure and benign light of Revelation, have had a meliorating influence on mankind and increased the blessings of Society. At this auspicious period, the United States came into existence as a Nation, and if their Citizens should not be completely free and happy, the fault will be intirely their own.

Such is our situation, and such are our prospects: but notwithstanding the cup of blessing is thus reached out to us, notwithstanding happiness is ours, if we have a disposition to seize the occasion and make it our own; yet, it appears to me there is an option still left to the United States of America, that it is in their choice, and depends upon their conduct, whether they will be respectable and prosperous, or contemptable and miserable as a Nation; This is the time of their political probation, this is the moment when the eyes of the whole World are turned upon them, this is the moment to establish or ruin their national Character forever, this is the favorable moment to give such a tone to our Federal Government, as will enable it to answer the ends of its institution, or this may be the ill-fated moment for relaxing the powers of the Union, annihilating the cement of the Confederation, and exposing us to become the sport of European politics, which may play one State against another to prevent their growing importance, and to serve their own interested purposes. For, according to the system of Policy the States shall adopt at this moment, they will stand or fall, and by their confirmation or lapse, it is yet to be decided, whether the Revolution must ultimately be considered as a blessing or a curse: a blessing or a curse, not to the present age alone, for with our fate will the destiny of unborn Millions be involved.

With this conviction of the importance of the present Crisis, silence in me would be a crime; I will therefore speak to your Excellency, the language of freedom and of sincerity, without disguise; I am aware, however, that those who differ from me in political sentiment, may perhaps remark, I am stepping out of the proper line of my duty, and they may possibly ascribe to arrogance or ostentation, what I know is alone the result of the purest intention, but the rectitude of my own heart, which disdains such unworthy motives, the part I have hitherto acted in life, the determination I have formed, of not taking any share in public business hereafter, the ardent desire I feel, and shall continue to manifest, of quietly enjoying in private life, after all the toils of War, the benefits of a wise and liberal Government, will, I flatter myself, sooner or later convince my Countrymen, that I could have no sinister views in delivering with so little reserve, the opinions contained in this Address.

There are four things, which I humbly conceive, are essential to the well being, I may even venture to say, to the existence of the United States as an Independent Power:

1st. An indissoluble Union of the States under one Federal Head.
2dly. A Sacred regard to Public Justice.

3dly. The adoption of a proper Peace Establishment, and

4thly. The prevalence of that pacific and friendly Disposition, among the People of the United States, which will induce them to forget their local prejudices and policies, to make those mutual concessions which are requisite to the general prosperity, and in some instances, to sacrifice their individual advantages to the interest of the Community.

These are the Pillars on which the glorious Fabrick of our Independency and National Character must be supported; Liberty is the Basis, and whoever would dare to sap the foundation, or overturn the Structure, under whatever specious pretexts he may attempt it, will merit the bitterest execration, and the severest punishment which can be inflicted by his injured Country.

On the three first Articles I will make a few observations, leaving the last to the good sense and serious consideration of those immediately concerned.

Under the first head, altho' it may not be necessary or proper for me in this place to enter into a particular disquisition of the principles of the Union, and to take up the great question which has been frequently agitated, whether it be expedient and requisite for the States to delegate a larger proportion of Power to Congress, or not, Yet it will be a part of my duty, and that of every true Patriot, to assert without reserve, and to insist upon the following positions, That unless the States will suffer Congress to exercise those prerogatives, they are undoubtedly invested with by the Constitution, every thing must very rapidly tend to Anarchy and confusion, That it is indispensable to the happiness of the individual States, that there should be lodged somewhere, a Supreme Power to regulate and govern the general concerns of the Confederated Republic, without which the Union cannot be of long duration. That there must be a faithfull and pointed compliance on the part of every State, with the late proposals and demands of Congress, or the most fatal consequences will ensue, That whatever measures have a tendency to dissolve the Union, or contribute to violate or lessen the Sovereign Authority, ought to be considered as hostile to the Liberty and Independency of America, and the Authors of them treated accordingly, and lastly, that unless we can be enabled by the concurrence of the States, to participate of the fruits of the Revolution, and enjoy the essential benefits of Civil Society, under a form of Government so free and uncorrupted, so happily guarded against the danger of oppression, as has been devised and adopted by the Articles of Confederation, it will be a subject of regret, that so much blood and treasure have been lavished for no purpose, that so many sufferings have been encountered without a compensation, and that so many sacrifices have been made in vain. Many other considerations might here be adduced to prove, that without an entire conformity to the Spirit of the Union, we cannot exist as an Independent Power; it will be sufficient for my purpose to mention but one or two which seem to me of the greatest importance. It is only in our united Character as an Empire, that our Independence is acknowledged, that our power can be regarded, or our Credit supported among Foreign Nations. The Treaties of the European Powers with the United States of America, will have no validity on a dissolution of the Union. We shall be left nearly in a state of Nature, or we may find by our own unhappy experience, that there is a natural and necessary progression, from the extreme of anarchy to the extreme of Tyranny; and that arbitrary power is most easily established on the ruins of Liberty abused to licentiousness.

As to the second Article, which respects the performance of Public Justice, Congress have, in their late Address to the United States, almost exhausted the subject, they have explained their Ideas so fully, and have enforced the obligations the States are under, to render compleat justice to all the Public Creditors, with so much dignity and energy, that in my opinion, no real friend to the honor and Independency of America, can hesitate a single moment respecting the propriety of complying with the just and honorable measures proposed; if their Arguments do not produce conviction, I know of nothing that will have greater influence; especially when we recollect that the System referred to, being the result of the collected Wisdom of the Continent, must be esteemed, if not perfect, certainly the least objectionable of any that could be devised; and that if it shall not be carried into immediate execution, a National Bankruptcy, with all its deplorable consequences will take place, before any different Plan can possibly be proposed and adopted; So pressing are the present circumstances! and such is the alternative now offered to the States!

The ability of the Country to discharge the debts which have been incurred in its defence, is not to be doubted, an inclination, I flatter myself, will not be wanting, the path of our duty is plain before us, honesty will be found on every experiment, to be the best and only true policy, let us then as a Nation be just, let us fulfil the public Contracts, which Congress had undoubtedly a right to make for the purpose of carrying on the War, with the same good faith we suppose ourselves bound to perform our private engagements; in the mean time, let an attention to the chearfull performance of their proper business, as Individuals, and as members of Society, be earnestly inculcated on the Citizens of America, that will they strengthen the hands of Government, and be happy under its protection: every one will reap the fruit of his labours, every one will enjoy his own acquisitions without molestation and without danger.

In this state of absolute freedom and perfect security, who will grudge to yield a very little of his property to support the common interest of Society, and insure the protection of Government? Who does not remember, the frequent declarations, at the commencement of the War, that we should be compleatly satisfied, if at the expence of one half, we could defend the remainder of our possessions? Where is the Man to be found, who wishes to remain indebted, for the defence of his own person and property, to the exertions, the bravery, and the blood of others, without making one generous effort to repay the debt of honor and of gratitude? In what part of the Continent shall we find any Man, or body of Men, who would not blush to stand up and propose measures, purposely calculated to rob the Soldier of his Stipend, and the Public Creditor of his due? and were it possible that such a flagrant instance of Injustice could ever happen, would it not excite the general indignation, and tend to bring down, upon the Authors of such measures, the aggravated vengeance of Heaven? If after all, a spirit of dis-union or a temper of obstinacy and perverseness, should manifest itself in any of the States, if such an ungracious disposition should attempt to frustrate all the happy effects that might be expected to flow from the Union, if there should be a refusal to comply with the requisitions for Funds to discharge the annual interest of the public debts, and if that refusal should revive again all those jealousies and produce all those evils, which are now happily removed, Congress, who have in all their Transaction shewn a great degree of magnanimity and justice, will stand justified in the sight of God and Man, and the State alone which puts itself in opposition to the aggregate Wisdom of the Continent, and follows such mistaken and pernicious Councils, will be responsible for all the consequences.

For my own part, conscious of having acted while a Servant of the Public, in the manner I conceived best suited to promote the real interests of my Country; having in consequence of my fixed belief in some measure pledged myself to the Army, that their Country would finally do them compleat and ample Justice; and not wishing to conceal any instance of my official conduct from the eyes of the World, I have thought proper to transmit to your Excellency the inclosed collection of Papers, relative to the half pay and commutation granted by Congress to the Officers of the Army; From these communications, my decided sentiment will be clearly comprehended, together with the conclusive reasons which induced me, at an early period, to recommend the adoption of the measure, in the most earnest and serious manner. As the proceedings of Congress, the Army, and myself are open to all, and contain in my opinion, sufficient information to remove the prejudices and errors which may have been entertained by any; I think it unnecessary to say any thing more, than just to observe, that the Resolutions of Congress, now alluded to, are undoubtedly as absolutely binding upon the United States, as the most solemn Acts of Confederation or Legislation. As to the Idea, which I am informed has in some instances prevailed, that the half pay and commutation are to be regarded merely in the odious light of a Pension, it ought to be exploded forever; that Provision, should be viewed as it really was, a reasonable compensation offered by Congress, at a time when they had nothing else to give, to the Officers of the Army, for services then to be performed. It was the only means to prevent a total dereliction of the Service, It was a part of their hire, I may be allowed to say, it was the price of their blood and of your Independency, it is therefore more than a common debt, it is a debt of honour, it can never be considered as a Pension or gratuity, nor be cancelled until it is fairly discharged.

With regard to a distinction between Officers and Soldiers, it is sufficient that the uniform experience of every Nation of the World, combined with our own, proves the utility and propriety of the discrimination. Rewards in proportion to the aids the public derives from them, are unquestionably due to all its Servants; In some Lines, the Soldiers have perhaps generally had as ample a compensation for their Services, by the large Bounties which have been paid to them, as their Officers will receive in the proposed Commutation, in others, if besides the donation of Lands, the payment of Arrearages of Cloathing and Wages (in which Articles all the component parts of the Army must be put upon the same footing) we take into the estimate, the Bounties many of the Soldiers have received and the gratuity of one Year's full pay, which is promised to all, possibly their situation (every circumstance being duly considered) will not be deemed less eligible than that of the Officers. Should a farther reward, however, be judged equitable, I will venture to assert, no one will enjoy greater satisfaction than myself, on seeing an exemption from Taxes for a limited time, (which has been petitioned for in some instances) or any other adequate immunity or compensation, granted to the brave defenders of their Country's Cause; but neither the adoption or rejection of this proposition will in any manner affect, much less militate against, the Act of Congress, by which they have offered five years full pay, in lieu of the half pay for life, which had been before promised to the Officers of the Army.

Before I conclude the subject of public justice, I cannot omit to mention the obligations this Country is under, to that meritorious Class of veteran Non-commissioned Officers and Privates, who have been discharged for inability, in consequence of the Resolution of Congress of the 23d of April 1782, on an annual pension for life, their peculiar sufferings, their singular merits and claims to that provision need only be known, to interest all the feelings of humanity in their behalf: nothing but a punctual payment of their annual allowance can rescue them from the most complicated misery, and nothing could be a more melancholy and distressing sight, than to behold those who have shed their blood or lost their limbs in the service of their Country, without a shelter, without a friend, and without the means of obtaining any of the necessaries or comforts of Life; compelled to beg their daily bread from door to door! suffer me to recommend those of this discription, belonging to your State, to the warmest patronage of your Excellency and your Legislature.

It is necessary to say but a few words on the third topic which was proposed, and which regards particularly the defence of the Republic, As there can be little doubt but Congress will recommend a proper Peace Establishment for the United States, in which a due attention will be paid to the importance of placing the Militia of the Union upon a regular and respectable footing; If this should be the case, I would beg leave to urge the great advantage of it in the strongest terms. The Militia of this Country must be considered as the Palladium of our security, and the first effectual resort in case of hostility; It is essential therefore, that the same system should pervade the whole; that the formation and discipline of the Militia of the Continent should be absolutely uniform, and that the same species of Arms, Accoutrements and Military Apparatus, should be introduced in every part of the United States; No one, (who has not learned it from experience, can conceive the difficulty, expence, and confusion which result from a contrary system, or the vague Arrangements which have hitherto prevailed.

If in treating of political points, a greater latitude than usual has been taken in the course of this Address, the importance of the Crisis, and the magnitude of the objects in discussion, must be my apology: It is, however, neither my wish or expectation, that the preceding observations should claim any regard, except so far as they shall appear to be dictated by a good intention, consonant to the immutable rules of Justice; calculated to produce a liberal system of policy, and founded on whatever experience may have been acquired by a long and close attention to public business. Here I might speak with the more confidence from my actual observations, and, if it would not swell this Letter (already too prolix) beyond the bounds I had prescribed myself: I could demonstrate to every mind open to conviction, that in less time and with much less expence than has been incurred, the War might have been brought to the same happy conclusion, if the resourses of the Continent could have been properly drawn forth, that the distresses and disappointments which have very often occurred, have in too many instances, resulted more from a want of energy, in the Continental Government, than a deficiency of means in the particular States. That the inefficiency of measures, arising from the want of an adequate authority in the Supreme Power, from a partial compliance with the Requisitions of Congress in some of the States, and from a failure of punctuality in others, while it tended to damp the zeal of those which were more willing to exert themselves; served also to accumulate the expences of the War, and to frustrate the best concerted Plans, and that the discouragement occasioned by the complicated difficulties and embarrassments, in which our affairs were, by this means involved, would have long ago produced the dissolution of any Army, less patient, less virtuous and less persevering, than that which I have had the honor to command. But while I mention these things, which are notorious facts, as the defects of our Federal Constitution, particularly in the prosecution of a War, I beg it may be understood, that as I have ever taken a pleasure in gratefully acknowledging the assistance and support I have derived from every Class of Citizens, so shall I always be happy to do justice to the unparalleled exertion of the individual States, on many interesting occasions.

I have thus freely disclosed what I wished to make known, before I surrendered up my Public trust to those who committed it to me, the task is now accomplished, I now bid adieu to your Excellency as the Chief Magistrate of your State, at the same time I bid a last farewell to the cares of Office, and all the imployments of public life.

It remains then to be my final and only request, that your Excellency will communicate these sentiments to your Legislature at their next meeting, and that they may be considered as the Legacy of One, who has ardently wished, on all occasions, to be useful to his Country, and who, even in the shade of Retirement, will not fail to implore the divine benediction upon it.

I now make it my earnest prayer, that God would have you, and the State over which you preside, in his holy protection, that he would incline the hearts of the Citizens to cultivate a spirit of subordination and obedience to Government, to entertain a brotherly affection and love for one another, for their fellow Citizens of the United States at large, and particularly for their brethren who have served in the Field, and finally, that he would most graciously be pleased to dispose us all, to do Justice, to love mercy, and to demean ourselves with that Charity, humility and pacific temper of mind, which were the Characteristicks of the Divine Author of our blessed Religion, and without an humble imitation of whose example in these things, we can never hope to be a happy Nation.

To Reverend John Rodgers, June 11, 1783

Dear Sir: I accept, with much pleasure your kind Congratulations on the happy Event of Peace, with the Establishment of our Liberties and Independence.

Glorious indeed has been our Contest: glorious, if we consider the Prize for which we have contended, and glorious in its Issue; but in the midst of our Joys, I hope we shall not forget that, to divine Providence is to be ascribed the Glory and the Praise.

Your proposition respecting Mr Aikins Bibles would have been particularly noticed by me, had it been suggested in Season; but the late Resolution of Congress for discharging Part of the Army, takg off near two thirds of our Numbers, it is now too late to make the Attempt. It would have pleased me, if Congress should have made such an important present, to the brave fellows, who have done so much for the Security of their Country's Rights and Establishment.

I hope it will not be long before you will be able to go peaceably to N York; some patience however will yet be necessary; but Patience is a noble Virtue, and when rightly exercised, does not fail of its Reward. With much Regard etc.

To the Mayor, Aldermen, and Commonalty of Albany, August 4, 1783

Gentlemen: I accept with heart-felt satisfaction your affectionate congratulations on the restoration of Peace, and the formal recognition of the Independence of the United States. We may indeed ascribe these most happy and glorious Events to the Smiles of Providence, the Virtue of our Citizens, and the bravery of our Troops, aided by the powerful interposition of our Magnanimous and illustrious Ally.

For the favorable Sentiments you are pleased to express of my Agency in this Revolution, and for your benevolent wishes for my personal felicity I entreat you, Gentlemen! to receive my warmest acknowledgments.

While I contemplate with inexpressible pleasure the future tranquillity and Glory of our common Country, I cannot but take a particular interest in the anticipation of the encreasing prosperity and greatness of this Antient and respectable City of Albany, from whose Citizens I have received such distinguished tokens of their approbation and Affection.

To the Massachusetts Senate and House of Representatives, August 10, 1783

Gentlemen: The Address of so respectable a Body as the Senate and House of Representatives of the Commonwealth of Massachusetts, congratulating me on so auspicious an Event as the Return of Peace, cannot fail to affect me with the highest pleasure and gratification.

Be assured Gentlemen, that, through the many and complicated vicissitudes of an arduous Conflict, I have ever turned my Eye, with a fixed Confidence on that superintendg. Providence which governs all Events: and the lively Gratitude I now feel, at the happy termination of our Contest, is beyond my Expression.

If, dependg on the Guidance of the same Allwise Providence, I have performed my part in this great Revolution, to the acceptance of my fellow Citizens, It is a source of high satisfaction to me; and forms an additional Motive of Praise to that Infinite Wisdom, which directs the Minds of Men. This Consideration will attend me in the Shades of retirement, and furnish one of the most pleasing Themes of my Meditation.

So great a revolution as this Country now experiences, doubtless ranks high in the Scale of human Events, and in the Eye of Omnipotence is introductive to some noble Scenes of future Grandeur to this happy fated Continent. May the States have Wisdom to discern their true Interests at this important period!

Impressed with sentiments of Gratitude for your benevolent Expressions for my personal Happiness and prosperity, I can make you no better return, than to pray, that Heaven, from the Stores of its Munificence, may shower its choisest blessings on you Gentlemen, and the People of the Commonwealth of Massachusetts, and to entreat that Our Liberties, now so happily established, may be continued in perfect Security, to the latest posterity. With Sentiments of high Veneration etc.

To the Countess of Huntingdon, August 10, 1783

My Lady: Within the course of a few days I have received the Letter you was pleased to Honor me with from Bath, of the 20th of febry. and have to express my respectful Thanks to your Goodness, for the marks of Confidence and Esteem contained therein.

Your Ladyships benevolent Designs toward the Indian Nations, claim my particular Attention, and to further so laudable an Undertakg will afford me much pleasure, so far as my Situation in Life, surrounded with many and arduous Cares will admit. To be named as an Execu-tor of your Intentions, may perhaps disappoint your Ladyships Views; but so far as my general Superintendence, or incidental Attention can contribute to the promotion of your Establishment, you may command my Assistance.

My Ancestry being derived from Yorkshire in England, it is more than probable that I am entitled to that honorable Connection, which you are pleased to mention; independent however of this privelidge, the Veneration with which your Ladyships Character, heretofore known, has impressed me, justly entitled you to rank high in my Esteem. The same Sentiments of respect and regard lead Mrs Washington to thank you for the distinguishd mention you are pleased to make of her. With great considn. etc.

To the Magistrates and Inhabitants of the Borough of Elizabeth, August 21, 1783

Gentlemen: It gives me the most pleasing sensations to find so cordial a welcome on my return, in peace, to this pleasant Town, after the vicissitudes of so long and obstinate a Contest.

On this happy occasion, suffer me, Gentlemen, to join you in grateful adoration to that divine Providence, which hath rescued our Country from the brink of destruction, which hath crowned our exertions with the fairest fruits of success, and which now (instead of the anxiety and distress occasioned by perpetual Alarms) permits you to enjoy, without molestation, the sweets of Peace and domestic happiness. May a spirit of Wisdom and Rectitude preside over all our Councils and Actions, and dispose us as a Nation to avail ourselves of the blessings which are placed before us, then shall we be happy indeed, and as a just reward for your liberal and virtuous sentiments, may the felicity of the Magistracy and Inhabitants of this Corporation, be only limited by the duration of time, and exceded by the fruition of a glorious immortality.

To the Inhabitants of Princeton and Neighborhood, Together with the President and Faculty of the College, August 25, 1783

Gentlemen: I receive with the utmost satisfaction and acknowledge with great sensibility your kind congratulations.

The prosperous situation of our public affairs, the flourishing state of this place and the revival of the Seat of Literature from the ravages of War, encrease to the highest degree, the pleasure I feel *in visiting* (at the return of Peace) the scene of our important military transactions, and *in recollecting* the period when the tide of adversity began to turn, and better fortune to smile upon us.

If in the execution of an arduous Office I have been so happy as to discharge my duty to the Public with fidelity and success, and to obtain the good opinion of my fellow Soldiers and fellow Citizens; I attribute all the glory to that Supreme Being, who hath caused the several parts, which have been employed in the production of the wonderful Events we now contemplate, to harmonize in the most perfect manner, and who was able by the humblest instruments as well as by the most powerful means to establish and secure the liberty and happiness of these United States.

I now return you Gentlemen my thanks for your benevolent wishes, and make it my earnest prayer to Heaven, that every temporal and divine blessing may be bestowed on the Inhabitants of Princeton, on the neighbourhood, and on the President and Faculty of the College of New Jersey, and that the usefulness of this Institution in promoting the interests of Religion and Learning may be universally extended.

Address to the Continental Congress, August 26, 1783

Mr. President: I am too sensible of the honorable reception I have now experienced not to be penetrated with the deepest feelings of gratitude.

Notwithstanding Congress appear to estimate the value of my life beyond any Services I have been able to render the U States, yet I must be permitted to consider the Wisdom and Unanimity of our National Councils, the firmness of our Citizens, and the patience and Bravery of our Troops, which have produced so happy a termination of the War, as the most conspicuous effect of the divine interposition, and the surest presage of our future happiness.

Highly gratified by the favorable sentiments which Congress are pleased to express of my past conduct, and amply rewarded by the confidence and affection of my fellow Citizens, I cannot hesitate to contribute my best endeavours, towards the establishment of the National security, in whatever manner the Sovereign Power may think proper to direct, until the ratification of the Definitive Treaty of Peace, or the final evacuation of our Country by the British Forces; after either of which events, I shall ask permission to retire to the peaceful shade of private life.

Perhaps, Sir, No occasion may offer more suitable than the present, to express my humble thanks to God, and my grateful acknowledgments to my Country, for the great and uniform support I have received in every vicissitude of Fortune, and for the many distinguished honors which Congress have been pleased to confer upon me in the course of the War.

Farewell Orders to the Continental Army, November 2, 1783

But before the Comdr in Chief takes his final leave of those he holds most dear, he wishes to indulge himself a few moments in calling to mind a slight review of the past. . . .

A contemplation of the compleat attainment (at a period earlier than could have been expected) of the object for which we contended against so formidable a power cannot but inspire us with astonishment and gratitude. The disadvantageous circumstances on our part, under which the war was undertaken, can never be forgotten. The singular interpositions of Providence in our feeble condition were such, as could scarcely escape the attention of the most unobserving; while the unparalleled perseverance of the Armies of the U States, through almost every possible suffering and discouragement for the space of eight long years, was little short of a standing miracle.

It is not the meaning nor within the compass of this address to detail the hardships peculiarly incident to our service, or to describe the distresses, which in several instances have resulted from the extremes of hunger and nakedness, combined with the rigours of an inclement season; nor is it necessary to dwell on the dark side of our past affairs. Every American Officer and Soldier must now console himself for any unpleasant circumstances which may have occurred by a recollection of the uncommon scenes in which he has been called to Act no inglorious part, and the astonishing events of which he has been a witness, events which have seldom if ever before taken place on the stage of human action, nor can they probably ever happen again. For who has before seen a disciplined Army form'd at once from such raw materials? Who, that was not a witness, could imagine that the most violent local prejudices would cease so soon, and that Men who came from the different parts of the Continent, strongly disposed, by the habits of education, to despise and quarrel with each other, would instantly become but one patriotic band of Brothers, or who, that was not on the spot, can trace the steps by which such a wonderful revolution has been effected, and such a glorious period put to all our warlike toils?

. . . .

. . . To the various branches of the Army the General takes this last and solemn opportunity of professing his inviolable attachment and friendship. He wishes more than bare professions were in his power, that he were really able to be useful to them all in future life. He flatters himself however, they will do him the justice to believe, that whatever could with propriety be attempted by him has been done, and being now to conclude these his last public Orders, to take his ultimate leave in a short time of the military character, and to bid a final adieu to the Armies he has so long had the honor to Command, he can only again offer in their behalf his recommendations to their grateful country, and his prayers to the God of Armies. May ample justice be done them here, and may the choicest of heaven's favours, both here and hereafter, attend those who, under the devine auspices, have secured innumerable blessings for others; with these wishes, and this benediction, the Commander in Chief is about to retire from Service. The Curtain of seperation will soon be drawn, and the military scene to him will be closed for ever.

To the Two United Dutch Reformed Churches of Hackensack and Schalenburgh and the Inhabitants of Hackensack, November 10, 1783

Gentn.: Your affectionate congratulations on the happy conclusion of the War, and the glorious prospect now opening to this extensive Country, cannot but be extremely satisfactory to me.

Having shared in common, the hardships and dangers of the War with my virtuous fellow Citizens in the field, as well as with those who on the Lines have been immediately exposed to the Arts and Arms of the Enemy, I feel the most lively sentiments of gratitude to that divine Providence which has graciously interposed for the protection of our Civil and Religious liberties.

In retireing from the field of Contest to the sweets of private life, I claim no merit, but if in that retirement my most earnest wishes and prayers can be of any avail, nothing will exceed the prosperity of our common Country, and the temporal and spiritual felicity of those who are represented in your Address.

To the Militia Officers of Bergen County, November 10, 1783

Gentn: I participate most sincerely in the joy you express at the conclusion of the War, and the re-establishment of the blessings of Peace.

Persuaded of the rectitude of our cause, and relying on the divine aid for its success, I accepted an arduous employment, the event has justified my most enlarged expectation; and if to the consciousness of having attempted faithfully to discharge my duty, I may add the approbation of my fellow Citizens, my happiness will be compleat.

To you, Gentn., who have experienced in no small degree the fatigues of a Military life, I must return these my last public thanks for the chearful and able assistance you have often afforded me. May you, as a reward of your virtuous conduct, enjoy the uninterrupted fruits of that Independence which has been procured at the hazard of our Lives.

To the Reformed German Congregation of New York, November 27, 1783

Gentlemen: The illustrious and happy event on which you are pleased to congratulate and wellcome me to this City, demands all our gratitude; while the favorable sentiments you have thought proper to express of my conduct, intitles you to my warmest acknowledgements.

Disposed, at every suitable opportunity to acknowledge publicly our infinite obligations to the Supreme Ruler of the Universe for rescuing our Country from the brink of destruction; I cannot fail at this time to ascribe all the honor of our late successes to the same glorious Being. And if my humble exertions have been made in any degree subservient to the execution of the divine purposes, a contemplation of the benediction of Heaven on our righteous Cause, the approbation of my virtuous Countrymen, and the testimony of my own Conscience, will be a sufficient reward and augment my felicity beyond anything which the world can bestow.

The establishment of Civil and Religious Liberty was the Motive which induced me to the Field; the object is attained, and it now remains to be my earnest wish and prayer, that the Citizens of the United States would make a wise and virtuous use of the blessings, placed before them; and that the reformed german Congregation in New York; may not only be conspicuous for their religious character, but as examplary, in support of our inestimable acquisitions, as their reverend Minister has been in the attainment of them.

To the Legislature of New Jersey, December 6, 1783

Gentlemen: I want Words to express the heart-felt pleasure I experience on receiving the congratulation and plaudit of so respectable a Body, as the Legislature of the State of New Jersey. I cannot however suppress the effusions of my gratitude for their flattering allusion to an event which hath signalized the name of Trenton; for the delicate manner of their recalling to mind none but grateful ideas; as well as for all their former assistance at the period of our deepest distress.

I am heartily disposed to join with you, Gentlemen, in adoration to that all-wise and most gracious Providence which hath so conspicuously interposed in the direction of our public affairs and the establishment of our national Independence.

The faithful page of History, will I doubt not, record all the patriotic sufferings and meritorious Services of the gallant little Army I have had the honor to command; nor, (if my testimony and the voice of truth can avail anything), shall the efficacious exertions of the State of New Jersey, or the almost unrivalled bravery of its Militia ever be forgotten. Let the fact be made known to the whole world, let it be remembered forever as an example to succeeding Ages, that, after a large extent of Country had been overrun by a formidable Enemy, and thousands of Citizens driven from their possessions; the virtuous freedom of New Jersey, recovering from the temporary shock, stungby the remembrance of what their wives, their children and Friends had already suffered, by the thought of losing all they yet held dear and sacred, animated by an enthusiastic hope of success, and bouyed, by a reliance on the aid of Heaven, above the fear of danger and death itself then began to stem the tide of adversity; and, in concert with our other force, recoiling like an impetuous torrent on our lately victorious foes, confined them within narrow limits 'till compelled to take their final departure from the State. For me, it is enough to have seen the divine Arm visibly outstretched for our deliverance, and to have recd the approbation of my Country, and my Conscience on account of my humble instrumentality in carrying the designs of Providence into effect; but for my gallant Associates in the Field, who have so essentially contributed to the establishment of our Independence and national glory, no rewards can be too great.

I am now to bid you a long farewell, and to recommend, you Gentlemen, and the State whose wellfare you are appointed to superintend, to the indulgent care of Heaven. May unanimity and wisdom ever prevail in your public Councils! May Justice and liberality distinguish the Administration of your Government! and may the Citizens of New Jersey be completely happy in the practice of Industry œconomy and every private Virtue.

To the Militia Officers of the City and Liberties of Philadelphia, December 12, 1783

Gentlemen: The honorable manner in which you are pleased to notice my return to this City, is particularly acceptable to me.

It would have been a proof of the want of Patriotism and every social Virtue not to have assumed the character of a Soldier when the exigency of the Public demanded, or not to have returned to the Class of Citizens when the necessity of farther Service ceased to exist. I can therefore claim no merit beyond that of having done my duty with fidelity.

While the various Scenes of the War, in which I have experienced the timely aid of the Militia of Philadelphia, recur to my mind, my ardent prayer ascends to Heaven that they may long enjoy the blessings of that Peace which has been obtained by the divine benediction on our common exertions.

To the Magistrates of the City and County of Philadelphia, December 13, 1783

Gentlemen: I have great occasion to be satisfied with the proofs you have now given of regard for my person, and approbation of my Services.

Nothing could have been more proper on this occasion than to attribute our glorious successes in the manner you have done, to the bravery of our Troops, the assistance of our Ally and the interposition of Providence. Having by such means acquired the inestimable blessings of Peace Liberty and Independence; the preservation of these important acquisitions must now, in a great measure, be committed to an able and faithful Magistracy. May the tranquility and good order of the City and County in which you are called to act in that respectable character, continue to exhibit your Example as worthy of universal imitation.

To the Learned Professions of Philadelphia, December 13, 1783

Gentlemen: I entreat you to accept my grateful thanks for your affectionate Address; and to be assured that the kindness and partiality of your sentiments respecting me, as well as the elegance and urbanity of your expressions, have made an impression on my mind never to be effaced.

Conscious of no impropriety in wishing to merit the esteem of my fellow Citizens in general; I cannot hesitate to acknowledge that I feel a certain pleasing sensation in obtaining the good opinion of men eminent for their virtue, knowledge and humanity; but I am sensible at the same time, it becomes me to receive with humility the warm commendations you are pleased to bestow on my conduct: for if I have been led to detest the folly and madness of unbounded ambition, if I have been induced from other motives to draw my sword and regulate my public behaviour, or if the management of the War has been conducted upon purer principles: let me not arrogate the merit to human imbecility, but rather ascribe whatever glory may result from our successful struggle to a higher and more efficient Cause. For the re-establishment of our once violated rights; for the confirmation of our Independence; for the protection of Virtue, Philosophy and Literature: for the present flourishing state of the Sciences, and for the enlarged prospect of human happiness, it is our common duty to pay the tribute of gratitude to the greatest and best of Beings.

Tho the military Scene is now closed and I am hastening with unspeakable delight to the still and placid walks of domestic Life; yet even there will my Country's happiness be ever nearest to my heart, and, while I cherish the fond idea I shall still retain, a pleasing remembrance of the able support the Public has often received from the learned Professions; whose prosperity is so essential to the preservation of the Liberties, as well as the augmentation of the happiness and glory of this extensive Empire.

To the Mayor, Recorder, Aldermen, and Common Council of Annapolis, December 22, 1783

Permit me, Gentlemen, to offer to you my sincere thanks for your Congratulations on the happy events, of Peace and the Establishment of our Independence.

If my Conduct throughout the War has merited the confidence of my fellow Citizens, and has been instrumental in obtaining for my Country the blessings of Peace and Freedom, I owe it to that Supreme being who guides the hearts of all; who has so signally interposed his aid in every Stage of the Contest and who has graciously been pleased to bestow on me the greatest of Earthly rewards: *the approbation and affections of a free people.*

Tho' I retire from the employments of public life I shall never cease to entertain the most anxious care for the welfare of my Country. May the Almighty dispose the heart of every Citizen of the United States to improve the great prospect of happiness before us, and may you Gentlemen, and the Inhabitants of this City long enjoy every felicity, this World can Afford.

Address to Congress on Resigning His Commission, December 23, 1783

Mr. President: The great events on which my resignation depended having at length taken place; I have now the honor of offering my sincere Congratulations to Congress and of presenting myself before them to surrender into their hands the trust committed to me, and to claim the indulgence of retiring from the Service of my Country.

Happy in the confirmation of our Independence and Sovereignty, and pleased with the oppertunity afforded the United States of becoming a respectable Nation, I resign with satisfaction the Appointment I accepted with diffidence. A diffidence in my abilities to accomplish so arduous a task, which however was superseded by a confidence in the rectitude of our Cause, the support of the Supreme Power of the Union, and the patronage of Heaven.

The Successful termination of the War has verified the most sanguine expectations, and my gratitude for the interposition of Providence, and the assistance I have received from my Countrymen, encreases with every review of the momentous Contest.

While I repeat my obligations to the Army in general, I should do injustice to my own feelings not to acknowledge in this place the peculiar Services and distinguished merits of the Gentlemen who have been attached to my person during the War. It was impossible the choice of confidential Officers to compose my family should have been more fortunate. Permit me Sir, to recommend in particular those, who have continued in Service to the present moment, as worthy of the favorable notice and patronage of Congress.

I consider it an indispensable duty to close this last solemn act of my Official life, by commending the Interests of our dearest Country to the protection of Almighty God, and those who have the superintendence of them, to his holy keeping.

Having now finished the work assigned me, I retire from the great theatre of Action; and bidding an Affectionate farewell to this August body under whose orders I have so long acted, I here offer my Commission, and take my leave of all the employments of public life.

✒

THREE

Father of a
New Nation
1784–1789

To the Countess of Huntingdon, February 27, 1785[1]

My Lady,

The very polite & obliging letter which you did me the honor to write to me on the 8th of April by Sir James Jay, never came to my hands until the 17th of last month; & is the best apology I can make for a silence, which might otherwise appear inattentive, if not disrespectful, to a correspondence which does me much honor.

The other letter which your Ladyship refers to, as having passed thro' the medium of our good friend Mr Fairfax—has never yet appeared; & it is matter of great regret, that letters are so often intercepted by negligence, curiosity or motives still more unworthy. I am persuaded that some of my letters to Mr Fairfax, as well as his (covering your Ladyships) to me, have miscarried, as I have never received an acknowledgment of some of mine to him, tho' long since written.

With respect to your humane & benevolent intentions towards the Indians; & the plan which your Ladyship has adopted to carry them into effect, they meet my highest approbation; & I should be very happy to find every possible encouragement given to them. It has ever been my opinion, since I have had opportunities to observe, & to reflect upon the ignorance, indolence & general pursuits of the Indians, that all attempts to reclaim, & introduce any system of religeon or morality among them, would prove fruitless, until they could be first brought into a state of greater civilization; at least that this attempt should accompany the other—& be enforced by example: & I am happy to find that it is made the ground work of your Ladyships plan.

With respect to the other parts of the plan, & the prospect of obtaining Lands for the Emigrants who are to be the instruments employed in the execution of it; my letter to Sir James Jay in answer to his to me on this subject, will convey every information, which is in my power, at this time to give your Ladyship; & therefore I take the liberty of enclosing a transcript of it. Agreeably to the assurance given in it, I have written fully to the President of Congress, with whom I have a particular intimacy, and transmitted copies of your Ladyships plan, addresses & letter to the several States therein mentioned, with my approving sentiments thereon. I have informed him, that tho' it comes to him as a private letter from me; it is nevertheless optional in him to make it a matter of private communication to the members individually, or officially to Congress, as his judgment shall dictate; giving it as my opinion, among other reasons, that I did not belive since the cession of Lands by individual States to the United States, any one of them (except New York) was in circumstances, however well inclined it might be, to carry your Ladyships plan into effect.

What may be the result of your Ladyships Addresses to the States of North Carolina, Virginia, Pennsylvania and New York, individually; or of my statemt of the matter in a friendly way to the President of Congress for the united deliberation of the whole—is not for me to anticipate, even were I acquainted with their sentiments. I have already observed, that neither of the States (unless Nw York may be in circumstances to do it) can in my opinion furnish good Lands in a body for such emigrants as your Ladyship seems inclin'd to provide for. That Congress can, if the treaty which is now depending with the Western Indians should terminate favourably & a cession of Lands be obtained from them, which I presume is one object for holding it, is certain; & unless the reasons which I have mentioned in my letter to Sir James Jay should be a let or bar, I have not a doubt but that they would do it; in which case, any quantity of Land (within such cession or purchase) might be obtained. If, ultimately, success should not attend any of these applications, I submit as a dernier resort, for your Ladyships information & consideration, a Gazette containing the terms upon which I have offered several tracts of Land (the quantity of which is since encreased) of my own in that country, & which lie as convenient to the Western Tribes of Indians, as any in that territory (appertaining to an individual State)—as your Ladyship may perceive by having recourse to Hutchens's, Evans's, or any other map of that Country, and comparing the descriptive Lands therewith; & being informed that Virginia has ceded all her claim to lands No. West of the Ohio, to the United States—& that the Western boundary of Pennsylvania is terminated by a meredian which crosses the river but a little distance from Fort Pitt.

It will appear evident, from the date of my publication, that I could not at the time it was promulgated, have had an eye to your Ladyships plan of emigration; and I earnestly pray that my communication of the matter at this time, may receive no other interpretation than what is really meant—that is, a last (if it should be thought an eligible) resort.

I have no doubt but that Lands, if to be had at all, may be obtained from the United States, or an individual State, upon easier terms than those upon which I have offered mine; but being equally persuaded that these of mine, from their situation & other local advantages, are worth what I ask, I should not incline to take less for them, unless the *whole* by good & responsible characters (after an agent in their behalf had previously examined into the quality & conveniency of the land) should be engaged upon either of the tenures that are published; especially as these Lands, from their particular situation, must become exceedingly valuable, by the Laws which have just passed the Assemblies of Virginia & Maryland for improving and extending the navigation of Potomac, as high as is practicable, & communicating it with the nearest western waters by good roads: & by the former assembly to do the same thing with James river, & the communication between it & the Great Kanhawa—by means of which the produce of the settlers on these Lands of mine, will come easily & cheaply to market. I am, &c. &c. &c.

To George Mason, October 3, 1785

Dr Sir

I have this moment received yours of yesterday's date enclosing a memorial & remonstrance against the assessment Bill, which I will read with attention; at *present* I am unable to do it, on account of company. The Bill itself I do not recollect ever to have read: with *attention* I am certain I never did—but will compare them together.

Altho' no mans sentiments are more opposed to *any kind* of restraint upon religious principles than mine are; yet I must confess, that I am not amongst the number of those who are so much alarmed at the thoughts of making people pay towards the support of that which they profess, if of the denominations of Christians; or declare themselves Jews, Mahomitans or otherwise, & thereby obtain proper relief. As the matter now stands, I wish an assessment had never been agitated—& as it has gone so far, that the Bill could die an easy death; because I think it will be productive of more quiet to the State, than by enacting it into a Law; which, in my opinion, wou'd be impolitic, admitting there is a decided majority for it, to the disgust of a respectable minority. In the first case the matter will soon subside; in the latter it will rankle, & perhaps convulse the State. The Dinner Bell rings, & I must conclude with an expression of my concern for your indisposition. Sincerely & affectionately I am &c. &c.

To Samuel Griffin, April 30, 1788

Dear Sir,

I am now to acknowledge to receipt of your letter of the 15th of April, in which you did me the favor to enclose an extract from the original Statute, designating the duties of the Office to which I had been appointed.

Influenced by a heart-felt desire to promote the cause of Science in general and the prosperity of the College of William and Mary in particular, I accept the office of Chancellor in the same; and request you will be pleased to give official notice thereof to the learned Body, who have thought proper to honor me with the appointment. I consider fully in their strenuous endeavour's for placing the system of Education on such a basis as will render it most beneficial to the State, and the Republic of letters, as well as to the more extensive interests of humanity and religion. In return, they will do me the Justice to believe that I shall not be tardy, in giving my chearful concurrence to such measures as may be best calculated for the attainment of those desirable and important objects. For the expressions of politeness and friendship blended with your communications, you are desired to receive my best acknowledgments. I am Dear Sir Yrs &c.

To John Ettwein, Bishop of the Moravian Church, May 2, 1788

Revd Sir, I have received your obliging letter of the 28th of March enclosing a copy of some remarks on the Customs, Languages &c. of the Indians, and a printed pamphlet containing the stated rules of a Society for propagating the Gospel among the Heathen, for which tokens of polite attention and kind remembrance I must beg you to accept of my best thanks.

So far as I am capable of Judging, the principles upon which the society is founded and the rules laid down for its government appear to be well calculated to promote so laudable and arduous an undertaking, and you will permit me to add that if an event so long and so earnestly desired as that of converting the Indians to Christianity and consequently to civilization, can be effected, the Society of Bethlehm bids fair to bear a very considerable part in it. I am, Revd Sir, With sentiments of esteem Yr most Obedt Hble Servant

President of the United States
Before the First Amendment

1789–1791

To William Hartshorne, April 1, 1789[1]

Sir,

As it seems that it will be my unavoidable lot to be again brought into publick life, however contrary to my inclinations, I must prepare myself to meet with many occurrences which will be painful and embarrassing; but I can truly say that few events would distress me more than the realizing of the apprehensions of so respectable a body of my fellow Citizens as the Quakers of Philadelphia; as mentioned in your letter of the 28th Ulto.

If I must go on to New-York, and my wishes & inclinations were consulted on the occasion, they would lead me to proceed in as quiet & peaceable a manner as possible. But, situated as I am at present, and knowing nothing of the intentions of the people respecting my passing through the several towns, more than what the publick papers inform me of—and these may be conjecture—I do not see how I can, with any degree of propriety or delicacy, interfere, at this moment, to prevent the ill effects which are feared from an illumination of the City of Philadelphia. Could any way be pointed out to me by which I might ward off the evil dreaded by the Quakers, I would, with peculiar pleasure, take every proper step to prevent it; for altho' I have no agency in these matters, yet nothing would be more painful to me than to be the *innocent* cause of distress or injury to any individual of my Country.

I must beg you to accept of my best thanks and warmest acknowledgments for your kind wishes for my happiness—and believe me to be—with very great esteem & regard Sir, Yr most Obedt Hble Servt

To the Citizens of Baltimore, April 17, 1789

Gentlemen,

The tokens of regard and affection, which I have often received from the Citizens of this Town, were always acceptable; because, I believed them, always sincere. Be pleased to receive my best acknowledgments for the renewal of them, on the present occasion.

If the affectionate partiality of my fellow Citizens has prompted them to ascribe greater effects to my conduct & character, than were justly due; I trust, the indulgent sentiment on their part, will not produce an overweening presumption on mine.

I cannot now, Gentlemen, resist my feelings so much, as to withhold the communication of my ideas, respecting the actual situation and prospect of our national affairs. It appears to me, that little more than common sense and common honesty, in the transactions of the community at large, would be necessary to make us a great and a happy Nation. For if the general Government, lately adopted, shall be arranged & administered in such a manner as to acquire the full confidence of the American People, I sincerely believe, they will have greater advantages, from their Natural, moral & political circumstances, for public felicity, than any other People ever possessed.

In the contemplation of those advantages, now soon to be realized, I have reconciled myself to the sacrifice of my fondest wishes, so far as to enter again upon the stage of Public life. I know the delicate nature of the duties incident to the part which I am called to perform; and I feel my incompetence, without the singular assistance of Providence to discharge them in a satisfactory manner. But having undertaken the task, from a sense of duty, no fear of encountering difficulties and no dread of losing popularity, shall ever deter me from pursuing what I conceive to be the true interests of my Country. Yet after a consciousness of having been actuated by the purest motives alone, and after having made use of the most persevering endeavors in my power to advance the public weal, I shall consider it as next to a miracle, if I may be so fortunate as to go out of office with a reputation as unsullied by the breath of obloquy, as that which I flatter myself I have hitherto maintained. In all contingencies you will remember, Gentlemen, when I was entering on the chief magistracy I told you "that it would be no unprecedated thing, if the close of a life, (mostly consumed in public cares) should be embittered by some ungrateful event" But in the present instance, that circumstance would be accounted by me of little moment, provided, in the mean time, I shall have been in the smallest degree instrumental in securing the liberties and promoting the happiness of the American People.

To the Officials of Wilmington, Delaware, April 19-20, 1789

Gentlemen,

In the respectful address of the Burgesses and common council of the Borough of Wilmington, I recognise the friendly dispositions towards myself, and the patriotic sentiments for the Community at large which have always distinguished the Citizens of Delaware.

When on a former occasion you intimated to me your expectation, that, if any event should again render my services necessary, I would not withhold them from the public, I did not conceive that such an event could exist. I have however been persuaded of the expediency of once more entering on the stage of public affairs. Heaven and my own heart are witnesses for me with how much reluctance I have yielded to that persuasion: But a sense of duty, in my conception, ought to supersede every personal consideration—and the promises of support which I am daily receiving from my fellow-citizens, together with a reliance upon that gracious Providence, which sustained us through our struggle for Liberty, encourage me, (notwithstanding a diffidence in my own abilities) to hope for a happy issue from my present arduous undertaking.

In the meantime, I am extremely obliged to you, Gentlemen, for your kind wishes respecting my individual felicity, as well as for your fervent supplications in behalf of the public prosperity.

To the Mayor, Recorder, Aldermen, and Common Council of Philadelphia,
April 20, 1789

I consider myself particularly obliged to you, Gentlemen, for your congratulatory address on my appointment to the Station of President of the United States.

Accustomed as I have been to pay a respectful regard to the Opinion of my Countrymen, I did not think myself at liberty to decline the Acceptance of the high Office, to which I had been called by their United suffrage—When I contemplate the Interposition of Providence, as it was visibly Manifested, in guiding us thro' the Revolution in preparing us for the Reception of a General Government, and in conciliating the Good will of the People of America, towards one another after its Adoption, I feel myself oppressed and almost overwhelmed with a sence of the Divine Munificence—I feel that nothing is due to my personal agency in all these complicated and wonderful Events, except what can simply be attributed to the exertions of an honest Zeal for the Good of my Country.

I thank you sincerely for your kind wishes that my Administration may be honorable and happy to myself and Country. I Pray you Gentlemen, will accept on your own behalf, as well as that of the Citizens you represent, my heartfelt acknowledgments for the polite welcome I have received upon my arrival in your City; In tendering these acknowledgments I must also desire it may be fully understood: that I entertain the same reciprocal Sensations of Attachment for the Good People of Philadelphia which they have on all occasions evinced in my favor.

To the Pennsylvania Supreme Court, April 20, 1789

Gentlemen,

It affords me the most sensible pleasure to be informed that my accession to the chief Magistracy of the United States has met the approbation of my fellow-citizens in general, and particularly that of the Judges of the supreme Court of Pennsylvania.

Your recapitulation of the deliverance in which almighty God hath been pleased, in some sort, to make use of me as his instrument, ought only to awaken my deepest gratitude for his mercies in the time past, and a humble reliance on them for the time to come. Feeling how greatly I shall stand in need of the patriotic assistance of every good citizen of America, the confidence they continue to express in the rectitude of my dispositions, will always be, as it ever has been, an unfailing source of consolation to me, in every hour of difficulty or distress—While the whole course of my past conduct will be a better security for my future transactions, than any verbal assurances I can give; I will only say that I should find myself singularly happy in contributing to realise the glorious work, which your partiality for me has been indulgent enough to anticipate, of establishing justice, ensuring tranquility, promoting the general welfare, and securing the blessings of Liberty and Independence to the good people of our native country, and their latest posterity.

I intreat you to be persuaded, Gentlemen, That, although it was with the utmost difficulty I could prevail upon myself to enter again on the Stage of Public Life, yet, since I have done it, the unequivocal encouragement of support, given by the most respectable citizens and Magistrates, will tend very much to remove my embarrassments, and, I hope to open the way for a prosperous Administration.

First Inaugural Address, April 30, 1789

Fellow Citizens of the Senate and of the House of Representatives

Among the vicissitudes incident to life, no event could have filled me with greater anxieties than that of which the notification was transmitted by your order, and received on the fourteenth day of the present month. On the one hand, I was summoned by my Country, whose voice I can never hear but with veneration and love, from a retreat which I had chosen with the fondest predilection, and, in my flattering hopes, with an immutable decision, as the asylum of my declining years: a retreat which was rendered every day more necessary as well as more dear to me, by the addition of habit to inclination, and of frequent interruptions in my health to the gradual waste committed on it by time. On the other hand, the magnitude and difficulty of the trust to which the voice of my Country called me, being sufficient to awaken in the wisest and most experienced of her citizens, a distrustful scrutiny into his qualifications, could not but overwhelm with despondence, one, who, inheriting inferior endowments from nature and unpractised in the duties of civil administration, ought to be peculiarly conscious of his own deficiencies. In this conflict of emotions, all I dare aver, is, that it has been my faithful study to collect my duty from a just appreciation of every circumstance, by which it might be affected. All I dare hope, is, that, if in executing this task I have been too much swayed by a grateful remembrance of former instances, or by an affectionate sensibility to this transcendent proof, of the confidence of my fellow-citizens; and have thence too little consulted my incapacity as well as disinclination for the weighty and untried cares before me; my *error* will be palliated by the motives which misled me, and its consequences be judged by my Country, with some share of the partiality in which they originated.

Such being the impressions under which I have, in obedience to the public summons, repaired to the present station; it would be peculiarly improper to omit in this first official Act, my fervent supplications to that Almighty Being who rules over the Universe, who presides in the Councils of Nations, and whose providential aids can supply every human defect, that his benediction may consecrate to the liberties and happiness of the People of the United States, a Government instituted by themselves for these essential purposes: and may enable every instrument employed in its administration, to execute with success, the functions allotted to his charge. In tendering this homage to the Great Author of every public and private good, I assure myself that it expresses your sentiments not less than my own; nor those of my fellow-citizens at large, less than either: No People can be bound to acknowledge and adore the invisible hand, which conducts the Affairs of men more than the People of the United States. Every step, by which they have advanced to the character of an independent nation, seems to have been distinguished by some token of providential agency. And in the important revolution just accomplished in the system of their United Government, the tranquil deliberations, and voluntary consent of so many distinct communities, from which the event has resulted, cannot be compared with the means by which most Governments have been established, without some return of pious gratitude along with an humble anticipation of the future blessings which the past seem to presage. These reflections, arising out of the present crisis, have forced themselves too strongly on my mind to be suppressed. You will join me I trust in thinking, that there are none under the influence of which, the proceedings of a new and free Government can more auspiciously commence.

By the article establishing the Executive Department, it is made the duty of the President "to recommend to your consideration, such measures as he shall judge necessary and expedient." The circumstances under which I now meet you, will acquit me from entering into that subject, farther than to refer to the Great Constitutional Charter under which you are assembled; and which, in defining your powers, designates the objects to which your attention is to be given. It will be more consistent with those circumstances, and far more congenial with the feelings which actuate me, to substitute, in place of a recommendation of particular measures, the tribute that is due to the talents, the rectitude, and the patriotism which adorn the characters selected to devise and adopt them. In these honorable qualifications, I behold the surest pledges, that as on one side, no local prejudices, or attachments; no seperate views, nor party animosities, will misdirect the comprehensive and equal eye which ought to watch over this great Assemblage of communities and interests: so, on another, that the foundations of our national policy, will be laid in the pure and immutable principles of private morality; and the pre-eminence of free Government, be exemplified by all the attributes which can win the affections of its Citizens, and command the respect of the world. I dwell on this prospect with every satisfaction which an ardent love for my Country can inspire: since there is no truth more thoroughly established, than that there exists in the œconomy and course of nature, an indissoluble union between virtue and happiness, between duty and advantage, between the genuine maxims of an honest and magnanimous policy, and the solid rewards of public prosperity and felicity: Since we ought to be no less persuaded that the propitious smiles of Heaven, can never be expected on a nation that disregards the eternal rules of order and right, which Heaven itself has ordained: And since the preservation of the sacred fire of liberty, and the destiny of the Republican model of Government, are justly considered as *deeply*, perhaps as *finally* staked, on the experiment entrusted to the hands of the American people.

Besides the ordinary objects submitted to your care, it will remain with your judgment to decide, how far an exercise of the occasional power delegated by the Fifth article of the Constitution is rendered expedient at the present juncture by the nature of objections which have been urged against the System, or by the degree of inquietude which has given birth to them. Instead of undertaking particular recommendations on this subject, in which I could be guided by no lights derived from official opportunites, I shall again give way to my entire confidence in your discernment and pursuit of the public good: For I assure myself that whilst you carefully avoid every alteration which might endanger the benefits of an United and effective Government, or which ought to await the future lessons of experience; a reverence for the characteristic rights of freemen, and a regard for the public harmony, will sufficiently influence your deliberations on the question how far the former can be more impregnably fortified, or the latter be safely and advantageously promoted.

To the preceding observations I have one to add, which will be most properly addressed to the House of Representatives. It concerns myself; and will therefore be as brief as possible. When I was first honoured with a call into the service of my Country, then on the eve of an arduous struggle for its liberties, the light in which I contemplated my duty required that I should renounce every pecuniary compensation. From this resolution I have in no instance departed—And being still under the impressions which produced it, I must decline as inapplicable to myself, any share in the personal emoluments, which may be indispensably included in a permanent provision for the Executive Department; and must accordingly pray that the pecuniary estimates for the Station in which I am placed, may, during my continuance in it, be limited to such actual expenditures as the public good may be thought to require.

Having thus imparted to you my sentiments, as they have been awakened by the occasion which brings us together, I shall take my present leave; but not without resorting once more to the benign Parent of the human race, in humble supplication that since he has been pleased to favour the American people, with opportunities for deliberating in perfect tranquility, and dispositions for deciding with unparellelled unanimity on a form of Government, for the security of their Union, and the advancement of their happiness; so this divine blessing may be equally *conspicuous* in the enlarged views—the temperate consultations, and the wise measures on which the success of this Government must depend.

To the German Lutherans of Philadelphia, April 1789

Gentlemen,

While I request you to accept my thanks for your kind address, I must profess myself highly gratified by the sentiments of esteem and consideration contained in it. The approbation my past conduct has received from so worthy a body of citizens, as that whose joy for my appointment you announce, is a proof of the indulgence with which my future transactions will be judged by them.

I could not, however, avoid apprehending that the partiality of my countrymen in favor of the measures now pursued has led them to expect too much from the present government; did not the same providence which has been visible in every stage of our progress to this interesting crisis, from a combination of circumstances, give us cause to hope for the accomplishment of all our reasonable desires.

Thus, partaking with you in the pleasing anticipation of the blessings of a wise and efficient government, I flatter myself opportunities will not be wanting for me to shew my disposition to encourage the domestic and public virtues of industry, œconomy, patriotism, philanthropy, and that righteousness which exalteth a nation.

I rejoice in having so suitable an occasion to testify the reciprocity of my esteem for the numerous people whom you represent. From the excellent character for diligence, sobriety, and virtue, which the Germans in general, who are settled in America, have ever maintained; I cannot forbear felicitating myself on receiving from so respectable a number of them such strong assurances of their affection for my person, confidence in my integrity, and zeal to support me in my endeavors for promoting the welfare of our common country.

So long as my conduct shall merit the approbation of the *wise and the good*, I hope to hold the same place in your affections, which your friendly declarations induce me to believe I possess at present; and amidst all the vicissitudes that may await me in this mutable state of existence, I shall earnestly desire the continuation of an interest in your intercessions at the Throne of Grace.

To the United States Senate, May 18, 1789

Gentlemen,

I thank you for your Address, in which the most affectionate sentiments are expressed in the most obliging terms. The coincidence of circumstances which led to this auspicious Crisis, the confidence reposed in me by my Fellow-citizens, and the assistance I may expect from counsels which will be dictated by an enlarged and liberal policy, seem to presage a more prosperous issue to my Administration, than a diffidence of my abilities had taught me to anticipate. I now feel myself inexpressibly happy in a belief, that Heaven which has done so much for our infant Nation will not withdraw its Providential influence before our political felicity shall have been completed; and in a conviction, that the Senate will at all times co-operate in every measure, which may tend to promote the welfare of this confederated Republic. Thus supported by a firm trust in the great Arbiter of the Universe, aided by the collected wisdom of the Union, and imploring the Divine benediction on our joint exertions in the service of our Country, I readily engage with you in the arduous, but pleasing, task, of attempting to make a Nation happy.

To the Bishops of the Methodist Episcopal Church, May 29, 1789

Gentlemen.

I return to you individually, and (through you) to your Society collectively in the United States my thanks for the demonstrations of affections, and the expressions of joy, offered in their behalf, on my late appointment. It shall still be my endeavor to manifest, by overt acts, the purity of my inclinations for promoting the happiness of mankind, as well as the sincerity of my desires to contribute whatever may be in my power towards the preservation of the civil and religious liberties of the American People. In pursuing this line of conduct, I hope, by the assistance of divine providence, not altogether to disappoint the confidence which you have been pleased to repose in me.

It always affords me satisfaction, when I find a concurrence in sentiment and practice between all conscientious men in acknowledgements of homage to the great Governor of the Universe, and in professions of support to a just civil government. After mentioning that I trust the people of every denomination, who demean themselves as good citizens, will have occasion to be convinced that I shall always strive to prove a faithful and impartial Patron of genuine, vital religion: I must assure you in particular that I take in the kindest part the promise you make of presenting your prayers at the Throne of Grace for me, and that I likewise implore the divine benedictions on yourselves and your religious community.

To the United Baptist Churches of Virginia, May 1789

Gentlemen,

I request that you will accept my best acknowledgments for your congratulation on my appointment to the first office in the nation. The kind manner in which you mention my past conduct equally claims the expression of my gratitude.

After we had, by the smiles of Heaven on our exertions, obtained the object for which we contended, I retired at the conclusion of the war, with an idea that my country could have no farther occasion for my services, and with the intention of never entering again into public life: But when the exigence of my country seemed to require me once more to engage in public affairs, an honest conviction of duty superseded my former resolution, and became my apology for deviating from the happy plan which I had adopted.

If I could have entertained the slightest apprehension that the Constitution framed in the Convention, where I had the honor to preside, might possibly endanger the religious rights of any ecclesiastical Society, certainly I would never have placed my signature to it; and if I could now conceive that the general Government might ever be so administered as to render the liberty of conscience insecure, I beg you will be persuaded that no one would be more zealous than myself to establish effectual barriers against the horrors of spiritual tyranny, and every species of religious persecution—For you, doubtless, remember that I have often expressed my sentiment, that every man, conducting himself as a good citizen, and being accountable to God alone for his religious opinions, ought to be protected in worshipping the Deity according to the dictates of his own conscience.

While I recollect with satisfaction that the religious Society of which you are Members, have been, throughout America, uniformly, and almost unanimously, the firm friends to civil liberty, and the persevering Promoters of our glorious revolution; I cannot hesitate to believe that they will be the faithful Supporters of a free, yet efficient general Government. Under this pleasing expectation I rejoice to assure them that they may rely on my best wishes and endeavors to advance their prosperity.

In the meantime be assured, Gentlemen, that I entertain a proper sense of your fervent supplications to God for my temporal and eternal happiness.

To the General Assembly of the Presbyterian Church, May 1789

Gentlemen,

I receive with great sensibility the testimonial, given by the General Assembly of the Presbyterian Church in the United States of America, of the live and unfeigned pleasure experienced by them on my appointment to the first office in the nation.

Although it will be my endeavor to avoid being elated by the too favorable opinion which your kindness for me may have induced you to express of the importance of my former conduct, and the effect of my future services: yet, conscious of the disinterestedness of my motive it is not necessary for me to conceal the satisfaction I have felt upon finding, that my compliance with the call of my country, and my dependence on the assistance of Heaven to support me in my arduous undertakings, have, so far as I can learn, met the universal approbation of my countrymen.

While I reiterate the possession of my dependence upon Heaven as the source of all public and private blessings; I will observe that the general prevalence of piety, philanthropy, honesty, industry and œconomy seems, in the ordinary course of human affairs are particularly necessary for advancing and confirming the happiness of our country. While all men within our territories are protected in worshipping the Deity according to the dictates of their consciences; it is rationally to be expected from them in return, that they will be emulous of evincing the sincerity of their profession by the innocence of their lives, and the beneficence of their actions: For no man, who is profligate in his morals, or a bad member of the civil community, can possibly be a true Christian, or a credit to his own religious society.

I desire you to accept my acknowledgements for your laudable endeavors to render men sober, honest, and good Citizens, and the obedient subjects of a lawful government; as well as for your prayers to Almighty God for his blessing on our common country and the humble instrument, which he has been pleased to make use of in the administration of it's government.

To the German Reformed Congregations, June 1789

Gentlemen,

I am happy in concurring with you in the sentiments of gratitude and piety towards Almighty-God, which are expressed with such fervency of devotion in your address; and in believing, that I shall always find in you, and the German Reformed Congregations in the United States a conduct correspondent to such worthy and pious expressions.

At the same time, I return you my thanks for the manifestation of your firm purpose to support in your persons a government founded in justice and equity, and for the promise that it will be your constant study to impress the minds of the People entrusted to your care with a due sense of the necessity of uniting reverence to such a government and obedience to its' laws with the duties and exercises of Religion.

Be assured, Gentlemen, it is, by such conduct, very much in the power of the virtuous Members of the community to alleviate the burden of the important office which I have accepted; and to give me Occasion to rejoice, in this world, for having followed therein the dictates of my conscience.

Be pleased also to accept my acknowledgements for the interest you so kindly take in the prosperity of my person, family, and administration.

May your devotions before the Throne of Grace be prevalent in calling down the blessings of Heaven upon yourselves and your country.

To the Massachusetts Senate and House of Representatives, July 9, 1789

Gentlemen,

Your Address, with which I have been honored, has made a most sensible impression upon me. That my acceptance of the Presidency of these United States should have given joy to the people of Massachusetts—and that my conduct through our late arduous struggle for Liberty and Independence hath met the approbation of the Citizens of that Commonwealth will be considered by me, as among the most pleasing circumstances of my life.

In executing the duties of my present important station I can promise nothing but purity of intentions—and in carrying these into effect, fidelity and diligence; if these, under the guidance of a superintending Providence, shall continue to me the approbation and affection of my fellow-citizens of the Union, it will be the highest gratification and the most ample reward that my mind can form any conception of in this life.

The adoption of the present Government by so large a majority of the States, and their Citizens—and the growing dispositions which are discoverable among all descriptions of men to give support and energy to it, are indications of its merit—auspicious of the future greatness and welfare of the Empire which will grow under it—and is the foundation on which I build my hopes of public felicity; the best efforts of mine towards the accomplishment of these great and glorious objects can only be secondary.

For the Benedictions you have been pleased to implore the Parent of the Universe on my person and family I have a grateful heart—and the most ardent wish that we may *all*, by rectitude of conduct and a perfect reliance on his beneficience, draw the smiles of Heaven on ourselves and posterity to the latest generation.

To the Moravian Society for Propagating the Gospel, August 15, 1789

Gentlemen,

I receive with satisfaction the congratulations of your Society and of the Brethren's Congregations in the United States of America. For you may be persuaded that the approbation and good wishes of such a peaceable and virtuous Community cannot be indifferent to me.

You will also be pleased to accept my thanks for the Treatise which you presented; and to be assured of my patronage in your laudable undertakings.

In proportion as the general Government of the United States shall acquire strength by duration, it is probable they may have it in their power to extend a salutary influence to the Aborigines in the extremities of their Territory. In the meantime, it will be a desirable thing for the protection of the Union to co-operate, as far as the circumstances may conveniently admit, with the disinterested endeavours of your society to civilize and Christianize the Savages of the Wilderness. Under these impressions, I pray Almighty God to have you always in his holy keeping.

To the Protestant Episcopal Church, August 19, 1789

Gentlemen,

I sincerely thank you for your affectionate congratulations on my election to the chief magistracy of the United States.

After having received from my fellow-citizens in general the most liberal treatment—after having found them disposed to contemplate in the most flattering point of view, the performance of my military services, and the manner of my retirement at the close of the war—I feel that I have a right to console myself in my present arduous undertakings, with a hope that they will still be inclined to put the most favorable construction on the motives which may influence me in my future public transactions. The satisfaction arising from the indulgent opinion entertained by the American People of my conduct, will, I trust, be some security for preventing me from doing any thing, which might justly incur the forfeiture of that opinion. And the consideration that human happiness and moral duty are inseparably connected, will always continue to prompt me to promote the progress of the former, by inculcating the practice of the latter.

On this occasion it would ill become me to conceal the joy I have felt in perceiving the fraternal affection which appears to encrease every day among the friends of genuine religion—It affords edifying prospects indeed to see Christians of different denominations dwell together in more charity, and conduct themselves in respect to each other with a more christian-like spirit than ever they have done in any former age, or in any other nation.

I receive with the greater satisfaction your congratulations on the establishment of the new constitution of government, because I believe its' mild, yet efficient, operations will tend to remove every remaining apprehension of those with whose opinions it may not entirely coincide, as well as to confirm the hopes of its' numerous friends; and because the moderation, patriotism, and wisdom of the present federal Legislature, seem to promise the restoration of Order, and our ancient virtues; the extension of genuine religion, and the consequent advancement of our respectability abroad, and of our substantial happiness at home.

I request most reverend and respected Gentlemen that you will accept my cordial thanks for your devout supplications to the Supreme Ruler of the Universe in behalf of me—May you, and the People whom you represent be the happy subjects of the divine benedictions both here and hereafter.

Thanksgiving Proclamation, October 3, 1789

By the President of the United States of America. a Proclamation.

Whereas it is the duty of all Nations to acknowledge the providence of Almighty God, to obey his will, to be grateful for his benefits, and humbly to implore his protection and favor—and whereas both Houses of Congress have by their joint Committee requested me "to recommend to the People of the United States a day of public thanksgiving and prayer to be observed by acknowledging with grateful hearts the many signal favors of Almighty God especially by affording them an opportunity peaceably to establish a form of government for their safety and happiness."

Now therefore I do recommend and assign Thursday the 26th day of November next to be devoted by the People of these States to the service of that great and glorious Being, who is the beneficent Author of all the good that was, that is, or that will be—That we may then all unite in rendering unto him our sincere and humble thanks—for his kind care and protection of the People of this Country previous to their becoming a Nation—for the signal and manifold mercies, and the favorable interpositions of his Providence which we experienced in the course and conclusion of the late war—for the great degree of tranquillity, union, and plenty, which we have since enjoyed—for the peaceable and rational manner, in which we have been enabled to establish constitutions of government for our safety and happiness, and particularly the national One now lately instituted—for the civil and religious liberty with which we are blessed; and the means we have of acquiring and diffusing useful knowledge; and in general for all the great and various favors which he hath been pleased to confer upon us.

and also that we may then unite in most humbly offering our prayers and supplications to the great Lord and Ruler of Nations and beseech him to pardon our national and other transgressions—to enable us all, whether in public or private stations, to perform our several and relative duties properly and punctually—to render our national government a blessing to all the people, by constantly being a Government of wise, just and constitutional laws, discreetly and faithfully executed and obeyed—to protect and guide all Sovereigns and Nations (especially such as have shewn kindness unto us) and to bless them with good government, peace, and concord—To promote the knowledge and practice of true religion and virtue, and the encrease of science among them and us and generally to grant unto all Mankind such a degree of temporal prosperity as he alone knows to be best.

Given under my hand at the City of New-York the third day of October in the year of our Lord 1789.

To the Congregational Ministers of New Haven, October 17, 1789

Gentlemen,

The Kind congratulations, contained in your address, claim and receive my grateful and affectionate thanks—respecting, as I do, the favorable opinions of Men distinguished for science and piety, it would be false delicacy to disavow the satisfaction, which I derive from their approbation of my public services, and private conduct.

Regarding that deportment, which consists with true religion, as the best security of temporal peace, and the sure mean of attaining eternal felicity, it will be my earnest endeavor (as far as human fraility can resolve) to inculcate the belief and practice of opinions, which lead to the consummation of those desireable objects.

The tender interest which you have taken in my personal happiness, and the obliging manner in which you express yourselves on the restoration of my health, are so forcibly impressed on my mind as to render language inadequate to the utterance of my feelings.

If it shall please the Great Disposer of events to listen to the pious supplication, which you have preferred in my behalf, I trust that the remainder of my days will evince the gratitude of a heart devoted to the advancement of those objects, which receive the approbation of Heaven, and promote the happiness of our fellow men.

My best prayers are offered to the Throne of Grace for your happiness, and that of the Congregations committed to your care.

To the Connecticut Legislature, October 17, 1789

Gentlemen,

Could any acknowledgement, which language might convey, do justice to the feelings excited by your partial approbation of my past services, and your affectionate wishes for my future happiness, I would endeavor to thank you: But, to minds disposed as yours are, it will suffice to observe that your address meets a grateful reception, and is reciprocated, in all its' wishes, with an unfeigned sincerity.

If the prosperity of our common country has in any degree been promoted by my military exertions, the toils which attended them have been amply rewarded by the approving voice of my fellow-citizens—I was but the humble Agent of favoring Heaven, whose benign interference was so often manifested in our behalf, and to whom the praise of victory alone is due.

In launching again on the ocean of events I have obeyed a summons, to which I can never be insensible—when my country demands the sacrifice, personal ease will always be a secondary consideration.

I cannot forego this opportunity to felicitate the Legislature of Connecticut on the pleasing prospect which an abundant harvest presents to its' citizens—May industry like theirs ever receive its' reward, and may the smile of Heaven crown all endeavors which are prompted by virtue—among which it is justice to estimate your assurance of supporting our equal government.

To the Citizens of Boston, October 27, 1789

Gentlemen

The obligations, which your goodness has imposed upon me, demand my grateful acknowledgements—Your esteem does me honor, and your affection communicates the truest pleasure—by endeavoring to deserve, I will indulge the hope of retaining them.

Over-rating my services, you have ascribed consequences to them, in which it would be injustice to deny a participation to the virtue and firmness of my worthy fellow-citizens of this respectable Town and Commonwealth.

If the exercise of my military commission has contributed to vindicate the rights of humanity, and to secure the freedom and happiness of my country, the purpose for which it was assumed has been completed, and I am amply rewarded—If, in the prosecution of my civil duties I shall be so fortunate as to meet the wishes of my fellow-citizens, and to promote the advantage of our common interests, I shall not regret the sacrifice which you are pleased to mention in terms so obliging.

The numerous sensations of heartfelt satisfaction, which a review of past scenes affords to my mind, in a comparison with the present happy hour, are far beyond my powers of utterance to express.

I rejoice with you, my fellow-citizens, in every circumstance that declares your prosperity—and I do so, most cordially, because you have well deserved to be happy.

Your love of liberty—your respect for the laws—your habits of industry—and your practice of the moral and religious obligations, are the strongest claims to national and individual happiness, and they will, I trust, be firmly and lastingly established.

Your wishes for my personal felicity impress a deep and affection-ate gratitude, and your prayer to the Almighty Ruler of the universe, in my behalf, calls forth my fervent supplication to that gracious and beneficent Being, for every blessing on your temporal pursuits, and for the perfection of your happiness hereafter.

To the Synod of the Dutch Reformed Church in North America, October 1789

Gentlemen,

I receive with a grateful heart your pious and affectionate address, and with truth declare to you that no circumstance of my life has affected me more sensibly or produced more pleasing emotions than the friendly congratulations, and strong assurances of support which I have received from my fellow-citizens of all descriptions upon my election to the Presidency of these United States.

I fear, Gentlemen, your goodness has led you to form too exalted an opinion of my virtues and merits—If such talents as I possess have been called into action by great events, and those events have terminated happily for our country, the glory should be ascribed to the manifest interposition of an over-ruling Providence. My military services have been abundantly recompensed by the flattering approbation of a grateful people; and, if a faithful discharge of my civil duties can ensure a like reward, I shall feel myself richly compensated for any personal sacrifice I may have made by engaging again in public life.

The Citizens of the United States of America have given as signal a proof of their wisdom and virtue in framing and adopting a constitution of government, without bloodshed or the intervention of force, as they, upon a former occasion, exhibited to the world of their valor, fortitude, and perseverance; and it must be a pleasing circumstance to every friend of good order and social happiness to find that our new government is gaining strength and respectability among the citizens of this country in proportion as it's operations are known, and its effects felt.

You, Gentlemen, act the part of pious Christians and good citizens by your prayers and exertions to preserve that harmony and good will towards men which must be the basis of every political establishment; and I readily join with you that "*while* just government protects all in their religious rights, true religion affords to government its surest support."

I am deeply impressed with your good wishes for my present and future happiness—and I beseech the Almighty to take you and yours under his special care.

To the Society of Quakers, October 1789

Gentlemen,

I receive with pleasure your affectionate address, and thank you for the friendly Sentiments & good wishes which you express for the Success of my administration, and for my personal Happiness.

We have Reason to rejoice in the prospect that the present National Government, which by the favor of Divine Providence, was formed by the common Counsels, and peaceably established with the common consent of the People, will prove a blessing to every denomination of them. To render it such, my best endeavors shall not be wanting.

Government being, among other purposes, instituted to protect the Persons and Consciences of men from oppression, it certainly is the duty of Rulers, not only to abstain from it themselves, but according to their Stations, to prevent it in others.

The liberty enjoyed by the People of these States of worshipping Almighty God agreable to their Consciences, is not only among the choicest of their *Blessings*, but also of their *Rights*—While men perform their social Duties faithfully, they do all that Society or the State can with propriety demand or expect; and remain responsible only to their

Maker for the Religion or modes of faith which they may prefer or profess.

Your principles & conduct are well known to me—and it is doing the People called Quakers no more than Justice to say, that (except their declining to share with others the burthen of the common defence) there is no Denomination among us who are more exemplary and useful Citizens.

I assure you very explicitly that in my opinion the Conscientious scruples of all men should be treated with great delicacy & tenderness, and it is my wish and desire that the Laws may always be as extensively accommodated to them, as a due regard to the Protection and essential Interests of the Nation may Justify, and permit.

To the Presbyterian Ministers of Massachusetts and New Hampshire, November 2, 1789

Gentlemen,

The affectionate welcome, which you are pleased to give me to the eastern parts of the union, would leave me without excuse, did I fail to acknowledge the sensibility, which it awakens, and to express the most sincere return that a grateful sense of your goodness can suggest.

To be approved by the praise-worthy is a wish as natural to becoming ambition, as its consequence is flattering to our self-love—I am, indeed, much indebted to the favorable sentiments which you entertain towards me, and it will be my study to deserve them.

The tribute of thanksgiving which you offer to "the gracious Father of lights" for his inspiration of our public-councils with wisdom and firmness to complete the national constitution, is worthy of men, who, devoted to the pious purposes of religion, desire their accomplishment by such means as advance the temporal happiness of their fellowmen—and, here, I am persuaded, you will permit me to observe that the path of true piety is so plain as to require but little political direction. To this consideration we ought to ascribe the absence of any regulation, respecting religion, from the Magna-Charta of our country.

To the guidance of the ministers of the gospel this important object is, perhaps, more properly committed—It will be your care to instruct the ignorant, and to reclaim the devious—and, in the progress of morality and science, to which our government will give every furtherance, we may confidently expect the advancement of true religion, and the completion of our happiness.

I pray the munificent Rewarder of virtue that your agency in this work may receive its compensation here and hereafter.

To the Governor and Legislature of New Hampshire, November 3, 1789

Allow me, Gentlemen, to assure you that grateful as my heart is for the affectionate regards which my fellow-citizens have manifested towards me, it has at no time been more sensibly impressed with a consciousness of their goodness than on the present occasion.

I am truly thankful for your expressions of attachment to my person, and approbation of my conduct—and I reciprocate your good wishes with unfeigned affection.

In exercising the vigilance and attention, with which you are pleased to compliment my military command, I did no more than what inclination prompted and duty enjoined.

In discharging the duties of my civil appointment, I can sincerely promise that the love of my country will be the ruling influence of my conduct.

The success, which has hitherto attended our united efforts, we owe to the gracious interposition of Heaven, and to that interposition let us gratefully ascribe the praise of victory, and the blessings of peace.

May the State, in whose councils you worthily preside, be happy under your administration, and may you, Gentlemen, partake of the blessings which your endeavors are intended to bestow.

To the Maryland Legislature, January 20, 1790

Gentlemen,

I receive with the liveliest emotions of satisfaction, your expressions of gratitude for my having accepted the Office of President of the United States, and your congratulations on that event.

From the enlightened policy of the Legislature of the Union, in conjunction with the patriotic measures of the State Assemblies, I anticipate the Blessings in reserve for these United States: and so far as my Administration may be conducive to their attainment, I dare pledge myself to co-operate with those distinguished Bodies, by constantly respecting and cherishing the rights of my fellow-Citizens.

Your mention of the place from whence you address me awakens a succession of uncommon reflections. In noticing the eventful period, since the resignation of my military command; I trace, with infinite gratitude, the agency of a Providence, which induced the People of America to substitute in the place of an inadequate confederacy, a general Government, eminently calculated to secure the safety and welfare of their Country.

The good dispositions of this People, and their increasing attachment to a Government of their own institution, with the aid of wisdom and firmness in their common Councils, afford a well founded hope, that the dangers of civil discord may be averted, and the Union established on so solid a basis that it may endure to the latest ages.

When I reflect on the critical situations to which this Country has been more than once reduced, I feel a kind of exultation in the character of my Countrymen, who have rescued it from threatened ruin by their virtue, fortitude, intelligence, and unanimity.

I thank you for the favorable sentiments which you are pleased to express of my public conduct, and for the affectionate interest which you have the goodness to take in the success of my measures and the preservation of my health. I pray for the Divine Benedictions on you, Gentlemen, and on your State.

To the Society of Free Quakers, March 1790

Gentlemen,

I desire to assure you of the sensibility with which I receive your congratulations on my appointment to the highest office and most extended trust which can be confided by a free People—and I thank you with sincerity for the obliging terms in which you express yourselves in my behalf.

Ever happy in being favored with the approbation of my fellow-citizens, the time at which yours is declared does not diminish my sense of the obligation it confers.

Having always considered the conscientious scruples of religious belief as resting entirely with the sects that profess, or the individuals who entertain them, I cannot, consistent with this uniform sentiment, otherwise notice the circumstances referred to in your address, than by adding the tribute of my acknowledgement, to that of our country, for those services which the members of your particular community rendered to the common cause in the course of our revolution—and by assuring you that, as our present government was instituted with an express view to general happiness, it will be my earnest endeavor, in discharging the duties confided to me with faithful impartiality, to realise the hope of common protection which you expect from the measures of that government.

Impressed with gratitude for your supplications to the supreme Being in my favor, I entreat his gracious beneficence in your behalf.

To Roman Catholics in America, March 1790

Gentlemen,

While I now receive with much satisfaction your congratulations on my being called, by an unanimous vote, to the first station in my Country; I cannot but duly notice your politeness in offering an apology for the unavoidable delay. As that delay has given you an opportunity of realizing, instead of anticipating, the benefits of the general Government; you will do me the justice to believe, that your testimony of the increase of the public prosperity, enhances the pleasure which I should otherwise have experienced from your affectionate address.

I feel that my conduct, in war and in peace, has met with more general approbation than could reasonably have been expected: and I find myself disposed to consider that fortunate circumstance, in a great degree, resulting from the able support and extraordinary candour of my fellow-citizens of all denominations.

The prospect of national prosperity now before us is truly animating, and ought to excite the exertions of all good men to establish and secure the happiness of their Country, in the permanent duration of its Freedom and Independence. America, under the smiles of a Divine Providence—the protection of a good Government—and the cultivation of manners, morals and piety, cannot fail of attaining an uncommon degree of eminence, in literature, commerce, agriculture, improvements at home and respectability abroad.

As mankind become more liberal they will be more apt to allow, that all those who conduct themselves as worthy members of the Community are equally entitled to the protection of civil Government. I hope ever to see America among the foremost nations in examples of justice and liberality. And I presume that your fellow-citizens will not forget the patriotic part which you took in the accomplishment of their Revolution, and the establishment of their Government: or the important assistance which they received from a nation in which the Roman Catholic faith is professed.

I thank you, Gentlemen, for your kind concern for me. While my life and my health shall continue, in whatever situation I may be, it shall be my constant endeavour to justify the favourable sentiments which you are pleased to express of my conduct. And may the members of your Society in America, animated alone by the pure spirit of Christianity, and still conducting themselves as the faithful subjects of our free Government, enjoy every temporal and spiritual felicity.

To the Savannah, Georgia, Hebrew Congregation, May 1790

Gentlemen,

I thank you with great sincerity for your congratulations on my appointment to the office, which I have the honor to hold by the unanimous choice of my fellow-citizens: and especially for the expressions which you are pleased to use in testifying the confidence that is reposed in me by your congregation.

As the delay which has naturally intervened between my election and your address has afforded an opportunity for appreciating the merits of the federal-government, and for communicating your sentiments of its administration—I have rather to express my satisfaction rather than regret at a circumstance, which demonstrates (upon experiment) your attachment to the former as well as approbation of the latter.

I rejoice that a spirit of liberality and philanthropy is much more prevalent than it formerly was among the enlightened nations of the earth; and that your brethren will benefit thereby in proportion as it shall become still more extensive. Happily the people of the United States of America have, in many instances, exhibited examples worthy of imitation—The salutary influence of which will doubtless extend much farther, if gratefully enjoying those blessings of peace which (under favor of Heaven) have been obtained by fortitude in war, they shall conduct themselves with reverence to the Deity, and charity towards their fellow-creatures.

May the same wonder-working Deity, who long since delivering the Hebrews from their Egyptian oppressors planted them in the promised land—whose providential agency has lately been conspicuous in establishing these United States as an independent nation—still continue to water them with the dews of Heaven and to make the inhabitants of every denomination participate in the temporal and spiritual blessings of that people whose God is Jehovah.

To the Convention of the Universal Church, August 9, 1790

Gentlemen,

I thank you cordially for the congratulations which you offer on my appointment to the office I have the honor to hold in the government of the United States.

It gives me the most sensible pleasure to find, that, in our nation, however different are the sentiments of citizens on religious doctrines, they generally concur in one thing, for their political professions and practices are almost universally friendly to the order and happiness of our civil institutions—I am also happy in finding this disposition particularly evinced by your society. It is moreover my earnest desire, that all the members of every association or community, throughout the United States, may make such use of the auspicious years of Peace, liberty and free enquiry, with which they are now favored, as they shall hereafter find occasion to rejoice for having done.

With great satisfaction I embrace this opportunity to express my acknowledgements for the interest my affectionate fellow-citizens have taken in my recovery from a late dangerous indisposition, and I assure you, Gentlemen, that in mentioning my obligations for the effusions of your benevolent wishes on my behalf, I feel animated with new zeal, that my conduct may ever be worthy of your favorable opinion, as well as such as shall in every respect best comport with the character of an intelligent and accountable Being.

To the Clergy of Newport, Rhode Island, August 18, 1790

Gentlemen,

The salutations of the Clergy of the Town of Newport on my arrival in the State of Rhode Island are rendered the more acceptable on account of the liberal sentiments and just ideas which they are known to entertain respecting civil and religious liberty.

I am inexpressibly happy that by the smiles of divine Providence, my weak but honest endeavors to serve my country have hitherto been crowned with so much success, and apparently given such satisfaction to those in whose cause they were exerted. The same benignant influence, together with the concurrent support of all real friends to their country will still be necessary to enable me to be in any degree useful to this numerous and free People over whom I am called to preside.

Wherefore I return you, Gentlemen, my hearty thanks for your solemn invocation of Almighty God that every temporal and spiritual blessing may be dispensed to me, and that, under my administration, the families of these States may enjoy peace and prosperity, with all the blessings attendant on civil and religious liberty—In the participation of which blessings may you have an ample Share.

To the Hebrew Congregation in Newport, Rhode Island, August 18, 1790

Gentlemen.

While I receive, with much satisfaction, your Address replete with expressions of affection and esteem; I rejoice in the opportunity of assuring you, that I shall always retain a grateful remembrance of the cordial welcome I experienced in my visit to Newport, from all classes of Citizens.

The reflection on the days of difficulty and danger which are past is rendered the more sweet, from a consciousness that they are succeeded by days of uncommon prosperity and security. If we have wisdom to make the best use of the advantages with which we are now favored, we cannot fail, under the just administration of a good Government, to become a great and a happy people.

The Citizens of the United States of America have a right to applaud themselves for having given to mankind examples of an enlarged and liberal policy: a policy worthy of imitation. All possess alike liberty of conscience and immunities of citizenship. It is now no more that toleration is spoken of, as if it was by the indulgence of one class of people, that another enjoyed the exercise of their inherent natural rights. For happily the Government of the United States, which gives to bigotry no sanction, to persecution no assistance requires only that they who live under its protection should demean themselves as good citizens, in giving it on all occasions their effectual support.

It would be inconsistent with the frankness of my character not to avow that I am pleased with your favorable opinion of my Administration, and fervent wishes for my felicity. May the Children of the Stock of Abraham, who dwell in this land, continue to merit and enjoy the good will of the other Inhabitants; while every one shall sit in safety under his own vine and figtree, and there shall be none to make him afraid. May the father of all mercies scatter light and not darkness in our paths, and make us all in our several vocations useful here, and in his own due time and way everlastingly happy.

To the Inhabitants of Providence, Rhode Island, August 19, 1790

Gentlemen

The Congratulations which you offer me, upon my arrival in this place, are received with no small degree of pleasure. For your attentions, and endeavours to render the town agreeable to me, and for your expressions of satisfaction at my election to the Presidency of the United States, I return my warmest thanks.

My sensibility is highly excited by your ardent declarations of attachment to my person, and the Constitution.

As, under the smiles of Heaven, America is indebted for Freedom and Independence, rather to the joint exertions of the Citizens of the several States; in which it may be your boast to have borne no inconsiderable share; than to the Conduct of her Commander in Chief, so is she indebted for their support, rather to a continuation of those exertions than to the Prudence and Ability manifested in the exercise of the powers delegated to the President of the United States.

Your hopes of the extension of Commerce, the encouragement of Agriculture and Manufactures, and the establishment of public faith, as reared upon our Constitution, are well founded; and it is my earnest wish that you may extensively enjoy the benefits arising from them.

I thank you, Gentlemen, for your prayer for my future welfare, and offer up my best wishes for your individual and collective happiness.

To the Hebrew Congregations of Philadelphia, New York, Charleston, and Richmond, December 13, 1790

Gentlemen,

The liberality of sentiment toward each other which marks every political and religious denomination of men in this Country, stands unparalleled in the history of Nations. The affection of such people is a treasure beyond the reach of calculation; and the repeated proofs which my fellow Citizens have given of their attachment to me, and approbation of my doings form the purest source of my temporal felicity. The affectionate expressions of your address again excite my gratitude, and receive my warmest acknowledgments.

The Power and Goodness of the Almighty were strongly Manifested in the events of our late glorious revolution; and his kind interposition in our behalf has been no less visible in the establishment of our present equal government. In war he directed the Sword; and in peace he has ruled our Councils. My agency in both has been guided by the best intentions, and a sense of the duty which I owe my Country: and as my exertions have hitherto been amply rewarded by the Approbation of my fellow Citizens, I shall endeavour to deserve a continuance of it by my future conduct.

May the same temporal and eternal blessings which you implore for me, rest upon your Congregations.

≈

FIVE

President of the United States
After the First Amendment

1792–1797

To Bishop John Carroll, April 10, 1792[1]

Sir,

I have recd, & duly considered your memorial of the 20th ultimo, on the subject of instructing the Indians, within and contiguous to the United States, in the principles & duties of Christianity.

The war now existing between the United States and some tribes of the Western Indians prevents, for the present, any intercourse of this nature with them. The Indians of the five nations are, in their religious concerns, under the immediate superintendance of the Revd Mr Kirkland; And those who dwell in the eastern extremity of the U.S. are, according to the best information that I can obtain, so situated as to be rather considered as a part of the inhabitants of the State of Massachusetts than otherwise, and that State has always considered them as under its immediate care & protection. Any application therefore relative to these Indians, for the purposes mentioned in your memorial, would seem most proper to be made to the Government of Massachusetts. The original letters on this subject, which were submitted to my inspection, have been returned to Charles Carroll, Esq. of Carrolton.

Impressed as I am with an opinion, that the most effectual means of securing the permanent attachment of our savage neighbors is to convince them that we are just, and to shew them that a proper & friendly intercourse with us would be for our mutual advantage, I cannot conclude without giving you my thanks for your pious & benevolent wishes to effect this desireable end upon the mild principles of Religion & Philanthropy. And when a proper occasion shall offer I have no doubt but such measures will be pursued as may seem best calculated to communicate liberal instruction & the blessings of society to their untoutered minds. With very great esteem & regard I am Sir.

To Edward Newenham, October 20, 1792

Dear Sir,

Where your Letter of the 21st of december last has been travelling since it left you, I cannot tell; but it did not get to my hands 'till within a few weeks past, when I likewise received yours of the 15th of July introducing Mr Anderson.

I was sorry to see the gloomy picture which you drew of the affairs of your country in your letter of december; but I hope events have not turned out so badly as you then apprehended. Of all the animosities which have existed among mankind those which are caused by a difference of sentiment in Religion appear to be the most inveterate and distressing and ought most to be deprecated. I was in hopes that the enlightened & liberal policy which has marked the present age would at least have reconciled *Christians* of every denomination so far that we should never again see their religious disputes carried to such a pitch as to endanger the peace of Society.

The affairs of this Country still wear a prosperous aspect. our agriculture, commerce & navigation are in a flourishing state. In some parts of the Country the crops of Indian corn (Maiz) have been injured by the drought in summer and early frosts in Autumn. We have, however, a happiness which is scarcely known in any other Country; for such is the extent of the U.S. and so great a variety of climate and soil do they embrace, that we never need apprehend an universal failure of our crops and a consequent famine.

I have spent part of the summer at Mount Vernon, & have but just returned to the seat of government, where I am so much engaged in attending to business which has accumulated during my absence—and in preparing such business as will be necessary to lay before the Legislature at their meeting early in next month, that I have but little time to attend to any affairs of a private or personal nature; I am therefore persuaded you will to these causes impute the shortness of this letter. Mrs Washington unites with me in respects & best wishes for Lady Newenham & yourself. I am Dear Sir with great esteem Your most Obedt Servt. &c.

To the New Jerusalem Church of Baltimore, January 27, 1793

Gentlemen,

It has ever been my pride to merit the approbation of my fellow citizens, by a faithful and honest discharge of the duties annexed to those stations on which they have been pleased to place me; and the dearest rewards of my services have been those testimonies of esteem and confidence with which they have honored me. But to the manifest interposition of an over-ruling Providence, and to the patriotic exertions of united America, are to be ascribed those events which have given us a respectable rank among the nations of the Earth.

We have abundant reason to rejoice, that in this land the light of truth and reason have triumphed over the power of bigotry and superstition, and that every person may here worship God according to the dictates of his own heart. In this enlightened age and in this land of equal liberty, it is our boast, that a man's religious tenets will not forfeit the protection of the laws, nor deprive him of the right of attaining and holding the highest offices that are known in the United States.

Your prayers for my present and future felicity are received with gratitude; and I sincerely wish, Gentlemen, that you may, in your social & individual capacities, taste those blessings which a gracious God bestows upon the righteous.

To the Inhabitants of the City of Hartford, August 4, 1793[2]

Fellow Citizens: The Address of the Inhabitants of the City of

Hartford contains sentiments too favorable to the public weal, too partial to myself not to claim and receive my affectionate acknowledgments.

It, at the same time, affords a new proof of that characteristic love of order and peace; of that virtuous and enlightened zeal, for the public good, which distinguishes the Inhabitants of Connecticut.

'Tis from dispositions like these that we may hope to avoid an interruption of the numerous blessings which demand our gratitude to Heaven; or that we may be encouraged to meet with firmness, confiding in the protection of a just Providence, any attempts to disturb them, which intemperance or injustice, from whatever quarter, may at any time make it our duty to encounter.

To the Inhabitants of Richmond, August 28, 1793

Fellow Citizens: Among the numerous expressions of the public sense in favor of the measures which have been adopted for the observance of neutrality in the present war of Europe, none is more grateful to me, than that of the Inhabitants of Richmond and its vicinity. The manner in which it is conveyed, lays claim to my affectionate acknowledgments.

In recollecting the anticipations wch. were entertained of a pacific policy, as most consonant with the situation of the United States and the genius of our Government, it is a pleasing reflection, that when the occasion for exemplifying it occurs, sentiments corresponding with it appear to pervade every part of the community. This steadiness of views, highly honorable to the national character is well calculated to support, in the administration of our affairs, a spirit constantly favorable to the great object of peace.

And tho' the best and sincerest endeavours to this end, may sometimes prove ineffectual; yet it will always be a source of consolation and encouragement, that the calamities of war, if at any time they shall be experienced, have been unsought and unprovoked. Every good citizen will then meet events with that firmness and perseverance which naturally accompany the consciousness of a good cause, the conviction that there is no ground for self-reproach.

True to our duties and interests as Americans, firm to our purpose as lovers of peace, let us unite our fervent prayers to the great ruler of the

Universe, that the justice and moderation of all concerned may permit us to continue in the uninterrupted enjoyment of a blessing, which we so greatly prize, and of which we ardently wish them a speedy and permanent participation.

To the Meeting of Inhabitants of Morris County, New Jersey, September 23, 1793

Sir: Your Letter, conveying to me the resolutions, agreed to by the Inhabitants of Morris County, the 10 inst: has reached my hands.

Their firm and manly sentiments, declared in the resolutions, and united determination to protect and defend the honor and dignity of our Country, are such as become the freemen and Citizens of the United States; and evince their firm and commendable resolution to preserve their liberty and independence inviolate. With such aid and support, under direction of Divine Providence, I trust the flourishing condition and inestimable blessings now enjoyed, will be long continued to our Country.

To the Meeting of Inhabitants of James City County, Virginia, September 23, 1793

Sir: Every well-wisher of the U. States must derive pleasure from the disposition which has been shewn generally, by the citizens thereof, to repel with firmness any attempts tending to disturb their present repose. It was with much satisfaction therefore that I received the Resolutions of the Inhabitants of James City County, enclosed in your Letter of the 16 instant, containing sentiments which accord with those which have been expressed by so many respectable Citizens in every part of the Union.

While such a disposition and such sentiments are retained by my Fellow Citizens, on whose aid and support, in the discharge of the trust which they have confided to me, I place entire confidence, we may expect, under the protection of a kind providence a continuation of those blessings which these States enjoy in a superior degree.

To the Trustees of the Public School of Germantown, November 6, 1793

Gentlemen: The readiness with which the Trustees of the public School of Germantown tender the buildings under their charge, for the use of Congress, is a proof of their zeal for furthering the public good; and doubtless the Inhabitants of Germantown generally, actuated by the same motives, will feel the same dispositions to accommodate, if necessary, these who assemble but for their service and that of their fellow Citizens.

Where it will be best for Congress to remain will depend on circumstances which are daily unfolding themselves, and for the issue of which, we can but offer up our prayers to the Sovereign Dispenser of life and health. His favor too on our endeavors, the good sense and firmness of our fellow Citizens, and fidelity in those they employ, will secure to us a permanence of good government.

If I have been fortunate enough, during the vicissitudes of my life, so to have conducted myself, as to have merited your approbation, it is a source of much pleasure; and shou'd my future conduct merit a continuance of your good opinion, especially at a time when our Country, and the City of Philada. in particular, is visited by so severe a calamity, it will add more than a little to my happiness.

To the Burgesses and the Citizens of Harrisburg, October 4, 1794

Gentlemen: In declaring to you the genuine satisfaction I derive from your very cordial address, I will not mingle any expression of the painful sensations which I experience from the occasion that has drawn me hither. You will be at no loss to do justice to my feelings. But relying on that kindness of providence towards our country which every adverse appearance hitherto has served to manifest and counting upon the tried good sense and patriotism of the great body of our fellow Citizens I do not hesitate to endulge with you the expectation of such an issue as will serve to confirm the blessings we enjoy under a constitution that well deserves the confidence, attachment and support of virtuous and enlightened men; to class the inhabitants of Harrisburgh among this number is only to bear testimony to the zealous and efficient exertions which they have made towards the defence of the laws.

To the Inhabitants of the Borough of Carlisle, October 6, 1794

Gentlemen: I thank you sincerely for your affectionate address. I feel as I ought what is personal to me; and I cannot but be particularly pleased with the enlightened and patriotic attachment which is manifested towards our happy constitution and the laws.

When we look round and behold the universally acknowledged prosperity, which blesses every part of the U States, facts no less unequivocal than those which are the lamented occasion of our present meeting were necessary to persuade us that any portion of our fellow citizens could be so deficient in descernment or virtue as to attempt to disturb a situation, which instead of murmurs and tumults calls for our warmest gratitude to heaven and our earnest endeavours to preserve and prolong so favoured a lot.

Let us hope that the delusion cannot be lasting, that reason will speedily regain her empire, and the laws their just authority where they have lost it. Let the wise and the virtuous unite their efforts to reclaim the misguided and to detect and defeat the acts of the factious. The union of good men is a basis on which the security of our internal peace and the stability of our government may safely rest. It will always prove an adequate rampart against the vicious and disorderly.

In any case in which it may be indispensable to raise the sword of Justice against obstinate offenders, I shall deprecate the necessity of deviating from a favourite aim, to establish the authority of the laws in the affections of all rather than in the fears of any.

Thanksgiving Proclamation, January 1, 1795[3]

When we review the calamities which afflict so many other nations, the present condition of the United States affords much matter of consolation and satisfaction. Our exemption hitherto from foreign war, an increasing prospect of the continuance of that exemption, the great degree of internal tranquillity we have enjoyed, the recent confirmation of that tranquillity by the suppression of an insurrection which so wantonly threatened it, the happy course of our public affairs in general, the unexampled prosperity of all classes of our citizens, are circumstances which peculiarly mark our situation with indications of the Divine beneficence toward us. In such a state of things it is in an especial manner our duty as a people, with devout reverence and affectionate gratitude, to acknowledge our many and great obligations to Almighty God and to implore Him to continue and confirm the blessings we experience.

Deeply penetrated with this sentiment, I, George Washington, President of the United States, do recommend to all religious societies and denominations, and to all persons whomsoever, within the United States to set apart and observe Thursday, the 19th day of February next, as a day of public thanksgiving and prayer, and on that day to meet together and render their sincere and hearty thanks to the Great Ruler of Nations for the manifold and signal mercies which distinguish our lot as a nation, particularly for the possession of constitutions of government which unite and by their union establish liberty with order; for the preservation of our peace, foreign and domestic; for the seasonable control which has been given to a spirit of disorder in the suppression of the late insurrection, and generally, for the prosperous course of our affairs, public and private; and at the same time humbly and fervently to beseech the kind Author of these blessings graciously to prolong them to us; to imprint on our hearts a deep and solemn sense of our obligations to Him for them; to teach us rightly to estimate their immense value; to preserve us from the arrogance of prosperity, and from hazarding the advantages we enjoy by delusive pursuits; to dispose us to merit the continuance of His favors by not abusing them; by our gratitude for them, and by a correspondent conduct as citizens and men; to render this country more and more a safe and propitious asylum for the unfortunate of other countries; to extend among us true and useful knowledge; to diffuse and establish habits of sobriety, order, morality, and piety, and finally, to impart all the blessings we possess, or ask for ourselves, to the whole family of mankind.

In testimony whereof I have caused the seal of the United States of

America to be affixed to these presents, and signed the same with my hand.

Done at the City of Philadelphia, the 1st day of January, 1795, and of the Independence of the United States of America the nineteenth.

Farewell Address, September 19, 1796[4]

Friends, & Fellow-Citizens.

The period for a new election of a Citizen, to Administer the Executive government of the United States, being not far distant, and the time actually arrived, when your thoughts must be employed in designating the person, who is to be cloathed with that important trust, it appears to me proper, especially as it may conduce to a more distinct expression of the public voice, that I should now apprise you of the resolution I have formed, to decline being considered among the number of those, out of whom a choice is to be made.

I beg you, at the sametime, to do me the justice to be assured, that this resolution has not been taken, without a strict regard to all the considerations appertaining to the relation, which binds a dutiful Citizen to his country—and that, in withdrawing the tender of service which silence in my Situation might imply, I am influenced by no diminution of zeal for your future interest, no deficiency of grateful respect for your past kindness; but am supported by a full conviction that the step is compatible with both.

The acceptance of, & continuance hitherto in, the Office to which your Suffrages have twice called me, have been a uniform sacrifice of inclination to the opinion of duty, and to a deference for what appeared to be your desire. I constantly hoped, that it would have been much earlier in my power, consistently with motives, which I was not at liberty to disregard, to return to that retirement, from which I had been reluctantly drawn. The strength of my inclination to do this, previous to the last Election, had even led to the preparation of an address to declare it to you; but mature reflection on the then perplexed & critical posture of our Affairs with foreign nations, and the unanimous advice of persons entitled to my confidence, impelled me to abandon the idea.

I rejoice, that the state of your concerns, external as well as internal, no longer renders the pursuit of inclination incompatible with the sentiment of duty, or propriety; & am persuaded whatever partiality may be retained for my services, that in the present circumstances of our country, you will not disapprove my determination to retire.

The impressions, with which, I first undertook the arduous trust, were explained on the proper occasion. In the discharge of this trust, I will only say, that I have, with good intentions, contributed towards the Organization and Administration of the government, the best exertions of which a very fallible judgment was capable. Not unconscious, in the outset, of the inferiority of my qualifications, experience in my own eyes, perhaps still more in the eyes of others, has strengthned the motives to diffidence of myself; and every day the encreasing weight of years admonishes me more and more, that the shade of retirement is as necessary to me as it will be welcome. Satisfied that if any circumstances have given peculiar value to my services, they were temporary, I have the consolation to believe, that while choice and prudence invite me to quit the political scene, patriotizm does not forbid it.

In looking forward to the moment, which is intended to terminate the career of my public life, my feelings do not permit me to suspend the deep acknowledgment of that debt of gratitude wch I owe to my beloved country, for the many honors it has conferred upon me; still more for the stedfast confidence with which it has supported me; and for the opportunities I have thence enjoyed of manifesting my inviolable attachment, by services faithful & persevering, though in usefulness unequal to my zeal. If benefits have resulted to our country from these services, let it always be remembered to your praise, and as an instructive example in our annals, that, under circumstances in which the Passions agitated in every direction were liable to mislead, amidst appearances sometimes dubious, viscissitudes of fortune often discouraging, in situations in which not unfrequently want of Success has countenanced the spirit of criticism, the constancy of your support was the essential prop of the efforts, and a guarantee of the plans by which they were effected. Profoundly penetrated with this idea, I shall carry it with me to my grave, as a strong incitement to unceasing vows that Heaven may continue to you the choicest tokens of its beneficence—that your Union & brotherly affection may be perpetual—that the free constitution, which is the work of your hands, may be sacredly maintained—that its Administration in every department may be stamped with wisdom and Virtue—that, in fine, the happiness of the people of these States, under the auspices of liberty, may be made complete, by so careful a preservation and so prudent a use of this blessing as will acquire to them the glory of recommending it to the applause, the affection—and adoption of every nation which is yet a stranger to it.

Here, perhaps, I ought to stop. But a solicitude for your welfare, which cannot end but with my life, and the apprehension of danger, natural to that solicitude, urge me on an occasion like the present, to offer to your solemn contemplation, and to recommend to your frequent review, some sentiments; which are the result of much reflection, of no inconsiderable observation, and which appear to me all important to the permanency of your felicity as a People. These will be offered to you with the more freedom as you can only see in them the disinterested warnings of a parting friend, who can possibly have no personal motive to biass his counsel. Nor can I forget, as an encouragement to it, your endulgent reception of my sentiments on a former and not dissimilar occasion.

Interwoven as is the love of liberty with every ligament of your hearts, no recommendation of mine is necessary to fortify or confirm the Attachment.

The Unity of Government which constitutes you one people is also now dear to you. It is justly so; for it is a main Pillar in the Edifice of your real independence, the support of your tranquility at home; your peace abroad; of your safety; of your prosperity; of that very Liberty which you so highly prize. But as it is easy to foresee, that from different causes & from different quarters, much pains will be taken, many artifices employed, to weaken in your minds the conviction of this truth; as this is the point in your political fortress against which the batteries of internal & external enemies will be most constantly and actively (though often covertly & insidiously) directed, it is of infinite moment, that you should properly estimate the immense value of your national Union to your collective & individual happiness; that you should cherish a cordial, habitual & immoveable attachment to it; accustoming yourselves to think and speak of it as of the Palladium of your political safety and prosperity; watching for its preservation with jealous anxiety; discountenancing whatever may suggest even a suspicion that it can in any event be abandoned, and indignantly frowning upon the first dawning of every attempt to alienate any portion of our Country from the rest, or to enfeeble the sacred ties which now link together the various parts.

For this you have every inducement of sympathy and interest. Citizens by birth or choice, of a common country, that country has a right to concentrate your affections. The name of American, which belongs to you, in your national capacity, must always exalt the just pride of Patriotism, more than any appellation derived from local discriminations. With slight shades of difference, you have the same Religeon, Manners, Habits & political Principles. You have in a common cause fought & triumphed together—The independence & liberty you possess are the work of joint councils, and joint efforts—of common dangers, sufferings and successes.

But these considerations, however powerfully they address themselves to your sensibility are greatly outweighed by those which apply more immediately to your Interest. Here every portion of our country finds the most commanding motives for carefully guarding & preserving the Union of the whole.

The *North*, in an unrestrained intercourse with the *South*, protected by the equal Laws of a common government, finds in the productions of the latter, great additional resources of Maratime & commercial enterprise and—precious materials of manufacturing industry. The *South* in the same Intercourse, benefitting by the Agency of the *North*, sees its agriculture grow & its commerce expand. Turning partly into its own channels the seamen of the North, it finds its particular navigation envigorated; and while it contributes, in different ways, to nourish & increase the general mass of the National navigation, it looks forward to the protection of a Maratime strength, to which itself is unequally adapted. The *East*, in a like intercourse with the *West*, already finds, and in the progressive improvement of interior communications, by land & water, will more & more find a valuable vent for the commodities which it brings from abroad, or manufactures at home. The *West* derives from the *East* supplies requisite to its growth & comfort—and what is perhaps of still greater consequence, it must of necessity owe the Secure enjoyment of indispensable *outlets* for its own productions to the weight, influence, and the future maritime strength of the Atlantic side of the Union, directed by an indissoluble community of Interest as *one Nation*. Any other tenure by which the *West* can hold this essential advantage, whether derived from its own seperate strength, or from an apostate & unnatural connection with any foreign Power, must be intrinsically precarious.

While then every part of our country thus feels an immediate & particular Interest in Union, all the parts combined cannot fail to find in the united mass of means & efforts greater strength, greater resource, proportionably greater security from external danger, a less frequent interruption of their Peace by foreign Nations; and, what is of inestimable value! they must derive from Union an exemption from those broils and Wars between themselves, which so frequently afflict neighbouring countries, not tied together by the same government; which their own rivalships alone would be sufficient to produce, but which opposite foreign alliances, attachments & intriegues would stimulate & imbitter. Hence likewise they will avoid the necessity of those overgrown Military establishments, which under any form of Government are inauspicious to liberty, and which are to be regarded as particularly hostile to Republican Liberty: In this sense it is, that your union ought to be considered as a main prop of your liberty, and that the love of the one ought to endear to you the preservation of the other.

These considerations speak a persuasive language to every reflecting & virtuous mind, and exhibit the continuance of the Union as a primary object of Patriotic desire. Is there a doubt, whether a common government can embrace so large a sphere? Let experience solve it. To listen to mere speculation in such a case were criminal. We are authorized to hope that a proper organization of the whole, with the auxiliary agency of governments for the respective Subdivisions, will afford a happy issue to the experiment. 'Tis well worth a fair and full experiment. With such powerful and obvious motives to Union, affecting all parts of our country, while experience shall not have demonstrated its impracticability, there will always be reason, to distrust the patriotism of those, who in any quarter may endeavor to weaken its bands.

In contemplating the causes wch may disturb our Union, it occurs as matter of serious concern, that any ground should have been furnished for characterizing parties by *Geographical* discriminations—*Northern* and *Southern*—*Atlantic* and *Western*; whence designing men may endeavour to excite a belief that there is a real difference of local interests and views. One of the expedients of Party to acquire influence, within particular districts, is to misrepresent the opinions & aims of other Districts. You cannot shield yourselves too much against the jealousies & heart burnings which spring from these misrepresentations. They tend to render Alien to each other those who ought to be bound together by fraternal Affection. The Inhabitants of our Western country have lately had a useful lesson on this head. They have Seen, in the Negociation by the Executive, and in the unanimous ratification by the Senate, of the Treaty with Spain, and in the universal satisfaction at that event, throughout the United States, a decisive proof how unfounded were the suspicions propagated among them of a policy in the General Government and in the Atlantic States unfriendly to their Interests in regard to the Mississippi. They have been witnesses to the formation of two Treaties, that with G: Britain and that with Spain, which secure to them every thing they could desire, in respect to our Foreign relations, towards confirming their prosperity. Will it not be their wisdom to rely for the preservation of these advantages on the Union by wch they were procured? Will they not henceforth be deaf to those Advisers, if such there are, who would sever them from their Brethren and connect them with Aliens?

To the efficacy and permanency of Your Union, a Government for the whole is indispensable. No Alliances however strict between the parts can be an adequate substitute. They must inevitably experience the infractions & interruptions which all Alliances in all times have experienced. Sensible of this momentous truth, you have improved upon your first essay, by the adoption of a Constitution of Government, better calculated than your former for an intimate Union, and for the efficacious management of your common concerns. This government, the offspring of our own choice uninfluenced and unawed, adopted upon full investigation & mature deliberation, completely free in its principles, in the distribution of its powers, uniting security with energy, and containing within itself a provision for its own amendment, has a just claim to your confidence and your support. Respect for its authority, compliance with its Laws, acquiescence in its measures, are duties enjoined by the fundamental maxims of true Liberty. The basis of our political Systems is the right of the people to make and to alter their Constitutions of Government. But the Constitution which at any time exists, 'till changed by an explicit and authentic act of the whole People, is sacredly obligatory upon all. The very idea of the power and the right of the People to establish Government presupposes the duty of every Individual to obey the established Government.

All obstructions to the execution of the Laws, all combinations and Associations, under whatever plausible character, with the real design to direct, controul counteract, or awe the regular deliberation and action of the Constituted authorities are distructive of this fundamental principle and of fatal tendency. They serve to Organize faction, to give it an artificial and extraordinary force—to put in the place of the delegated will of the Nation, the will of a party; often a small but artful and enterprizing minority of the Community; and, according to the alternate triumphs of different parties, to make the public Administration the Mirror of the ill concerted and incongruous projects of faction, rather than the Organ of consistent and wholesome plans digested by common councils and modefied by mutual interests. However combinations or Associations of the above description may now & then answer popular ends, they are likely, in the course of time and things, to become potent engines, by which cunning, ambitious and unprincipled men will be enabled to subvert the Power of the People, & to usurp for themselves the reins of Government; destroying afterwards the very engines which have lifted them to unjust dominion.

Towards the preservation of your Government and the permanency of your present happy state, it is requisite, not only that you steadily discountenance irregular oppositions to its acknowledged authority, but also that you resist with care the spirit of innovation upon its principles however specious the pretexts. One method of assault may be to effect, in the forms of the Constitution, alterations which will impair the energy of the system, and thus to undermine what cannot be directly overthrown. In all the changes to which you may be invited, remember that time and habit are at least as necessary to fix the true character of Governments, as of other human institutions—that experience is the surest standard, by which to test the real tendency of the existing Constitution of a Country—that facility in changes upon the credit of mere hypotheses & opinion exposes to perpetual change, from the endless variety of hypotheses and opinion: and remember, especially, that for the efficient management of your common interests, in a country so extensive as ours, a Government of as much vigour as is consistent with the perfect security of Liberty is indispensable—Liberty itself will find in such a Government, with powers properly distributed and adjusted, its surest Guardian. It is indeed little else than a name, where the Government is too feeble to withstand the enterprises of faction, to confine each member of the Society within the limits prescribed by the laws & to maintain all in the secure & tranquil enjoyment of the rights of person & property.

I have already intimated to you the danger of Parties in the State, with particular reference to the founding of them on Geographical discriminations. Let me now take a more comprehensive view, & warn you in the most solemn manner against the baneful effects of the Spirit of Party, generally.

This Spirit, unfortunately, is inseperable from our nature, having its root in the strongest passions of the human Mind. It exists under different shapes in all Governments, more or less stifled, controuled, or repressed; but in those of the popular form it is seen in its greatest rankness and is truly their worst enemy.

The alternate domination of one faction over another, sharpened by the spirit of revenge natural to party dissention, which in different ages & countries has perpetrated the most horrid enormities, is itself a frightful despotism. But this leads at length to a more formal and permanent despotism. The disorders & miseries, which result, gradually incline the minds of men to seek security & repose in the absolute power of an Individual: and sooner or later the chief of some prevailing faction more able or more fortunate than his competitors, turns this disposition to the purposes of his own elevation, on the ruins of Public Liberty.

Without looking forward to an extremity of this kind (which nevertheless ought not to be entirely out of sight) the common & continual mischiefs of the spirit of Party are sufficient to make it the interest and the duty of a wise People to discourage and restrain it.

It serves always to distract the Public Councils and enfeeble the Public Administration. It agitates the Community with ill founded Jealousies and false alarms, kindles the animosity of one part against another, foments occasionally riot & insurrection. It opens the door to foreign influence & corruption, which find a facilitated access to the government itself through the channels of party passions. Thus the policy and the will of one country, are subjected to the policy and will of another.

There is an opinion that parties in free countries are useful checks upon the Administration of the Government and serve to keep alive the spirit of Liberty. This within certain limits is probably true—and in Governments of a Monarchical cast Patriotism may look with endulgence, if not with favour, upon the spirit of party. But in those of the popular character, in Governments purely elective, it is a spirit not to be encouraged. From their natural tendency, it is certain there will always be enough of that spirit for every salutary purpose. And there being constant danger of excess, the effort ought to be, by force of public opinion, to mitigate & assuage it. A fire not to be quenched; it demands a uniform vigilance to prevent its bursting into a flame, lest instead of warming it should consume.

It is important, likewise, that the habits of thinking in a free Country should inspire caution in those entrusted with its Administration, to confine themselves within their respective Constitutional Spheres; avoiding in the exercise of the Powers of one department to encroach upon another. The spirit of encroachment tends to consolidate the powers of all the departments in one, and thus to create whatever the form of government, a real despotism. A just estimate of that love of power, and proneness to abuse it, which predominates in the human heart, is sufficient to satisfy us of the truth of this position. The necessity of reciprocal checks in the exercise of political power; by dividing and distributing it into different depositories, & constituting each the Guardian of the Public Weal against invasions by the others, has been evinced by experiments ancient & modern; some of them in our country & under our own eyes. To preserve them must be as necessary as to institute them. If in the opinion of the People, the distribution or modification of the Constitutional powers be in any particular wrong, let it be corrected by an amendment in the way which the Constitution designates. But let there be no change by usurpation; for though this, in one instance, may be the instrument of good, it is the customary weapon by which free governments are destroyed. The precedent must always greatly overbalance in permanent evil any partial or transient benefit which the use can at any time yield.

Of all the dispositions and habits which lead to political prosperity, Religion and morality are indispensable supports. In vain would that man claim the tribute of Patriotism, who should labour to subvert these great Pillars of human happiness, these firmest props of the duties of Men & citizens. The mere Politician, equally with the pious man ought to respect & to cherish them. A volume could not trace all their connections with private & public felicity. Let it simply be asked where is the security for property, for reputation, for life, if the sense of religious obligation *desert* the Oaths, which are the instruments of investigation in Courts of Justice? And let us with caution indulge the supposition, that morality can be maintained without religion. Whatever may be conceded to the influence of refined education on minds of peculiar structure—reason & experience both forbid us to expect that National morality can prevail in exclusion of religious principle.

'Tis substantially true, that virtue or morality is a necessary spring of popular government. The rule indeed extends with more or less force to every species of Free Government. Who that is a sincere friend to it, can look with indifference upon attempts to shake the foundation of the fabric.

Promote then as an object of primary importance, Institutions for the general diffusion of knowledge. In proportion as the structure of a government gives force to public opinion, it is essential that public opinion should be enlightened.

As a very important source of strength & security, cherish public credit. One method of preserving it is to use it as sparingly as possible: avoiding occasions of expence by cultivating peace, but remembering also that timely disbursements to prepare for danger frequently prevent much greater disbursements to repel it—avoiding likewise the accumulation of debt, not only by shunning occasions of expence, but by vigorous exertions in time of Peace to discharge the Debts which unavoidable wars may have occasioned, not ungenerously throwing upon posterity the burthen which we ourselves ought to bear. The execution of these maxims belongs to your Representatives, but it is necessary that public opinion should cooperate. To facilitate to them the performance of their duty, it is essential that you should practically bear in mind, that towards the payment of debts there must be Revenue—that to have Revenue there must be taxes—that no taxes can be devised which are not more or less inconvenient & unpleasant—that the intrinsic embarrassment inseperable from the Selection of the proper objects (which is always a choice of difficulties) ought to be a decisive motive for a candid construction of the Conduct of the Government in making it, and for a spirit of acquiescence in the measures for obtaining Revenue which the public exigencies may at any time dictate.

Observe good faith & justice towds all Nations. Cultivate peace & harmony with all—Religion & morality enjoin this conduct; and can it be that good policy does not equally enjoin it? It will be worthy of a free, enlightened, and, at no distant period, a great Nation, to give to mankind the magnanimous and too novel example of a People always guided by an exalted justice & benevolence. Who can doubt that in the course of time and things the fruits of such a plan would richly repay any temporary advantages wch might be lost by a steady adherence to it? Can it be, that Providence has not connected the permanent felicity of a Nation with its virtue? The experiment, at least, is recommended by every sentiment which ennobles human Nature. Alas! is it rendered impossible by its vices?

In the execution of such a plan nothing is more essential than that permanent inveterate antipathies against particular Nations and passionate attachments for others should be excluded; and that in place of them just & amicable feelings towards all should be cultivated. The Nation, which indulges towards another an habitual hatred, or an habitual fondness, is in some degree a slave. It is a slave to its animosity or to its affection, either of which is sufficient to lead it astray from its duty and its interest. Antipathy in one Nation against another—disposes each more readily to offer insult and injury, to lay hold of slight causes of umbrage, and to be haughty and intractable, when accidental or trifling occasions of dispute occur. Hence frequent collisions, obstinate

envenomed and bloody contests. The Nation, prompted by ill will &
resentment sometimes impels to War the Government, contrary to the
best calculations of policy. The Government sometimes participates in
the national propensity, and adopts through passion what reason would
reject; at other times, it makes the animosity of the Nation subservient
to projects of hostility instigated by pride, ambition and other sinister
& pernicious motives. The peace often, sometimes perhaps the Liberty,
of Nations has been the victim.

So likewise, a passionate attachment of one Nation for another
produces a variety of evils. Sympathy for the favourite nation, facilitat-
ing the illusion of an imaginary common interest, in cases where no
real common interest exists, and infusing into one the enmities of the
other, betrays the former into a participation in the quarrels & Wars of
the latter, without adequate inducement or justification: It leads also
to concessions to the favourite Nation of priviledges denied to others,
which is apt doubly to injure the Nation making the concessions—by
unnecessarily parting with what ought to have been retained—& by
exciting jealousy, ill will, and a disposition to retaliate, in the parties
from whom eql priviledges are withheld: And it gives to ambitious,
corrupted, or deluded citizens (who devote themselves to the favourite
Nation) facility to betray, or sacrifice the interests of their own country,
without odium, sometimes even with popularity; gilding with the appearances of a virtuous sense of obligation a commendable deference for
public opinion, or a laudable zeal for public good, the base or foolish
compliances of ambition corruption or infatuation.

As avenues to foreign influence in innumerable ways, such attachments are particularly alarming to the truly enlightened and independent
Patriot. How many opportunities do they afford to tamper with domestic
factions, to practice the arts of seduction, to mislead public opinion, to
influence or awe the public Councils! Such an attachment of a small
or weak, towards a great & powerful Nation, dooms the former to be
the satellite of the latter.

Against the insidious wiles of foreign influence, (I conjure you to
believe me fellow citizens), the jealousy of a free people ought to be
constantly awake; since history and experience prove that foreign influence is one of the most baneful foes of Republican Government. But

that jealousy to be useful must be impartial; else it becomes the instrument of the very influence to be avoided, instead of a defence against
it. Excessive partiality for one foreign nation and excessive dislike of
another, cause those whom they actuate to see danger only on one side,
and serve to veil and even second the arts of influence on the other.
Real Patriots, who may resist the intriegues of the favourite, are liable
to become suspected and odious; while its tools and dupes usurp the
applause & confidence of the people, to surrender their interests.

The Great rule of conduct for us, in regard to foreign Nations is
in extending our comercial relations to have with them as little *political*
connection as possible. So far as we have already formed engagements
let them be fulfilled, with perfect good faith. Here let us stop.

Europe has a set of primary interests, which to us have none, or a
very remote relation. Hence she must be engaged in frequent controversies, the causes of which are essentially foreign to our concerns. Hence
therefore it must be unwise in us to implicate ourselves, by artificial ties,
in the ordinary vicissitudes of her politics, or the ordinary combinations
& collisions of her friendships, or enmities.

Our detached & distant situation invites and enables us to pursue
a different course. If we remain one People, under an efficient government, the period is not far off, when we may defy material injury from
external annoyance; when we may take such an attitude as will cause
the neutrality we may at any time resolve upon to be scrupulously respected; when belligerent nations, under the impossibility of making
acquisitions upon us, will not lightly hazard the giving us provocation;
when we may choose peace or War, as our interest guided by justice
shall Counsel.

Why forego the advantages of so peculiar a situation? Why quit our
own to stand upon foreign ground? Why, by interweaving our destiny
with that of any part of Europe, entangle our peace and prosperity in the
toils of European Ambition, Rivalship, Interest, Humour or Caprice?

'Tis our true policy to steer clear of permanent Alliances, with any
portion of the foreign World—So far, I mean, as we are now at liberty
to do it—for let me not be understood as capable of patronising infidil-
ity to existing engagements, (I hold the maxim no less applicable to

public than to private affairs, that honesty is always the best policy)—I repeat it therefore, Let those engagements be observed in their genuine sense. But in my opinion, it is unnecessary and would be unwise to extend them.

Taking care always to keep ourselves, by suitable establishments, on a respectably defensive posture, we may safely trust to temporary alliances for extraordinary emergencies.

Harmony, liberal intercourse with all Nations, are recommended by policy, humanity and interest. But even our Commercial policy should hold an equal and impartial hand: neither seeking nor granting exclusive favours or preferences; consulting the natural course of things; diffusing & deversifying by gentle means the streams of Commerce, but forcing nothing; establishing with Powers so disposed—in order to give to trade a stable course, to define the rights of our Merchants, and to enable the Government to support them—conventional rules of intercourse; the best that present circumstances and mutual opinion will permit, but temporary, & liable to be from time to time abandoned or varied, as experience and circumstances shall dictate; constantly keeping in view, that 'tis folly in one Nation to look for disinterested favors from another—that it must pay with a portion of its Independence for whatever it may accept under that character—that by such acceptance, it may place itself in the condition of having given equivalents for nominal favours and yet of being reproached with ingratitude for not giving more. There can be no greater error than to expect, or calculate upon real favours from Nation to Nation. 'Tis an illusion which experience must cure, which a just pride ought to discard.

In offering to you, my Countrymen, these counsels of an old and affectionate friend, I dare not hope they will make the strong and lasting impression, I could wish—that they will controul the usual current of the passions, or prevent our Nation from running the course which has hitherto marked the Destiny of Nations: But if I may even flatter myself, that they may be productive of some partial benefit, some occasional good; that they may now & then recur to moderate the fury of party spirit, to warn against the mischiefs of foreign Intriegue, to guard against the Impostures of pretended patriotism—this hope will be a full recompence for the solicitude for your welfare, by which they have been dictated.

How far in the discharge of my Official duties, I have been guided by the principles which have been delineated, the public Records and other evidences of my conduct must witness to You and to the world. To myself, the assurance of my own conscience is, that I have at least believed myself to be guided by them.

In relation to the still subsisting War in Europe, my Proclamation of the 22d of April 1793 is the index to my Plan. Sanctioned by your approving voice and by that of Your Representatives in both Houses of Congress, the spirit of that measure has continually governed me; uninfluenced by any attempts to deter or divert me from it.

After deliberate examination with the aid of the best lights I could obtain I was well satisfied that our Country, under all the circumstances of the case, had a right to take, and was bound in duty and interest, to take a Neutral position. Having taken it, I determined, as far as should depend upon me, to maintain it, with moderation, perseverence & firmness.

The considerations, which respect the right to hold this conduct, it is not necessary on this occasion to detail. I will only observe, that according to my understanding of the matter, that right, so far from being denied by any of the Belligerent Powers has been virtually admitted by all.

The duty of holding a neutral conduct may be inferred, without any thing more, from the obligation which justice and humanity impose on every Nation, in cases in which it is free to act, to maintain inviolate the relations of Peace and amity towards other Nations.

The inducements of interest for observing that conduct will best be referred to your own reflections & experience. With me, a predominant motive has been to endeavour to gain time to our country to settle & mature its yet recent institutions, and to progress without interruption, to that degree of strength & consistency, which is necessary to give it, humanly speaking, the command of its own fortunes.

Though in reviewing the incidents of my Administration, I am unconscious of intentional error—I am nevertheless too sensible of my defects not to think it probable that I may have committed many errors. Whatever they may be I fervently beseech the Almighty to avert or mitigate the evils to which they may tend. I shall also carry with me the hope that my Country will never cease to view them with indulgence; and that after forty five years of my life dedicated to its Service, with an upright zeal, the faults of incompetent abilities will be consigned to oblivion, as myself must soon be to the Mansions of rest.

Relying on its kindness in this as in other things, and actuated by that fervent love towards it, which is so natural to a Man, who views in it the native soil of himself and his progenitors for several Generations; I anticipate with pleasing expectation that retreat, in which I promise myself to realize, without alloy, the sweet enjoyment of partaking, in the midst of my fellow Citizens, the benign influence of good Laws under a free Government—the ever favourite object of my heart, and the happy reward, as I trust, of our mutual cares, labours and dangers.

To the Inhabitants of Shepherds Town and Its Vicinity, October 12, 1796

Gentlemen: With great sensibility I receive your polite and affectionate Address of the 6th. instant.

That Beneficent Providence, which, hitherto, has preserved us in Peace, and increased our prosperity, will not, I trust, withdraw its protecting hand; while we, on our part, endeavour to merit a continuance of its favors.

Equally persuaded am I, that no inconvenience will result from my retreat to the walks of private life. The good sense of my Countrymen will always discern, and can never be at a loss to choose, a fit character to administer the Executive Government of these United States.

If it has been my good fortune, through the course of my Civil and Military employment, to have met the approbation of my Countrymen, my wishes will be consummated; and I shall have found the only reward I ever had in view.

For the favorable sentiments you have expressed for me, and for your kind wishes, I sincerely thank you, and reciprocate with great cordiality my vows for your welfare.

Address to Congress, December 7, 1796

Fellow Citizens of the Senate and House of Representatives: In recurring to the internal situation of our Country, since I had last the pleasure to Address you, I find ample reason for a renewed expression of that gratitude to the ruler of the Universe, which a continued series of prosperity has so often and so justly called forth.

. . . .

The situation in which I now stand, for the last time, in the midst of the Representatives of the People of the United States, naturally recalls the period when the Administration of the present form of Government commenced; and I cannot omit the occasion, to congratulate you and my Country, on the success of the experiment; nor to repeat my fervent supplications to the Supreme Ruler of the Universe, and Sovereign Arbiter of Nations, that his Providential care may still be extended to the United States; that the virtue and happiness of the People, may be preserved; and that the Government, which they have instituted, for the protection of their liberties, may be perpetual.

To the Pennsylvania House of Representatives, February 17, 1797

Gentlemen: The kindness of my fellow Citizens has given me frequent occasion to make my acknowledgments for their expressions of confidence, attachment and affection; and for their honourable testimonies that my public cares and labours have been useful to my Country.

With great satisfaction I receive your additional testimonies, that as a public man I have not lived in vain.

Though now seeking that repose which retirement and the tranquil pursuit of rural affairs are calculated to afford, and which my time of life requires, the love of my Country will indeed suffer no abatement: its safety and prosperity will be essential to the enjoyment of my remaining years. And I confide in the discernment and patriotism of my fellow Citizens for the choice of wise and virtuous men who will successively administer every branch of the Government in such manner, as under divine providence, to enforce the general happiness.

For your affectionate wishes for my present and future happiness, accept, Gentlemen, my cordial thanks.

To the United Episcopal Churches of Christ Church and St. Peter's, March 2, 1797

Gentlemen: To this public testimony of your approbation of my conduct and affection for my person I am not insensible, and your prayers for my present and future happiness merit my warmest acknowledgments. It is with peculiar satisfaction I can say, that, prompted by a high sense of duty in my attendance on public worship, I have been gratified, during my residence among you, by the liberal and interesting discourses which have been delivered in your Churches.

Believing that that Government alone can be approved by Heaven, which promotes peace and secures protection to its Citizens in every thing that is dear and interesting to them, it has been the great object of my administration to insure those invaluable ends; and when, to a consciousness of the purity of intentions, is added the approbation of my fellow Citizens, I shall experience in my retirement that heartfelt satisfaction which can only be exceeded by the hope of future happiness.

To the Clergy of Different Denominations Residing in and Near the City of Philadelphia, March 3, 1797

Gentlemen: Not to acknowledge with gratitude and sensibility the affectionate addresses and benevolent wishes of my fellow Citizens on my retiring from public life, would prove that I have been unworthy of the Confidence which they have been pleased to repose in me.

And, among those public testimonies of attachment and approbation, none can be more grateful than that of so respectable a body as yours.

Believing, as I do, that *Religion* and *Morality* are the essential pillars of Civil society, I view, with unspeakable pleasure, that harmony and brotherly love which characterizes the Clergy of different denominations, as well in this, as in other parts of the United States; exhibiting to the world a new and interesting spectacle, at once the pride of our Country and the surest basis of universal Harmony.

That your labours for the good of Mankind may be crowned with success; that your temporal enjoyments may be commensurate with your merits; and that the future reward of good and faithful Servants may be your's, I shall not cease to supplicate the Divine Author of life and felicity.

Notes

AUTHORS' NOTE

1. The database can be found at http://memory.loc.gov/ammem/gwhtml/gwhome. html.
2. *See generally* THE WRITINGS OF GEORGE WASHINGTON FROM THE ORIGINAL MANUSCRIPT SOURCES 1745-1799 (John C. Fitzpatrick ed., 1931-44).
3. More information on this project can be found at http://gwpapers.virginia.edu.

INTRODUCTION

1. *E.g.*, McCreary County v. ACLU of Ky., 545 U.S. 844 (2005); Van Orden v. Perry, 545 U.S. 677 (2005); County of Allegheny v. ACLU, 492 U.S. 573 (1989); Lynch v. Donnelly, 465 U.S. 668 (1984); Stone v. Graham, 449 U.S. 39 (1980).
2. *See* Elk Grove Unified Sch. Dist. v. Newdow, 542 U.S. 1 (2004); Newdow v. Cong. of the United States, 383 F. Supp. 2d 1229 (E.D. Cal. 2005); Jennifer Coleman, *Federal Judge Sets Stage for Pledge Case to Move to Appeals Court*, ASSOCIATED PRESS, Oct. 5, 2005; David Kravets, *Atheist Now Sues to Take Motto Off Money*, ASSOCIATED PRESS, Nov. 18, 2005.
3. *See, e.g.*, Santa Fe Indep. Sch. Dist. v. Doe, 530 U.S. 290 (2000); Lee v. Weisman, 505 U.S. 577 (1992); Wallace v. Jaffree, 472 U.S. 38 (1985); Sch. Dist. v. Schempp, 374 U.S. 203 (1963); Engel v. Vitale, 370 U.S. 421 (1962).
4. In hearing these cases, the Court applies different legal tests, depending on whether a case involves the first of the First Amendment's religion clauses or the second. The first clause, often referred to as the Establishment Clause, provides that "Congress shall make no law respecting an establishment of religion . . ." U.S. CONST. amend. I. The second clause, often referred to as the Free Exercise Clause, concludes " . . . or prohibiting the free exercise thereof." *Id.* Establishment Clause cases tend to rely more heavily upon Jefferson's "wall of separation" phase; thus, this Introduction will focus on sample cases that are (or will be) decided by the Court under its Establishment Clause jurisprudence. Generally speaking, however, the different legal standards used for each clause are not relevant for purposes of

this book and will not be discussed in depth. For an excellent summary of these legal standards, however, see THE HERITAGE GUIDE TO THE CONSTITUTION 302-11 (David F. Forte & Matthew Spalding eds., 2005).

5.   *E.g.*, John Antczak, *ACLU Demands Removal of Cross from Los Angeles County Seal*, ASSOCIATED PRESS, May 25, 2004; *LA County to Remove Cross from County Seal After ACLU Challenge*, ASSOCIATED PRESS, June 3, 2004; Hugo Martin, *Facing ACLU Complaint, City to Drop Seal's Cross*, L.A. TIMES, Apr. 29, 2004, at B1; *see also* Laurie Goodstein, *Judge Orders a City to Remove Fish Symbol From Official Seal*, N.Y. TIMES, July 14, 1999, at A19 (ichthus on city seal); Joyce Howard Price, *Federal Judge Rules Fish on Town's Seal Unconstitutional*, WASH. TIMES, July 15, 1999, at A6 (same); Editorial, *The KU Seal Issue*, KAN. CITY STAR, Oct. 4, 1999, at B4 (Moses on university seal).

6.   *E.g.*, Scott Duke Harris, Op-Ed., *Rebuilding: A Righteous Mission For Your Tax Dollars*, L.A. TIMES, Sept. 25, 2005, at M1; Editorial, *Mission Miscues*, PRESS-ENTERPRISE (Riverside, CA.), Mar. 27, 2006, at B4; Douglas Quan & Bettye Wells Miller, *Suit Targeting Missions Funding Dropped*, PRESS-ENTERPRISE (Riverside, CA.), Jan. 19, 2006, at B5; David Whitney, *No Prop. 40 Aid for Mission: Quake-Hit Site Barred Because It Has Active Church*, SACRAMENTO BEE, Mar. 23, 2006, at A3.

7.   *E.g.*, Nat Hentoff, Op-Ed., *Lesson Plan for the Nation*, WASH. TIMES, Dec. 20, 2004, at A21; *Judge Tosses Bulk of Christian Teacher's Suit*, ASSOCIATED PRESS, Apr. 29, 2005; Dean E. Murphy, *God, American History and a Fifth-Grade Class*, N.Y. TIMES, Dec. 5, 2004, § 4, at 4.

8.   *E.g.*, Richard Benedetto, *Faith-Based Programs Flourishing, Bush Says*, USA TODAY, Mar. 10, 2006, at 5A; *Judge Gets Prison-Program Dispute*, RICH. TIMES-DISPATCH, Feb. 26, 2006, at A17; *Lawsuit Over Prison Religion Program Goes to Judge*, ASSOCIATED PRESS, Feb. 17, 2006.

9.   *E.g.*, Zachary Coile, *Atheist Unable to Block Bush Inauguration Blessing*, S.F. CHRON., Jan. 15, 2005, at A3; Julia Duin, *Faithful Bush Calls on God's Blessings*, WASH. TIMES, Jan. 21, 2005, at A1; Jon Ward, *Atheist Sues to Ban Hand on Bible*, WASH. TIMES, Jan. 8, 2005, at A1.

10. Another interesting dynamic is at play in cases that are filed based upon one of the First Amendment's two religion clauses. On the one hand, those who seek to drive religion out of public life often file cases that rely heavily upon the First Amendment's Establishment Clause. Examples are cited in the text and often rely heavily upon Jefferson's "separation of church and state" terminology. *See* discussion *supra* note 4 and accompanying text. On the other hand, Americans who wish to preserve America's religious heritage tend to file lawsuits that rely heavily on the First Amendment's Free Exercise Clause (perhaps in conjunction with the Free Speech Clause). For instance, a lawsuit was recently filed on behalf of an elementary school student in Plano, Texas. His public school had forbidden him from handing out gift bags with candy cane pens at Christmas, because an explanation of the religious symbolism of the candy canes was included in the gift bag. The school eventually relented. Paula Lavigne, *Holiday Parties Go on at Schools*, DALLAS MORNING NEWS, Dec. 18, 2004, at 1B. Other plaintiffs seek to avoid laws that violate their religious convictions. For instance, pharmacists have sought the courts' protection from laws that would require them to dispense the

"morning after pill" despite their religious beliefs against abortion. *E.g.*, Jim Suhr, *Advocacy Group Sues to Halt Illinois Rule on Contraceptive Prescriptions*, Associated Press, Dec. 20, 2005; *see also* Todd C. Frankel, *Pharmacists Allege Religious Bias in Pill Dispute*, St. Louis Post-Dispatch, Dec. 8, 2005, at C9; *Walgreen Accused of Religious Bias*, Chi. Trib., Dec. 8, 2005, at C23.

11. Religion has played a role in American civic life for centuries. In 1620, when the Pilgrims landed in the new world, they established a government for Plymouth Colony by entering into the Mayflower Compact, which declared:

> having undertaken, for the glory of God, and advancement of the Christian faith, and honour of our king and country, a voyage to plant the first colony in the Northerne parts of Virginia, doe, by these presents, solemnly and mutually in the presence of God, and one of another, covenant and combine ourselves together into a civill body politick, for our better ordering and preservation and furtherance of the ends aforesaid.

American Historical Documents: 1000-1904, at 59 (Harvard Classics, Charles W. Eliot, LL.D. ed., 1910). More than 150 years later, the American colonies declared their independence from Great Britain. As they did so, they declared that all men are "*endowed by their Creator* with certain unalienable Rights." The Declaration of Independence para. 2 (U.S. 1776) (emphasis added). The Declaration concludes with an appeal to the "Supreme Judge of the World for the Rectitude of our Intentions," along with a "firm Reliance on the Protection of divine Providence." *Id.* para. 32.

In recent years, it has become fashionable among some academics to describe the founding generation as irreligious, atheist, or deist. Yet, in all likelihood, most in the founding generation would not have recognized this description of themselves and would have instead called themselves a religious people. *See* Michael Novak, On Two Wings: Humble Faith and Common Sense at the American Founding (2002); *cf.* Frank Lambert, The Founding Fathers and the Place of Religion in America (2003) (noting that many in the founding generation sought religious freedom because they wanted a free "religious marketplace" in which religion could flourish); Michael W. McConnell, *The Origins and Historical Understanding of Free Exercise of Religion*, 103 Harv. L. Rev. 1409, 1437-43 (1990) (discussing the manner in which religiosity, not secularism, drove the effort for religious freedom at the founding).

12. On the other hand, non-Christians sometimes file suit alleging bias against their religions as well. For instance, in North Carolina, the ACLU filed a lawsuit arguing that witnesses in courtrooms should be allowed to take their oaths on religious texts other than the Bible. *E.g.*, Yonat Shimron, *Whose Holy Scriptures?*, News & Observer (Raleigh, N.C.), Jan. 6, 2006, at E1; *State Seeks Dismissal of Oath-Text Lawsuit*, Myrtle Beach Sun-News, Sept. 30, 2005, at C4. As another example, Rastafarian and Muslim inmates have sought exemption from prison policies that would require them to shave their beards or cut their hair. *E.g.*, Guillermo Contreras, *Muslim Sues Bexar, Guards Over Detainment*, San Antonio Express-News, July 27, 2005, at 3B; Frank Green, *Inmates: Grooming Rules Violate Faith*, Rich. Times-Dispatch, Sept. 28, 2005, at B4. Policemen and firefighters have also fought for the right to keep beards in accordance with their religious beliefs.

E.g., Laurie Asseo, *Court Says Muslim Police Officers Can Have Beards*, ASSOCIATED PRESS, Oct. 4, 1999; Del Quentin Wilber, *Judge Could Resolve Debate Over Firefighters' Facial Hair*, WASH. POST, July 31, 2005, at C4.

13. Office of the Clerk, Chaplains of the House (1789 to Present), http://clerk.house.gov/art_history/house_history/chaplains.html (last visited May 1, 2007); U.S. Senate, Chaplain's Office, http://www.senate.gov/reference/office/chaplain.htm (last visited May 1, 2007); *see also* 2 U.S.C. §§ 61d, 84-2 (2000); Marsh v. Chambers, 463 U.S. 783, 787-88 (1983).

14. LONNELLE AIKMAN, U.S. CAPITOL HISTORICAL SOC'Y, WE, THE PEOPLE: THE STORY OF THE UNITED STATES CAPITOL ITS PAST AND ITS PROMISE 122-23 (3d ed. 1965). The prayer room was established in 1954. *Id.* at 123.

15. *E.g.*, City of Elkhart v. Books, 532 U.S. 1058, 1062 (2001) (Rehnquist, C.J., dissenting); *see also* Lynch v. Donnelly, 465 U.S. 668, 677 (1984).

16. U.S. Supreme Court, The Court and Its Procedures, http://www.supremecourtus.gov/about/procedures.pdf (last visited May 1, 2007).

17. U.S. CONST. amend I. While these clauses refer only to "Congress," since the 1940s they have been held to apply equally to state governments, by operation of the Fourteenth Amendment to the United States Constitution. *See* Everson v. Bd. of Educ., 330 U.S. 1 (1947); Cantwell v. Connecticut, 310 U.S. 296 (1940); *see also* U.S. CONST. amend XIV; McCollum v. Bd. of Educ., 333 U.S. 203, 211 (1948).

18. *See* Letter from Thomas Jefferson to the Danbury Baptist Association (Jan. 1, 1802), *in* DANIEL L. DREISBACH, THOMAS JEFFERSON AND THE WALL OF SEPARATION BETWEEN CHURCH AND STATE 148, 148 (2002). Although Jefferson's letter was the first notable appearance of the "separation" phrase in reference to the First Amendment, others had used the term in other contexts before. For an excellent history of the concept of "separation of church and state," see PHILIP HAMBURGER, SEPARATION OF CHURCH AND STATE (2002); *see also* DREISBACH, *supra*, at 71-82.

19. *E.g.*, DREISBACH, *supra* note 18, at 98-99; *see also* Arlin M. Adams & Charles J. Emmerich, *A Heritage of Religious Liberty*, 137 U. PA. L. REV. 1559, 1584-85 (1989).

20. Wallace v. Jaffree, 472 U.S. 38, 92 (1985) (Rehnquist, J., dissenting). Rehnquist's opinion erroneously states that Jefferson was absent from the country at the time the First Amendment was ratified. *See id.* at 92. In fact, Jefferson returned from France in November 1789, after Congress approved the final text of the First Amendment, but before the states had completed ratification. The latter action was completed on December 15, 1791. DREISBACH, *supra* note 18, at 98-99 & 229 n.69.

21. *See, e.g.*, Vincent Phillip Muñoz, *Religion and the Common Good: George Washington on Church and State*, *in* THE FOUNDERS ON GOD AND GOVERNMENT 1, 1 (Daniel L. Dreisbach et al. eds., 2004); NOVAK, *supra* note 11, at 129; James R. Stoner, *Catholic Politics and Religious Liberty in America: The Carrolls of Maryland*, *in* THE FOUNDERS ON GOD AND GOVERNMENT, *supra*, at 251, 251-52. For empirical evidence that the Supreme Court has disproportionately relied upon Jefferson and Madison, to the exclusion of the other Founders, see Mark David Hall, *Jeffersonian Walls and Madisonian Lines: The Supreme Court's Use of History in Religion Clause Cases*, 85 OR. L. REV. 563, 567-69 & 568 tbl.1 (2006).

22. Washington biographer Marcus Cunliffe notes that Washington was practically idolized, even within his lifetime. MARCUS CUNLIFFE, GEORGE WASHINGTON: MAN AND MONUMENT 15-16 (1958); *see also* PAUL F. BOLLER, JR., GEORGE WASH-

INGTON & RELIGION viii (1963); JOSEPH J. ELLIS, FOUNDING BROTHERS: THE REVOLUTIONARY GENERATION 120 (2000) [hereinafter ELLIS, FOUNDING BROTHERS]; BARRY SCHWARTZ, GEORGE WASHINGTON: THE MAKING OF AN AMERICAN SYMBOL 41-89 (1987). After his death in 1799, the legend of George Washington grew still more, taking on a life of its own. Stories were fabricated, exaggerating his goodness, virtue, and honesty. CUNLIFFE, *supra*, at 17-29; *see also generally* SCHWARTZ, *supra*. One early Washington biographer, Parson Weems, is especially notorious for the stories that he created. His book was the source, for instance, of the well-known tale about Washington cutting down a cherry tree. ("I can't tell a lie, Pa.") CUNLIFFE, *supra*, at 17-20; JOSEPH J. ELLIS, HIS EXCELLENCY: GEORGE WASHINGTON 7 (2004) [hereinafter ELLIS, HIS EXCELLENCY]; MICHAEL NOVAK & JANA NOVAK, WASHINGTON'S GOD: RELIGION, LIBERTY, AND THE FATHER OF OUR COUNTRY 8 (2006); FRANKLIN STEINER, THE RELIGIOUS BELIEFS OF OUR PRESIDENTS: FROM WASHINGTON TO F.D.R. 14 (Prometheus Books 1995) (1936).

23. JAMES MADISON, NOTES OF DEBATES IN THE FEDERAL CONVENTION OF 1787, at 23-24 (W.W. Norton & Co. 1987).

24. U.S. CONST. art. II., § 1, cl. 8.

25. ELLIS, FOUNDING BROTHERS, *supra* note 22, at 121.

26. Washington's practical approach and tendency to learn through experience are not surprising. He did not have as much formal education as many of his contemporaries. *See, e.g.*, ELLIS, HIS EXCELLENCY, *supra* note 22, at 8-9; PAUL JOHNSON, GEORGE WASHINGTON: THE FOUNDING FATHER 8-9 (Eminent Lives Series, James Atlas ed., 2005) [hereinafter JOHNSON, FOUNDING FATHER]; PAUL K. LONGMORE, THE INVENTION OF GEORGE WASHINGTON 214 (1988). However, Washington also read a great deal more than many of his peers realized, perhaps in his efforts to make up for his lack of formal schooling. *See* RICHARD BROOKHISER, FOUNDING FATHER: REDISCOVERING GEORGE WASHINGTON 139-40 (1997); PETER R. HENRIQUES, REALISTIC VISIONARY: A PORTRAIT OF GEORGE WASHINGTON 32 (2006); LONGMORE, *supra*, at 213-26; *cf.* JOHNSON, FOUNDING FATHER, *supra*, at 8 (discussing Washington's large library at his death).

27. A lengthy analysis of Washington's views on church-state relations has not been completed prior to publication of this book. *See* discussion *infra* note 30 and accompanying text. However, a few scholars have completed essay or chapter-length pieces that generally agree with the observations made in this paragraph. *See, e.g.*, BOLLER, *supra* note 22, at 45-65, 116-62; FRANK E. GRIZZARD, JR., THE WAYS OF PROVIDENCE: RELIGION & GEORGE WASHINGTON 9-14 (2005); Muñoz, *supra* note 21, at 6-10; NOVAK & NOVAK, *supra* note 22, at 13-15, 111-17, 144-60.

28. The editors of *The Papers of George Washington* have not yet published the final volumes of their Presidential Series. The text of the Farewell Address, however, has been made available at http://gwpapers.virginia.edu/documents/farewell/transcript.html#top; *see also* Farewell Address (Sept. 19, 1796), *reprinted in* 35 THE WRITINGS OF GEORGE WASHINGTON FROM THE ORIGINAL MANUSCRIPT SOURCES 1745-1799, at 214, 229 (John C. Fitzpatrick ed., 1940) [the collection is hereinafter to as WRITINGS].

29. *See* SCHWARTZ, *supra* note 22, at 85; *cf.* BOLLER, *supra* note 22, at 116-62 (discussing Washington's relations with minority religious groups, such as Jews, Quakers, and Catholics, and noting the generally high esteem in which he was held); FRITZ

HIRSCHFELD, GEORGE WASHINGTON AND THE JEWS 16 (2005) (noting special relationship between the Jews and Washington).

30. Several new biographies have been released in recent years. Few focus on Washington's personal religious views, much less his views on the narrower issue of church-state relations. *See, e.g.*, JAMES MACGREGOR BURNS & SUSAN DUNN, GEORGE WASHINGTON (American Presidents Series, Arthur M. Schlesinger, Jr. ed., 2004); ELLIS, HIS EXCELLENCY, *supra* note 22; JOHNSON, FOUNDING FATHER, *supra* note 26; EDWARD G. LENGEL, GENERAL GEORGE WASHINGTON: A MILITARY LIFE (2005). A few exceptions to this general trend have recently been released. *See* JANICE CONNELL, FAITH OF OUR FOUNDING FATHER: THE SPIRITUAL JOURNEY OF GEORGE WASHINGTON (2004); GRIZZARD, *supra* note 27; NOVAK & NOVAK, *supra* note 22. All three books, however, focus primarily on Washington's personal religious views. His perspective on church-state relations is discussed to some degree (particularly in *Washington's God*, by Novak and Novak), but it is not the focus. Another somewhat recent book describes itself as a "moral biography" of George Washington, but it also does not discuss Washington's views on church-state matters in depth. BROOKHISER, *supra* note 26, at 11; *see also* HENRIQUES, *supra* note 26. In addition, the recent book *George Washington and the Jews* focuses on the contributions of the Jewish people to the creation of the American nation and the friendly relationship between Washington and the Jews. *See* HIRSCHFELD, *supra* note 29. The book includes only scattered mentions of Washington's perspective on church-state matters.

31. WRITINGS, *supra* note 28, at 93 n.65.

32. *E.g.*, BOLLER, *supra* note 22, at 26; BROOKHISER, *supra* note 26, at 144; GRIZZARD, *supra* note 27, at 1; HENRIQUES, *supra* note 26, at 173; JOHN C. McCOLLISTER, PH.D., GOD AND THE OVAL OFFICE: THE RELIGIOUS FAITH OF OUR 43 PRESIDENTS 2-3 (2005); *see also, e.g.*, JOHN SUTHERLAND BONNELL, PRESIDENTIAL PROFILES: RELIGION IN THE LIFE OF AMERICAN PRESIDENTS 18 (1971); DAVID L. HOLMES, THE FAITHS OF THE FOUNDING FATHERS 59-60 (2006); ALF J. MAPP, JR., THE FAITHS OF OUR FATHERS: WHAT AMERICA'S FOUNDERS REALLY BELIEVED 66 (2003).

33. *E.g.*, BOLLER, *supra* note 22, at 26-27; NOVAK & NOVAK, *supra* note 22, at 216-17; *see also, e.g.*, GRIZZARD, *supra* note 27, at 1; HENRIQUES, *supra* note 26, at 173-74; HOLMES, *supra* note 32, at 59; MAPP, *supra* note 32, at 66. Paul Boller notes that the position of vestryman was "as much civil as religious." BOLLER, *supra* note 22, at 26.

34. *See* discussion *infra* Chapter One, notes 50-56 and accompanying text.

35. BOLLER, *supra* note 22, at 67; *see also* HENRIQUES, *supra* note 26, at 168-69.

36. HENRIQUES, *supra* note 26, at 174; *see also* BOLLER, *supra* note 22, at 75.

37. HENRIQUES, *supra* note 26, at 174.

38. For arguments that Washington was probably a Christian, see CONNELL, *supra* note 30; WILLIAM J. JOHNSON, GEORGE WASHINGTON THE CHRISTIAN (Christian Liberty Press 1992) (1919); PETER A. LILLBACK, GEORGE WASHINGTON'S SACRED FIRE (2006). In their recent book, *Washington's God*, Michael Novak and Jana Novak seem unwilling to categorically state that Washington was a Christian, but they argue that he was definitely more than a Deist and was probably a Christian. *See generally* NOVAK & NOVAK, *supra* note 22; *see also* BOLLER, *supra* note 22, at 89-91; BROOKHISER, *supra* note 26, at 144-49; RICHARD NORTON SMITH, PATRIARCH:

GEORGE WASHINGTON AND THE NEW AMERICAN NATION 148 (1993); BONNELL, *supra* note 32, at 18-24. Others state that Washington was a Deist. *E.g.*, JAMES THOMAS FLEXNER, WASHINGTON: THE INDISPENSABLE MAN 216 (Back Bay ed. 1974); JOHNSON, FOUNDING FATHER, *supra* note 26, at 102-03; SCHWARTZ, *supra* note 22, at 174-75; STEINER, *supra* note 22, at 14-41; *see also* ELLIS, HIS EXCELLENCY, *supra* note 22, at 45, 151; LONGMORE, *supra* note 26, at 169.

39. *See* discussion *infra* Chapter Five, notes 9-10 and accompanying text.

40. Washington's busy schedule caused him to rely upon several aides for help with his correspondence. These aides would draft documents, relying upon written or oral directions from Washington. *E.g.*, 1 THE PAPERS OF GEORGE WASHINGTON: PRESIDENTIAL SERIES xviii (W.W. Abbot et al. eds., 1987); 1 THE PAPERS OF GEORGE WASHINGTON: REVOLUTIONARY WAR SERIES xvii-xix (W.W. Abbot et al. eds., 1985) [hereinafter WAR SERIES]; 1 WRITINGS, *supra* note 28, at xliii-xlv. Washington's reliance on such aides has caused some academics to question the extent to which Washington can be held responsible for the language in his public statements. Historians can debate who drafted or influenced various letters or speeches, but the outcomes of these intellectual exercises will not change one fact that no one seriously disputes: Washington was a man who knew, fairly early on, that his words were being preserved for posterity. At least as early as 1781, arrangements were being made to have his papers preserved. 1 THE PAPERS OF GEORGE WASHINGTON: CONFEDERATION SERIES 2-3 n. (W.W. Abbot et al. eds., 1992); *see also* WAR SERIES, *supra*, at xix-xx; 1 WRITINGS, *supra* note 28, at xlvi-xlviii. As a result, Washington was conscientious about his correspondence, and he carefully reviewed it before it went out. The ideas expressed were his own, even if someone else wrote the initial draft. Indeed, John C. Fitzpatrick, editor of the George Washington Bicentennial Commission collection of Washington writings, claims that Washington "dominated his correspondence," noting that the literary style is consistent across his writings, regardless of which aide drafted any particular document. 1 WRITINGS, *supra* note 28, at xlv. If Washington had not maintained personal control over his public statements, Fitzpatrick notes, such consistency could not have come about, particularly because Washington's aides were strong, thoughtful individuals in their own right. *Id.*

This book assumes that Washington is responsible for his statements and speeches, even if they were originally drafted by someone else. Washington bears ultimate responsibility for the ideas expressed in his writings, a fact that seems to have been clear to him as well.

PART ONE

ONE

1. Letter from George Washington to John Augustine Washington (July 18, 1755), *in* 1 THE PAPERS OF GEORGE WASHINGTON: COLONIAL SERIES 343, 343 (W.W. Abbot et al. eds., 1983) [the collection is hereinafter referred to as COLONIAL SERIES].

2. *Id.*

3. Washington biographer Douglas Southall Freeman lists the number of troops at 1,459. 2 DOUGLAS SOUTHALL FREEMAN, GEORGE WASHINGTON, A BIOGRAPHY: YOUNG WASHINGTON 86 (1948). Biographer Joseph Ellis states that there were about

1,300. Joseph J. Ellis, His Excellency: George Washington 22 (2004).

4. Descriptions of the day's events can be found at Ellis, *supra* note 3, at 21-23; James Thomas Flexner, Washington: The Indispensable Man 24-26 (Back Bay ed. 1974); 2 Freeman, *supra* note 3, at 64-102; Bernhard Knollenberg, George Washington: The Virginia Period, 1732-1775, at 29-35 (1964); Michael Novak & Jana Novak, Washington's God: Religion, Liberty, and the Father of Our Country 55-58 (2006).

5. 2 Freeman, *supra* note 3, at 86; *see also* Ellis, *supra* note 3, at 22.

6. Letter from George Washington to John Augustine Washington (July 18, 1755), *supra* note 1, at 343.

7. *Id.*; *see also* Letter from George Washington to Robert Jackson (Aug. 2, 1755), *in* 1 Colonial Series, *supra* note 1, at 349, 350.

8. *See, e.g.,* Ellis, *supra* note 3, at 23; Knollenberg, *supra* note 4, at 35; Novak & Novak, *supra* note 4, at 56, 58; *see also* 1 The Writings of George Washington from the Original Manuscript Sources 1745-1799, at 153 n.45 (John C. Fitzpatrick ed., 1931).

9. Douglas Southall Freeman states that this acceptance occurred on August 13, 1755. 2 Freeman, *supra* note 3, at 113. The editors of *The Papers of George Washington* opine that the acceptance occurred later, but by or on September 1. *See* 2 Colonial Series, *supra* note 1, at 1-3.

10. Letter from George Washington to Robert Dinwiddie (Sept. 23, 1756), *in* 3 Colonial Series, *supra* note 1, at 414, 417.

11. *Id.*

12. Letter from Robert Dinwiddie to George Washington (Sept. 30, 1756), *in* 3 Colonial Series, *supra* note 1, at 424, 425.

13. *Id.*

14. *See* 3 Colonial Series, *supra* note 1, at 425 & 426 n.5.

15. *See, e.g.,* Letter from George Washington to John Robinson (Aug. 5, 1756), *in* 3 Colonial Series, *supra* note 1, at 323, 326; *see also* 3 Colonial Series, *supra* note 1, at 202 n.8.

16. Letter from George Washington to Robert Dinwiddie (Nov. 9, 1756), *in* 4 Colonial Series, *supra* note 1, at 1, 6.

17. Letter from George Washington to John Robinson (Nov. 9, 1756), *in* 4 Colonial Series, *supra* note 1, at 11, 16.

18. Letter from Robert Dinwiddie to George Washington (Nov. 16, 1756), *in* 4 Colonial Series, *supra* note 1, at 24, 26.

19. Letter from George Washington to Robert Dinwiddie (Nov. 24, 1756), *in* 4 Colonial Series, *supra* note 1, at 29, 31.

20. Letter from George Washington to Robert Dinwiddie (Apr. 29, 1757), *in* 4 Colonial Series, *supra* note 1, at 144, 147.

21. Letter from George Washington to Robert Dinwiddie (June 12, 1757), *in* 4 Colonial Series, *supra* note 1, at 203, 204.

22. Letter from Robert Dinwiddie to George Washington (June 24, 1757), *in* 4 Colonial Series, *supra* note 1, at 254, 255.

23. *See* 5 Colonial Series, *supra* note 1, at 82 n.

24. *Id.* at 130 n.5. While it is hard to know, with any degree of certainty, what delayed the authorization of military chaplains and why they were finally approved, appointment of Anglican clergy, generally speaking, was a major point of contention during

Dinwiddie's governorship. Perhaps the two issues were related, as hypothesized by Philander D. Chase, Senior Editor of *The Papers of George Washington*, in an email written to the authors. *See also* JOHN RICHARD ALDEN, ROBERT DINWIDDIE: SERVANT OF THE CROWN 23-25 (1973).

25. Letter from George Washington to John Blair (Apr. 17, 1758), *in* 5 COLONIAL SERIES, *supra* note 1, at 129, 130.

26. Letter from Robert Dinwiddie to George Washington (Apr. 8, 1756), *in* 2 COLONIAL SERIES, *supra* note 1, at 343, 343.

27. Letter from George Washington to Robert Dinwiddie (Apr. 18, 1756), *in* 3 COLONIAL SERIES, *supra* note 1, at 13, 13-14.

28. Letter from John Robinson to George Washington (Apr. 17, 1756), *in* 3 COLONIAL SERIES, *supra* note 1, at 12, 12.

29. Letter from George Washington to John Robinson (Apr. 24, 1756), *in* 3 COLONIAL SERIES, *supra* note 1, at 48, 48; *see also* Letter from George Washington to John Robinson (Apr. 18, 1756), *in* 3 COLONIAL SERIES, *supra* note 1, at 15, 15.

30. A discussion of the events discussed in this paragraph can be found at 2 FREEMAN, *supra* note 3, at 174-207; KNOLLENBERG, *supra* note 4, at 42-43.

31. The events surrounding the article are discussed at 2 FREEMAN, *supra* note 3, at 208-31.

32. *Id.* at 210 (citation omitted).

33. *Id.* (citation omitted).

34. Letter from George Washington to John Augustine Washington (July 18, 1755), *supra* note 1, at 343.

35. According to the authors' review of *The Papers of George Washington*, Washington's first specific orders in this regard were issued on August 21, 1756. *See* Orders (Aug. 21, 1756), *in* 3 COLONIAL SERIES, *supra* note 1, at 372, 372. Similar orders followed in subsequent months, concluding with a November 1756 order that provided "this to be a standing order for the future." Orders (Nov. 13, 1756), *in* 4 COLONIAL SERIES, *supra* note 1, at 23, 23. Washington may have relied upon public prayers at an earlier point in his career as well. Jared Sparks reports that "it was Washington's custom to have prayers in the camp, while he was at Fort Necessity." 2 THE WRITINGS OF GEORGE WASHINGTON BEING HIS CORRESPONDENCE, ADDRESSES, MESSAGES, AND OTHER PAPERS, OFFICIAL AND PRIVATE 51-54 n.† (Jared Sparks ed., 1837). Unfortunately, the only source that Sparks cites is a letter written by William Fairfax while Washington was encamped at the Great Meadows. Fairfax urged Washington: "'I will not doubt your having public prayers in the camp, especially when the Indian families are your guests.'" *Id.* (citation omitted in original).

36. *Cf.* NOVAK & NOVAK, *supra* note 4, at 64 (discussing the lessons that Washington learned when he was with the Virginia Regiment, including the need for "discipline—especially moral discipline").

37. 3 COLONIAL SERIES, *supra* note 1, at 104 n.4 (citation omitted); *see also* 2 FREEMAN, *supra* note 3, at 192.

38. Letter from George Washington to Robert Dinwiddie (June 25, 1756), *in* 3 COLONIAL SERIES, *supra* note 1, at 222, 224 & 225 n.8. At least two more Quakers were drafted in 1757. *See* 4 COLONIAL SERIES, *supra* note 1, at 361 n.2. No information on the fate of these two men has been found, but Washington presumably implemented toward them the same principles established toward Quakers during the 1756 draft.

39. Letter from George Washington to Robert Dinwiddie (June 25, 1756), *supra* note 38, at 224.
40. *Id.*
41. Letter from Robert Dinwiddie to George Washington (July 1, 1756), *in* 3 COLONIAL SERIES, *supra* note 1, at 232, 232.
42. Letter from George Washington to Robert Dinwiddie (Aug. 4, 1756), *in* 3 COLONIAL SERIES, *supra* note 1, at 312, 315.
43. Letter from Robert Dinwiddie to George Washington (Aug. 19, 1756), *in* 3 COLONIAL SERIES, *supra* note 1, at 358, 360.
44. Letter from George Washington to Robert Dinwiddie (Sept. 8, 1756), *in* 3 COLONIAL SERIES, *supra* note 1, at 396, 397. The draftees were due to be released on December 1, 1756. *See* 3 COLONIAL SERIES, *supra* note 1, at 225 n.8.
45. *See, e.g.*, General Court-Martial (July 25-26, 1757), *in* 4 COLONIAL SERIES, *supra* note 1, at 329, 329-34; Court-Martial (May 18, 1756), *in* 3 COLONIAL SERIES, *supra* note 1, at 152, 152-53; Court-Martial (May 3, 1756), *in* 3 COLONIAL SERIES, *supra* note 1, at 77, 77-79; *see also* Letter from George Washington to Adam Stephen (May 18, 1756), *in* 3 COLONIAL SERIES, *supra* note 1, at 157, 158; 2 FREEMAN, *supra* note 3, at 137-38, 258, 372.
46. PAUL F. BOLLER, JR., GEORGE WASHINGTON & RELIGION 129 (1963).
47. Consider the process by which Henry Campbell and James Thomas were tried and punished for their desertion at about the time of this incident with the Quakers. First, Washington ordered a court martial. *See* Court-Martial (May 18, 1756), *supra* note 45, at 152-53. The court martial sentenced both men to death. *Id.* Washington wrote Dinwiddie, informing him, for the first time, of the proceedings against these men. *See* Letter from George Washington to Robert Dinwiddie (May 23, 1756), *in* 3 COLONIAL SERIES, *supra* note 1, at 171, 171-72. Dinwiddie wrote back, approving Campbell's death sentence but remitting the punishment for Thomas, per Washington's recommendation. *See* Letter from Robert Dinwiddie to George Washington (May 27, 1756), *in* 3 COLONIAL SERIES, *supra* note 1, at 178, 178-79.
48. *See, e.g.*, 2 FREEMAN, *supra* note 3, at 137. Although note that Dinwiddie appears to have sent blank death warrants to Washington, at least occasionally. Washington sometimes filled these warrants out and used them, as needed, without first notifying Dinwiddie. *See id.* at 139, 259 n.30.
49. Letter from George Washington to Robert Dinwiddie (Aug. 4, 1756), *supra* note 42, at 315.
50. *E.g.*, MAJOR J. HUGO TATSCH, THE FACTS ABOUT GEORGE WASHINGTON AS A FREEMASON 1-2 (1931); *see also* WILLIAM MOSELEY BROWN, P.G.M., GEORGE WASHINGTON: FREEMASON 10, 140 (1952); CHARLES H. CALLAHAN, WASHINGTON: THE MAN AND THE MASON 265 (1913); MARK A. TABBERT, AMERICAN FREEMASONS: THREE CENTURIES OF BUILDING COMMUNITIES 36 (2005).
51. *See generally, e.g.*, BROWN, *supra* note 50; CALLAHAN, *supra* note 50; TATSCH, *supra* note 50.
52. The authors would suggest, however, that the choice is not necessarily between two extremes: wholehearted, diligent, active support of Freemasonry versus total rejection of Masonic principles. A third option is often overlooked: Perhaps Washington supported Freemasonry, but saw it as just one of many good institutions crying for his attention. The Freemasons may have cherished their association with Washington more than Washington valued his membership with them. In

the Introduction to his book, *George Washington: Freemason*, William Moseley Brown practically admits as much:

> From 1755 to 1777 [Washington] appears not to have been active at all. Then, from his taking public part in the Christ Church Procession in Philadelphia in 1778 until his death in 1799, Masonic events occur one after another, and in every year. But to an outsider they have the look of being a succession of unrelated events, born of chance or temporary circumstances, *and it is most likely that they appeared as unrelated events to his own eye, as he viewed them from within.*
>
> But to a Masonic historian . . . who can see Washington in the perspective of the vast and complex history of the Fraternity . . . the circumstances, and the accidents, and the episodes melt together into a single picture.

BROWN, *supra* note 50, at vii (emphasis added). Freemasons cherish evidence of Washington's attendance at Masonic functions, letters that he wrote to lodges, and various honorary tributes and titles that were given to Washington. *See generally* BROWN, *supra* note 50; TATSCH, *supra* note 50. However, most of these events seem to have occurred at the instigation of individual Freemasons or a Masonic Lodge, not because Washington initiated the contact. Washington received similar overtures from churches and other groups; the diligence with which he answered letters from Freemasons did not differ from the diligence with which he answered letters from other types of organizations. Moreover, while records exist of Washington's attendance at several dinners, meetings, or Masonic celebrations, the number of confirmed events is fairly small, all things considered. If Washington sought out opportunities to be with Freemasons on a regular basis, then the confirmed evidentiary record of this behavior is unusually scant.

53. *See, e.g.*, TABBERT, *supra* note 50, at 11-12.
54. *See, e.g.*, 6 THE PAPERS OF GEORGE WASHINGTON: PRESIDENTIAL SERIES 287 n. (Dorothy Twohig et al. eds., 1996).
55. Admittedly, neither of the authors is a Freemason. As such, we can speak only as to what Freemasons themselves have told us. We have not been inside a Masonic meeting to see these activities for ourselves, nor would we be allowed in if we asked for permission to do so. Only Freemasons may attend meetings. Much of the authors' information about Freemasons comes from an interview with Mark Tabbert, Director of Collections at the George Washington Masonic National Memorial in Alexandria, Virginia, and the former Curator of Masonic and Fraternal Collections at the National Heritage Museum in Lexington, Massachusetts.
56. *See, e.g.*, TABBERT, *supra* note 50, at 18; *cf. id.* at 22-23 (discussing the fact that Solomon's Temple "became a theologically neutral symbol for Freemasonry's spirituality and brotherly love to which all believers in a Supreme Being could relate").

TWO

1. 3 THE DIARIES OF GEORGE WASHINGTON 254 (Donald Jackson & Dorothy Twohig eds., 1978) [hereinafter DIARIES].
2. *See, e.g.*, 2 DOUGLAS SOUTHALL FREEMAN, GEORGE WASHINGTON, A BIOGRAPHY: YOUNG WASHINGTON 147 (1948); PAUL K. LONGMORE, THE INVENTION OF GEORGE WASHINGTON 36-37 (1988).

3. *See* 2 FREEMAN, *supra* note 2, at 147.

4. Freeman reports the following tally: Washington (309 votes), Thomas Bryan Martin (239 votes), Hugh West (199 votes), and Thomas Swearingen (45 votes). *Id.* at 320. Bernhard Knollenberg and Paul Longmore report slightly different figures, not only from Freeman, but also from each other. *See* BERNHARD KNOLLENBERG, GEORGE WASHINGTON: THE VIRGINIA PERIOD, 1732-1775, at 102 (1964); LONGMORE, *supra* note 2, at 60.

5. *See* 2 FREEMAN, *supra* note 2, at 322-67; 3 DOUGLAS SOUTHALL FREEMAN, GEORGE WASHINGTON, A BIOGRAPHY: PLANTER AND PATRIOT 1 (1951).

6. 3 FREEMAN, *supra* note 5, at 1.

7. LONGMORE, *supra* note 2, at 56.

8. KNOLLENBERG, *supra* note 4, at 101.

9. *See* JOURNALS OF THE HOUSE OF BURGESSES OF VIRGINIA: 1758-1761, at 57 (H.R. McIlwaine ed., 1908) [hereinafter JOURNALS OF 1758-61]; *see also* KNOLLENBERG, *supra* note 4, at 102-03; LONGMORE, *supra* note 2, at 61-62.

10. *See, e.g.*, JOURNALS OF THE HOUSE OF BURGESSES OF VIRGINIA: 1770-1772, at 204, 210 (John Pendleton Kennedy ed., 1906) [hereinafter JOURNALS OF 1770-72]; JOURNALS OF THE HOUSE OF BURGESSES OF VIRGINIA: 1761-1765, at 92, 111, 175-76 (John Pendleton Kennedy ed., 1907) [hereinafter JOURNALS OF 1761-65]; *see also, e.g.*, Report to the House of Burgesses (Nov. 14, 1759), *in* 6 THE PAPERS OF GEORGE WASHINGTON: COLONIAL SERIES 372, 372 (W.W. Abbot et al. eds., 1988) [the collection is hereinafter referred to as COLONIAL SERIES]; Report to the House of Burgesses (Nov. 10, 1759), *in* 6 COLONIAL SERIES, *supra*, at 371, 371-72.

11. *See* JOURNALS OF THE HOUSE OF BURGESSES OF VIRGINIA: 1766-1769, at 190, 211 (John Pendleton Kennedy ed., 1906); *see also* 3 FREEMAN, *supra* note 5, at 218; KNOLLENBERG, *supra* note 4, at 103, 105; LONGMORE, *supra* note 2, at 81, 92-93.

12. JOURNALS OF THE HOUSE OF BURGESSES OF VIRGINIA: 1773-1776, at 75 (John Pendleton Kennedy ed., 1905) [hereinafter JOURNALS OF 1773-76]. In the quotation in the text, the long s, which resembles an f, has been updated.

13. The Committee was first asked to draft legislation protecting dissenters when it was four days old; however, the governor dissolved the legislature before a bill was drafted. Paul K. Longmore, *"All Matters and Things Relating to Religion and Morality": The Virginia Burgesses' Committee for Religion, 1769 to 1775*, 38 J. CHURCH & STATE 775, 782-83 (1996) [hereinafter Longmore, *Committee for Religion*]. Longmore characterizes the proposed legislation as a "limited call for exemption from legal penalties" that would "yield as little ground as necessary to dissenters." *Id.* at 782.

14. LONGMORE, *supra* note 2, at 93; *see also* Longmore, *Committee for Religion*, *supra* note 13, at 777. *But see* PETER A. LILLBACK, GEORGE WASHINGTON'S SACRED FIRE 288 (2006) (claiming that the purpose of the committee was to "check the growing menace of Deism in Anglican Virginia").

15. *See, e.g.*, JOURNALS OF 1773-76, *supra* note 12, at 31; JOURNALS OF 1770-72, *supra* note 10, at 5-6, 78-79, 81, 125, 287-88, 300; JOURNALS OF 1761-65, *supra* note 10, at 10, 97, 99, 117-18, 218-19; JOURNALS OF 1758-61, *supra* note 9, at xviii, 73.

16. *See* JOURNALS OF 1761-65, *supra* note 10, at 218; JOURNALS OF 1758-61, *supra* note 9, at 165.

17. *See, e.g.*, JOURNALS OF 1773-76, *supra* note 12, at 8, 32; JOURNALS OF 1758-61, *supra* note 9, at 56, 151.

18. *See, e.g.*, THE LIBRARY OF VIRGINIA, THE HISTORY OF THE LIBRARY OF VIR-GINIA, http://www.lva.lib.va.us/whatwehave/notes/timeline.pdf (last visited May 3, 2007).

19. The colonists were also upset about a new legislative policy that essentially gave the East India Company a monopoly on the trade in tea. These events are discussed at 3 FREEMAN, *supra* note 5, at 339-58; KNOLLENBERG, *supra* note 4, at 107-08; LONGMORE, *supra* note 2, at 111-16.

20. JOURNALS OF 1773-76, *supra* note 12, at 124. In the quotation in the text, the long s, which resembles an f, has been updated.

21. 3 FREEMAN, *supra* note 5, at 351-52. Paul Boller argues that Washington's decision to observe the day of fasting was a political action, not a religious one. PAUL F. BOLLER, JR., GEORGE WASHINGTON & RELIGION 32 (1963). Either way, Washington found the public call for the day to be permissible, not only in establishment Virginia, but later as president, following passage of the First Amendment.

22. 3 FREEMAN, *supra* note 5, at 352-53 (citation omitted).

23. Letter from George Washington to George William Fairfax (June 10-15, 1774), *in* 10 COLONIAL SERIES, *supra* note 10, at 94, 96.

24. 3 DIARIES, *supra* note 1, at 254.

25. Paul K. Longmore has, however, written an analysis of the work of the entire Committee for Religion, without focusing on any individual member of that Committee. *See generally* Longmore, *Committee for Religion, supra* note 13.

26. 3 FREEMAN, *supra* note 5, at 353-54 (citation omitted).

27. *Id.* at 370.

28. 1 JOURNALS OF THE CONTINENTAL CONGRESS, 1774-89, at 26 & n.1 (Worthington Chauncey Ford ed., Government Printing Office 1904) [hereinafter CONTINENTAL JOURNALS]; *see also* 3 FREEMAN, *supra* note 5, at 375; 1 ANSON PHELPS STOKES, CHURCH AND STATE IN THE UNITED STATES 448-49 (1950).

29. 1 STOKES, *supra* note 28, at 449 (citation omitted).

30. *Id.* (citation omitted).

31. 1 CONTINENTAL JOURNALS, *supra* note 28, at 26; 1 STOKES, *supra* note 28, at 449.

32. 1 STOKES, *supra* note 28, at 450 (citation omitted).

33. 5 CONTINENTAL JOURNALS, *supra* note 28, at 530; 1 STOKES, *supra* note 28, at 450.

34. 1 CONTINENTAL JOURNALS, *supra* note 28, at 108; *see also* 1 STOKES, *supra* note 28, at 458-59.

35. 1 CONTINENTAL JOURNALS, *supra* note 28, at 112.

36. 1 STOKES, *supra* note 28, at 459.

37. 1 CONTINENTAL JOURNALS, *supra* note 28, at 87-88.

38. 1 STOKES, *supra* note 28, at 459-60.

39. 3 FREEMAN, *supra* note 5, at 389-90.

40. 2 CONTINENTAL JOURNALS, *supra* note 28, at 87.

41. *Id.*

42. *Id.* at 88.

43. General Orders (July 16, 1775), *in* 1 THE PAPERS OF GEORGE WASHINGTON: REVO-LUTIONARY WAR SERIES 122, 122 (W.W. Abbot et al. eds., 1985).

THREE

1. General Orders (Feb. 15, 1783), *in* 26 THE WRITINGS OF GEORGE WASHINGTON
    FROM THE ORIGINAL MANUSCRIPT SOURCES 1745-1799, at 135, 135 (John C. Fitz-
    patrick ed., 1938) [the collection is hereinafter referred to as WRITINGS].

2. When Washington's army was first formed, it was referred to in a variety of ways:
    Continental army, New England army, or the Troops of the United Provinces of
    North America, to name a few. *E.g.*, DAVID MCCULLOUGH, 1776, at 24 (2005). For
    the reader's convenience, this book will use only one term: "Continental Army."

3. *See* MICHAEL NOVAK & JANA NOVAK, WASHINGTON'S GOD: RELIGION, LIBERTY,
    AND THE FATHER OF OUR COUNTRY 148-53 (2006); *see also, e.g.*, Letter from
    George Washington to Thomas McKean (Nov. 15, 1781), *in* 23 WRITINGS, *supra*
    note 1, at 342, 343; Letter from George Washington to Philip Schuyler (Mar. 23,
    1781), *in* 21 WRITINGS, *supra* note 1, at 360, 361; Letter from George Washington
    to Reverend William Gordon (Mar. 9, 1781), *in* 21 WRITINGS, *supra* note 1, at 332,
    332; Letter from George Washington to Robert R. Livingston (Jan. 31, 1781), *in* 21
    WRITINGS, *supra* note 1, at 163, 164; Letter from George Washington to Edmund
    Pendleton (Nov. 1, 1779), *in* 17 WRITINGS, *supra* note 1, at 51, 51; Letter from George
    Washington to President Joseph Reed (July 29, 1779), *in* 16 WRITINGS, *supra* note
    1, at 7, 10; Letter from George Washington to John Augustine Washington (July 4,
    1778), *in* 16 THE PAPERS OF GEORGE WASHINGTON: REVOLUTIONARY WAR SERIES
    25, 25 (Theodore J. Crackel et al. eds., 2006) [the collection is hereinafter referred
    to as WAR SERIES]; Letter from George Washington to Landon Carter (May
    30, 1778), *in* 15 WAR SERIES, *supra*, at 267, 267; Letter from George Washington
    to Landon Carter (Oct. 27, 1777), *in* 12 WAR SERIES, *supra*, at 25, 27; Letter from
    George Washington to Brigadier General James Potter (Oct. 18, 1777), *in* 11 WAR
    SERIES, *supra*, at 547, 547; Letter from George Washington to Major General Israel
    Putnam (Oct. 15, 1777), *in* 11 WAR SERIES, *supra*, at 522, 522; Letter from George
    Washington to Brigadier General John Armstrong (July 4, 1777), *in* 10 WAR SERIES,
    supra, at 181, 182; Letter from George Washington to John Parke Custis (Jan. 22,
    1777), *in* 8 WAR SERIES, *supra*, at 123, 123; Letter from George Washington to John
    Augustine Washington (May 31-June 4, 1776), *in* 4 WAR SERIES, *supra*, at 411, 413;
    Letter from George Washington to William Gordon (May 13, 1776), *in* 4 WAR
    SERIES, *supra*, at 285, 286; Letter from George Washington to Josiah Quincy (Mar.
    24, 1776), *in* 3 WAR SERIES, *supra*, at 528, 528-29; Letter from George Washington
    to Lieutenant Colonel Joseph Reed (Nov. 30, 1775), *in* 2 WAR SERIES, *supra*, at
    463, 463; Letter from George Washington to the Portsmouth Committee of Safety
    (Oct. 5, 1775), *in* 2 WAR SERIES, *supra*, at 113, 113; Address from George Washington
    to the Inhabitants of Canada (Sept. 14, 1775), *in* 1 WAR SERIES, *supra*, at 461, 461;
    Address from George Washington to the Inhabitants of Bermuda (Sept. 6, 1775),
    in 1 WAR SERIES, *supra*, at 419, 419.

    Washington also wrote of times that went poorly for the American troops,
    stating, for instance, that "Providence—or some unaccountable something, designd
    it otherwise." Letter from George Washington to John Augustine Washington
    (Oct. 18, 1777), *in* 11 WAR SERIES, *supra*, at 551, 551; *see also* Letter from George
    Washington to Joseph Reed (Nov. 27, 1778), *in* 13 WRITINGS, *supra* note 1, at 347,
    348; Letter from George Washington to John Augustine Washington (Mar. 31,

1776), *in* 3 WAR SERIES, *supra*, at 566, 567; Letter from George Washington to Landon Carter (Mar. 27, 1776), *in* 3 WAR SERIES, *supra*, at 544, 545.

4. The army's escape from Brooklyn Heights during the summer of 1776 is one example. *See, e.g.*, 4 DOUGLAS SOUTHALL FREEMAN, GEORGE WASHINGTON, A BIOGRAPHY: LEADER OF THE REVOLUTION 171-75 (1951); MCCULLOUGH, *supra* note 2, at 182-91; NOVAK & NOVAK, *supra* note 3, at 76-78.

5. One such instance occurred during the American attempt to seize and fortify Dorchester Heights. *See* discussion *infra* note 7.

6. *See* Letter from George Washington to President Joseph Reed (Oct. 18, 1780), *in* 20 WRITINGS, *supra* note 1, at 213, 213; Letter from George Washington to Lieutenant Colonel John Laurens (Oct. 13, 1780), *in* 20 WRITINGS, *supra* note 1, at 172, 173.

7. As an example, the troops completed "'a most astonishing night's work,'" MC-CULLOUGH, *supra* note 2, at 93 (citation omitted), when they seized and fortified Dorchester Heights. *E.g., id.* at 90-94; *see also* 4 FREEMAN, *supra* note 4, at 27-59; NOVAK & NOVAK, *supra* note 3, at 68-69.

8. *See* discussion *infra* note 12 and accompanying text.

9. Letter from George Washington to Brigadier General Thomas Nelson, Jr. (Aug. 20, 1778), *in* 16 WAR SERIES, *supra* note 3, at 340, 341.

10. Letter from George Washington to Major General John Armstrong (Mar. 26, 1781), *in* 21 WRITINGS, *supra* note 1, at 377, 378.

11. Letter from George Washington to Governor Thomas Jefferson (Aug. 14, 1780), *in* 19 WRITINGS, *supra* note 1, at 373, 374.

12. These personal references appeared both in his private and his official correspondence. In some instances, it can be difficult to ascertain the boundary between his personal expressions of reliance on Providence and his official exhortations for others to follow in his path. In addition to the other writings cited in this chapter, see, for example, Letter from George Washington to Major General William Heath (Sept. 23, 1781), *in* 23 WRITINGS, *supra* note 1, at 129, 130; Letter from George Washington to the Minister, Elders, and Deacons of the Dutch Reformed Church at Raritan (June 2, 1779), *in* 15 WRITINGS, *supra* note 1, at 210, 210; Letter from George Washington to John Armstrong (May 18, 1779), *in* 15 WRITINGS, *supra* note 1, at 96, 99; Letter from George Washington to Thomas Nelson (Mar. 15, 1779), *in* 14 WRITINGS, *supra* note 1, at 246, 246; Letter from George Washington to Jonathan Trumbull, Sr. (Sept. 6, 1778), *in* 16 WAR SERIES, *supra* note 3, at 533, 533; Letter from George Washington to Brigadier General Thomas Nelson, Jr. (Nov. 8, 1777), *in* 12 WAR SERIES, *supra* note 3, at 170, 171; Letter from George Washington to Major General Israel Putnam (Oct. 19, 1777), *in* 11 WAR SERIES, *supra* note 3, at 558, 558; Letter from George Washington to Colonel Arendt (Oct. 18, 1777), *in* 11 WAR SERIES, *supra* note 3, at 542, 542; Letter from George Washington to John Page (Oct. 3, 1777), *in* 11 WAR SERIES, *supra* note 3, at 385, 386; Letter from George Washington to Brigadier General Thomas Nelson, Jr. (Sept. 27, 1777), *in* 11 WAR SERIES, *supra* note 3, at 332, 333; Letter from George Washington to Major General Israel Putnam (Sept. 10, 1777), *in* 11 WAR SERIES, *supra* note 3, at 185, 186; Letter from George Washington to Edmund Pendleton (Apr. 12, 1777), *in* 9 WAR SERIES, *supra* note 3, at 140, 141; Letter from George Washington to James Bowdoin (Dec. 18, 1776), *in* 7 WAR SERIES, *supra* note 3, at 364, 365; Letter from George Washington to Major General Horatio Gates (Dec. 14, 1776), *in* 7 WAR SERIES, *supra* note 3, at 333, 333; Letter from George Washington to Major General William

Heath (Oct. 9, 1776), *in* 6 WAR SERIES, *supra* note 3, at 516, 517; General Orders (Sept. 2, 1776), *in* 6 WAR SERIES, *supra* note 3, at 198, 198-99; Letter from George Washington to John Hancock (Aug. 22, 1776), *in* 6 WAR SERIES, *supra* note 3, at 102, 102; Letter from George Washington to Jonathan Trumbull, Sr. (Aug. 18, 1776), *in* 6 WAR SERIES, *supra* note 3, at 70, 70; Proclamation for the Evacuation of New York (Aug. 17, 1776), *in* 6 WAR SERIES, *supra* note 3, at 45, 46; Letter from George Washington to Major General Horatio Gates (Aug. 14, 1776), *in* 6 WAR SERIES, *supra* note 3, at 20, 21; Letter from George Washington to James Bowdoin (Aug. 14, 1776), *in* 6 WAR SERIES, *supra* note 3, at 18, 19; Letter from George Washington to Major General Philip Schuyler (Aug. 13, 1776), *in* 6 WAR SERIES, *supra* note 3, at 9, 11; Letter from George Washington to Colonel Thomas McKean (Aug. 13, 1776), *in* 6 WAR SERIES, *supra* note 3, at 6, 6; General Orders (Aug. 9, 1776), *in* 5 WAR SERIES, *supra* note 3, at 644, 645; General Orders (July 21, 1776), *in* 5 WAR SERIES, *supra* note 3, at 411, 412; Letter from George Washington to Colonel Adam Stephen (July 20, 1776), *in* 5 WAR SERIES, *supra* note 3, at 408, 409; Letter from George Washington to Major General Philip Schuyler (July 11, 1776), *in* 5 WAR SERIES, *supra* note 3, at 273, 274; Orders and Instructions to Major General Horatio Gates (June 24, 1776), *in* 5 WAR SERIES, *supra* note 3, at 84, 86; Letter from George Washington to John Adams (Apr. 15, 1776), *in* 4 WAR SERIES, *supra* note 3, at 67, 67; Address from George Washington to the Massachusetts General Court (Apr. 1, 1776), *in* 4 WAR SERIES, *supra* note 3, at 8, 9; Letter from George Washington to Major General Philip Schuyler (Jan. 27, 1776), *in* 3 WAR SERIES, *supra* note 3, at 201, 203; Letter from George Washington to Lieutenant Colonel Joseph Reed (Jan. 14, 1776), *in* 3 WAR SERIES, *supra* note 3, at 87, 89; Letter from George Washington to Lieutenant Colonel Joseph Reed (Jan. 4, 1776), *in* 3 WAR SERIES, *supra* note 3, at 23, 24; Circular Letter from George Washington to the General Officers (Sept. 8, 1775), *in* 1 WAR SERIES, *supra* note 3, at 432, 432-33.

13. General Orders (July 4, 1775), *in* 1 WAR SERIES, *supra* note 3, at 54, 54-55.

14. Letter from George Washington to Jonathan Trumbull, Sr. (July 18, 1775), *in* 1 WAR SERIES, *supra* note 3, at 131, 131.

15. Letter from George Washington to Lieutenant General Thomas Gage (Aug. 19, 1775), *in* 1 WAR SERIES, *supra* note 3, at 326, 327.

16. *E.g.*, Letter from George Washington to the Officers of the Somerset County Militia (Nov. 7, 1783), *in* 27 WRITINGS, *supra* note 1, at 234, 235; Letter from George Washington to Governor Jonathan Trumbull (Nov. 28, 1781), *in* 23 WRITINGS, *supra* note 1, at 359, 360; General Orders (Sept. 15, 1781), *in* 23 WRITINGS, *supra* note 1, at 114, 114; Letter from George Washington to Colonel Fisher Gay (Sept. 4, 1776), *in* 6 WAR SERIES, *supra* note 3, at 214, 214; Orders from George Washington to Major General Israel Putnam (Aug. 25, 1776), *in* 6 WAR SERIES, *supra* note 3, at 126, 126; General Orders (July 9, 1776), *in* 5 WAR SERIES, *supra* note 3, at 245, 246; General Orders (July 2, 1776), *in* 5 WAR SERIES, *supra* note 3, at 179, 180; General Orders (June 30, 1776), *in* 5 WAR SERIES, *supra* note 3, at 154, 155; Letter from George Washington to John Hancock (Apr. 18, 1776), *in* 4 WAR SERIES, *supra* note 3, at 80, 80; Letter from George Washington to the Massachusetts Council (Feb. 26, 1776), *in* 3 WAR SERIES, *supra* note 3, at 368, 368; General Orders (Jan. 1, 1776), *in* 3 WAR SERIES, *supra* note 3, at 1, 1; General Orders (Dec. 10, 1775), *in* 2 WAR SERIES, *supra* note 3, at 525, 525; Instructions from George Washington

to Colonel Benedict Arnold (Sept. 14, 1775), *in* 1 WAR SERIES, *supra* note 3, at 457, 457; *see also* General Orders (Apr. 18, 1783), *in* 26 WRITINGS, *supra* note 1, at 334, 335; Letter from George Washington to Reverend Samuel Cooper (Sept. 24, 1782), *in* 25 WRITINGS, *supra* note 1, at 200, 200; Circular Letter from George Washington to the States (Jan. 31, 1782), *in* 23 WRITINGS, *supra* note 1, at 476, 478; Letter from George Washington to Major General Nathanael Greene (Sept. 4, 1781), *in* 23 WRITINGS, *supra* note 1, at 84, 86; General Orders (Dec. 17, 1777), *in* 12 WAR SERIES, *supra* note 3, at 620, 620; Letter from George Washington to John Hancock (Oct. 10-11, 1777), *in* 11 WAR SERIES, *supra* note 3, at 473, 475; General Orders (Aug. 23, 1776), *in* 6 WAR SERIES, *supra* note 3, at 109, 110; Letter from George Washington to John Hancock (July 10, 1776), *in* 5 WAR SERIES, *supra* note 3, at 258, 258; Letter from George Washington to Brigadier General John Sullivan (June 13, 1776), *in* 4 WAR SERIES, *supra* note 3, at 519, 519.

17. Letter from George Washington to Israel Evans (Mar. 13, 1778), *in* 14 WAR SERIES, *supra* note 3, at 169, 169; *see also* PETER A. LILLBACK, GEORGE WASHINGTON'S SACRED FIRE 384 (2006).

18. Washington's emphases on morality and virtue complemented the practical need for order and discipline. "Next to the favour of divine providence," Washington told his soldiers, "nothing is more essentially necessary to give this Army the victory of all its enemies, than Exactness of discipline, Alertness when on duty, and Cleanliness in their arms and persons." General Orders (Feb. 27, 1776), *in* 3 WAR SERIES, *supra* note 3, at 379, 380; *see also, e.g.,* Letter from George Washington to Colonel Fisher Gay (Sept. 4, 1776), *supra* note 16, at 214-15; General Orders (Jan. 1, 1776), *supra* note 16, at 1.

19. Letter from George Washington to Andrew Lewis (Oct. 15, 1778), *in* 13 WRITINGS, *supra* note 1, at 79, 80.

20. *Id.*; *see also* General Orders (Sept. 19, 1776), *in* 6 WAR SERIES, *supra* note 3, at 340, 340.

21. Letter from George Washington to Colonel Fisher Gay (Sept. 4, 1776), *supra* note 16, at 214; *see also, e.g.,* General Orders (Sept. 4, 1777), *in* 11 WAR SERIES, *supra* note 3, at 141, 142; General Orders (Jan. 21, 1777), *in* 8 WAR SERIES, *supra* note 3, at 119, 119; Letter from George Washington to John Hancock (Sept. 22, 1776), *in* 6 WAR SERIES, *supra* note 3, at 368, 368-69; General Orders (Sept. 18, 1776), *in* 6 WAR SERIES, *supra* note 3, at 328, 328; General Orders (Sept. 6, 1776), *in* 6 WAR SERIES, *supra* note 3, at 229, 229; General Orders (Apr. 27, 1776), *in* 4 WAR SERIES, *supra* note 3, at 140, 140-41; Proclamation on the Occupation of Boston (Mar. 21, 1776), *in* 3 WAR SERIES, *supra* note 3, at 501, 502.

22. *E.g.,* General Orders (Apr. 18, 1783), *supra* note 16, at 336; General Orders (Oct. 21, 1778), *in* 13 WRITINGS, *supra* note 1, at 118, 119; General Orders (Feb. 18, 1778), *in* 13 WAR SERIES, *supra* note 3, at 576, 576-77; General Orders (Jan. 8, 1778), *in* 13 WAR SERIES, *supra* note 3, at 171, 171; Circular Instructions from George Washington to the Brigade Commanders (May 26, 1777), *in* 9 WAR SERIES, *supra* note 3, at 532, 533; General Orders (May 8, 1777), *in* 9 WAR SERIES, *supra* note 3, at 368, 368; General Orders (Oct. 8, 1776), *in* 6 WAR SERIES, *supra* note 3, at 502, 503; Proclamation on the Occupation of Boston (Mar. 21, 1776), *supra* note 21, at 502; General Orders (Feb. 26, 1776), *in* 3 WAR SERIES, *supra* note 3, at 362, 362; General Orders (Oct. 3, 1775), *in* 2 WAR SERIES, *supra* note 3, at 81, 81; General Orders (July 4, 1775), *supra* note 13, at 54-55.

23. *E.g.*, General Orders (July 29, 1779), *in* 16 WRITINGS, *supra* note 1, at 11, 13; General Orders (Oct. 21, 1778), *supra* note 22, at 119; General Orders (May 31, 1777), *in* 9 WAR SERIES, *supra* note 3, at 567, 567-58; General Orders (Aug. 3, 1776), *in* 5 WAR SERIES, *supra* note 3, at 551, 551. Michael Novak and Jana Novak note that Washington's orders against immoral behavior were issued partly for practical, rather than moral, considerations: moral behavior would help the soldiers to obtain the respect and support of the American people. Without this support, the war would be lost. *See* NOVAK & NOVAK, *supra* note 3, at 30-31.

24. Letter from George Washington to the Pennsylvania Associators (Aug. 8, 1776), *in* 5 WAR SERIES, *supra* note 3, at 637, 638 (emphasis added); *see also, e.g.*, Letter from George Washington to Reverend Samuel Cooper (Sept. 24, 1782), *supra* note 16, at 200; General Orders (Apr. 9, 1778), *in* 14 WAR SERIES, *supra* note 3, at 431, 431; General Orders (Aug. 12, 1776), *in* 5 WAR SERIES, *supra* note 3, at 672, 674.

25. Letter from George Washington to Jonathan Trumbull, Sr. (Aug. 7, 1776), *in* 5 WAR SERIES, *supra* note 3, at 615, 616 (emphasis added).

26. Letter from George Washington to Brigadier General Samuel Holden Parsons (Apr. 23-25, 1777), *in* 9 WAR SERIES, *supra* note 3, at 248, 248 (emphasis added).

27. Circular Letter from George Washington to the States (Jan. 31, 1782), *supra* note 16, at 478; *see also* PETER R. HENRIQUES, REALISTIC VISIONARY: A PORTRAIT OF GEORGE WASHINGTON 172 (2006).

28. General Orders (Sept. 3, 1776), *in* 6 WAR SERIES, *supra* note 3, at 204, 205. In the days and weeks before the escape, Washington had exhorted his men to behave with bravery, trusting the outcome to heaven. *See* General Orders (Aug. 23, 1776), *supra* note 16, at 110; General Orders (Aug. 14, 1776), *in* 6 WAR SERIES, *supra* note 3, at 17, 18; General Orders (Aug. 13, 1776), *in* 6 WAR SERIES, *supra* note 3, at 1, 1; General Orders (July 2, 1776), *supra* note 16, at 180.

29. General Orders (Oct. 5, 1777), *in* 11 WAR SERIES, *supra* note 3, at 390, 391.

30. *Id.* at 391 (emphasis added); *see also* General Orders (Dec. 17, 1777), *supra* note 16, at 620; Letter from George Washington to Colonel Fisher Gay (Sept. 4, 1776), *supra* note 16, at 214-15; General Orders (Dec. 10, 1775), *supra* note 16, at 525.

31. Letter from George Washington to the President of Congress (July 21, 1781), *in* 22 WRITINGS, *supra* note 1, at 404, 405.

32. Letter from George Washington to Reverend Samuel Cooper (Sept. 24, 1782), *supra* note 16, at 200.

33. Circular Letter from George Washington to New Jersey, Delaware, and Maryland (Sept. 3, 1781), *in* 23 WRITINGS, *supra* note 1, at 81, 82; *see also* Circular Letter from George Washington to the States (May 4-8, 1782), *in* 24 WRITINGS, *supra* note 1, at 234, 236; Letter from George Washington to Governor Jonathan Trumbull (Nov. 28, 1781), *supra* note 16, at 359-60; Letter from George Washington to the Inhabitants of Providence (Mar. 14, 1781), *in* 21 WRITINGS, *supra* note 1, at 337, 338.

34. Letter from George Washington to Brigadier General Thomas Nelson, Jr. (May 15, 1778), *in* 15 WAR SERIES, *supra* note 3, at 128, 129.

35. Washington was appointed commander-in-chief of the Continental Army on June 15, 1775, but he did not join his army in Boston until July 2. 3 DOUGLAS SOUTHALL FREEMAN, GEORGE WASHINGTON, A BIOGRAPHY: PLANTER AND PATRIOT 436-37, 475-77 (1951).

36. General Orders (July 4, 1775), *supra* note 13, at 55.

37. *E.g.*, 1 WAR SERIES, *supra* note 3, at 57 n.4.

38. 2 JOURNALS OF THE CONTINENTAL CONGRESS, 1774-89, at 112 (Worthington Chauncey Ford ed., Government Printing Office 1905) [hereinafter CONTINENTAL JOURNALS].

39. The committee of five men was appointed on June 14. 2 CONTINENTAL JOURNALS, *supra* note 38, at 90; 1 WAR SERIES, *supra* note 3, at 46 n.3. Washington was appointed commander-in-chief one day later, on June 15. *See supra* note 35. According to the editors of the most recent collection of Washington's papers, Washington "apparently attended at least one meeting" of the committee before his appointment. 1 WAR SERIES, *supra* note 3, at 46 n.3.

40. *See* Letter from John Hancock to George Washington (July 5, 1775), *in* 1 WAR SERIES, *supra* note 3, at 64, 64 & n.

41. PAUL F. BOLLER, JR., GEORGE WASHINGTON & RELIGION 49 (1963).

42. General Orders (July 9, 1776), *supra* note 16, at 246.

43. Letter from Colonel George Baylor to George Washington (May 13, 1777), *in* 9 WAR SERIES, *supra* note 3, at 408, 408.

44. Letter from George Washington to Colonel George Baylor (May 23, 1777), *in* 9 WAR SERIES, *supra* note 3, at 502, 502.

45. General Orders (May 31, 1777), *supra* note 23, at 567-58.

46. *E.g.*, General Orders (Feb. 15, 1783), *supra* note 1, at 136; General Orders (June 9, 1777), *in* 9 WAR SERIES, *supra* note 3, at 651, 651; *see also* 8 CONTINENTAL JOURNALS, *supra* note 38, at 753-54.

47. *E.g.*, Letter from George Washington to Sir Guy Carleton (Aug. 18, 1782), *in* 25 WRITINGS, *supra* note 1, at 38, 38; Letter from George Washington to the Secretary at War (Aug. 16, 1782), *in* 25 WRITINGS, *supra* note 1, at 25, 26; Letter from George Washington to Reverend John Hurt (Sept. 25, 1781), *in* 23 WRITINGS, *supra* note 1, at 139, 139-40; Letter from George Washington to the Board of War (July 9, 1781), *in* 22 WRITINGS, *supra* note 1, at 343, 344; Letter from George Washington to John Beatty (Apr. 4, 1780), *in* 18 WRITINGS, *supra* note 1, at 216, 216; Letter from George Washington to Major General Arthur St. Clair (Apr. 2, 1780), *in* 18 WRITINGS, *supra* note 1, at 201, 202.

48. Letter from George Washington to Colonel George Baylor (May 23, 1777), *supra* note 44, at 502.

49. Letter from George Washington to the First Church of Woodstock (Mar. 24, 1776), *in* 3 WAR SERIES, *supra* note 3, at 531, 531; *see also* General Orders (July 9, 1776), *supra* note 16, at 246; Letter from George Washington to Jonathan Trumbull, Sr. (Dec. 15, 1775), *in* 2 WAR SERIES, *supra* note 3, at 555, 555-56.

50. *E.g.*, General Orders (Feb. 15, 1783), *supra* note 1, at 135; General Orders (Oct. 20, 1781), *in* 23 WRITINGS, *supra* note 1, at 244, 247; General Orders (May 2, 1778), *in* 15 WAR SERIES, *supra* note 3, at 13, 13; General Orders (Sept. 27, 1777), *in* 11 WAR SERIES, *supra* note 3, at 329, 329; General Orders (July 5, 1777), *in* 10 WAR SERIES, *supra* note 3, at 194, 195; General Orders (June 28, 1777), *in* 10 WAR SERIES, *supra* note 3, at 135, 135; General Orders (May 31, 1777), *supra* note 23, at 567-58; Circular Instructions from George Washington to the Brigade Commanders (May 26, 1777), *supra* note 22, at 533; General Orders (May 24, 1777), *in* 9 WAR SERIES, *supra* note 3, at 513, 513; General Orders (May 17, 1777), *in* 9 WAR SERIES, *supra* note 3, at 448, 448; General Orders (Apr. 19, 1777), *in* 9 WAR SERIES, *supra* note 3, at 207, 208; General Orders (Apr. 12, 1777), *in* 9 WAR SERIES, *supra* note 3, at 126, 126; General

Orders (Aug. 3, 1776), *supra* note 23, at 551; General Orders (July 9, 1776), *supra* note 16, at 246; General Orders (May 16, 1776), *in* 4 WAR SERIES, *supra* note 3, at 310, 310; General Orders (Aug. 5, 1775), *in* 1 WAR SERIES, *supra* note 3, at 245, 246; General Orders (July 4, 1775), *supra* note 13, at 55.

51. *See* General Orders (Oct. 7, 1777), *in* 11 WAR SERIES, *supra* note 3, at 415, 416; *see also* General Orders (Feb. 15, 1783), *supra* note 1, at 135; General Orders (May 2, 1778), *supra* note 50, at 13.

52. General Orders (June 28, 1777), *supra* note 50, at 135 (emphasis added); *see also* General Orders (Mar. 22, 1783), *in* 26 WRITINGS, *supra* note 1, at 249, 250.

53. General Orders (June 28, 1777), *supra* note 50, at 135.

54. General Orders (May 2, 1778), *supra* note 50, at 13.

55. 2 CONTINENTAL JOURNALS, *supra* note 38, at 220; *see also* BOLLER, *supra* note 41, at 51.

56. Letter from George Washington to John Hancock (Dec. 31, 1775), *in* 2 WAR SERIES, *supra* note 3, at 622, 624.

57. *Id.*

58. *See* 4 CONTINENTAL JOURNALS, *supra* note 38, at 61; 3 WAR SERIES, *supra* note 3, at 11 n.1.

59. General Orders (Feb. 7, 1776), *in* 3 WAR SERIES, *supra* note 3, at 258, 258.

60. *See* 3 WAR SERIES, *supra* note 3, at 11 n.1; *see also* BOLLER, *supra* note 41, at 51-52.

61. Letter from George Washington to John Hancock (June 28, 1776), *in* 5 WAR SERIES, *supra* note 3, at 132, 134.

62. *Id.*

63. Congress voted to authorize one chaplain per regiment on July 5, 1776. The chaplains were still to receive "thirty three dollars and one third of a dollar a month." 5 CONTINENTAL JOURNALS, *supra* note 38, at 522; 5 WAR SERIES, *supra* note 3, at 136 n.8; 3 WAR SERIES, *supra* note 3, at 11 n.1; *see also* Letter from George Washington to Major General Artemas Ward (July 9, 1776), *in* 5 WAR SERIES, *supra* note 3, at 254, 255; General Orders (July 9, 1776), *supra* note 16, at 246.

64. On April 11, 1777, Congress increased the pay of regiment chaplains to $40 per month. 7 CONTINENTAL JOURNALS, *supra* note 38, at 256; 9 WAR SERIES, *supra* note 3, at 207 n.3; *see also* Letter from George Washington to Brigadier General Samuel Holden Parsons (Apr. 19, 1777), *in* 9 WAR SERIES, *supra* note 3, at 212, 212; Letter from George Washington to Brigadier General Alexander McDougall (Apr. 18, 1777), *in* 9 WAR SERIES, *supra* note 3, at 206, 207; Letter from George Washington to Major General William Heath (Apr. 18-19, 1777), *in* 9 WAR SERIES, *supra* note 3, at 205, 205. Several weeks after the pay increase, Congress resolved that "for the future, there be only one chaplain allowed to each brigade in the army." 8 CONTINENTAL JOURNALS, *supra* note 38, at 390. Congress added that "each brigade chaplain be allowed the same pay, rations, and forage that is allowed to a colonel in the same corps." *Id.*

65. Letter from George Washington to John Hancock (May 29, 1777), *in* 9 WAR SERIES, *supra* note 3, at 553, 553; *see also* General Orders (June 8, 1777), *in* 9 WAR SERIES, *supra* note 3, at 642, 643.

66. Letter from George Washington to John Hancock (June 8, 1777), *in* 9 WAR SERIES, *supra* note 3, at 644, 644-45.

67. Vincent Phillip Muñoz, *George Washington on Religious Liberty*, 65 REV. POL. 11, 21 (2003).

68. *See id.* For a discussion of Washington's preference for regiment chaplains, rather than brigade chaplains, see BOLLER, *supra* note 41, at 51-53, 127-28.

69. A committee of Congress met with Washington on July 17 to discuss this and other matters. The committee's August 5 report stated that the "'appointment of Brigade Chaplains has in some measure been suspended until the Sense of Congress is more fully known on the Matter.'" 10 WAR SERIES, *supra* note 3, at 339 n.1 (citation omitted); *see also* Letter from George Washington to Major General William Heath (July 19, 1777), *in* 10 WAR SERIES, *supra* note 3, at 338, 339. However, Congress continued to push for the change to brigade chaplains in subsequent years. *See* 10 CONTINENTAL JOURNALS, *supra* note 38, at 40; *see also* General Orders (May 30, 1781), *in* 22 WRITINGS, *supra* note 1, at 135, 135-36.

70. Sentiments on a Peace Establishment (May 2, 1783), *in* 26 WRITINGS, *supra* note 1, at 374, 380. Interestingly, Washington opined later in the same letter that the chaplains' pay had been too high at the end of the Revolution. *See id.* at 384. When taken in conjunction with his request for pay increases at the beginning of the war, such a position suggests that Washington may have wanted chaplains' pay to be high enough to "encourage men of Abilities," but not so high that Congress could not afford a sufficient number of chaplains for the army.

71. General Orders (Feb. 15, 1783), *supra* note 1, at 136 (emphasis added).

72. General Orders (July 16, 1775), *in* 1 WAR SERIES, *supra* note 3, at 122, 122.

73. *See* 1 WAR SERIES, *supra* note 3, at 123 n.1.

74. *See* General Orders (Nov. 27, 1782), *in* 25 WRITINGS, *supra* note 1, at 374, 375; General Orders (Nov. 14, 1782), *in* 25 WRITINGS, *supra* note 1, at 343, 344-45; General Orders (Apr. 22, 1782), *in* 24 WRITINGS, *supra* note 1, at 151, 151; General Orders (Apr. 27, 1781), *in* 22 WRITINGS, *supra* note 1, at 2, 2; General Orders (Apr. 6, 1780), *in* 18 WRITINGS, *supra* note 1, at 222, 225; Letter from George Washington to the President of Congress (Mar. 23, 1780), *in* 18 WRITINGS, *supra* note 1, at 145, 146; General Orders (Nov. 27, 1779), *in* 17 WRITINGS, *supra* note 1, at 189, 189-90; General Orders (May 5, 1779), *in* 14 WRITINGS, *supra* note 1, at 504, 504; General Orders (Apr. 12, 1779), *in* 14 WRITINGS, *supra* note 1, at 369, 369; Letter from George Washington to the President of Congress (Apr. 2, 1779), *in* 14 WRITINGS, *supra* note 1, at 328, 328; General Orders (Dec. 22, 1778), *in* 13 WRITINGS, *supra* note 1, at 448, 450-51; Letter from George Washington to Major General John Sullivan (Dec. 20, 1778), *in* 13 WRITINGS, *supra* note 1, at 440, 441; General Orders (Apr. 12, 1778), *in* 14 WAR SERIES, *supra* note 3, at 483, 483; General Orders (Dec. 17, 1777), *supra* note 16, at 621; General Orders (Nov. 30, 1777), *in* 12 WAR SERIES, *supra* note 3, at 444, 444; General Orders (May 15, 1776), *in* 4 WAR SERIES, *supra* note 3, at 305, 305.

75. *See* General Orders (Feb. 5, 1777), *in* 8 WAR SERIES, *supra* note 3, at 247, 247; General Orders (Feb. 4, 1777), *in* 8 WAR SERIES, *supra* note 3, at 240, 240; General Orders (Mar. 6, 1776), *in* 3 WAR SERIES, *supra* note 3, at 413, 413; General Orders (Nov. 18, 1775), *in* 2 WAR SERIES, *supra* note 3, at 392, 393.

76. General Orders (Apr. 18, 1783), *supra* note 16, at 334; General Orders (June 30, 1778), *in* 15 WAR SERIES, *supra* note 3, at 590, 590; General Orders (May 5, 1778), *in* 15 WAR SERIES, *supra* note 3, at 38, 38-39; General Orders (Oct. 18, 1777), *in* 11 WAR SERIES, *supra* note 3, at 541, 541; *see also* BOLLER, *supra* note 41, at 54-55.

77. The quotes in this sentence can be found at General Orders (May 15, 1776), *supra* note 74, at 305; General Orders (Mar. 6, 1776), *supra* note 75, at 413; General Orders

(Nov. 18, 1775), *supra* note 75, at 393; *see also* General Orders (Apr. 27, 1781), *supra* note 74, at 2; General Orders (Dec. 17, 1777), *supra* note 16, at 621.

78. General Orders (Apr. 12, 1779), *supra* note 74, at 369.

79. General Orders (Nov. 14, 1782), *supra* note 74, at 345; *see also* General Orders (Dec. 22, 1778), *supra* note 74, at 451; General Orders (Apr. 12, 1778), *supra* note 74, at 483.

80. General Orders (Oct. 18, 1777), *supra* note 76, at 541.

81. General Orders (May 5, 1778), *supra* note 76, at 38-39; *see also* General Orders (Oct. 20, 1781), *supra* note 50, at 247; General Orders (June 30, 1778), *supra* note 76, at 590.

82. General Orders (Oct. 18, 1777), *supra* note 76, at 541.

83. General Orders (May 5, 1778), *supra* note 76, at 39.

84. General Orders (Nov. 14, 1775), *in* 2 WAR SERIES, *supra* note 3, at 369, 369.

85. General Orders (Nov. 28, 1775), *in* 2 WAR SERIES, *supra* note 3, at 443, 443-44.

86. General Orders (May 2, 1778), *supra* note 50, at 13.

87. General Orders (June 30, 1776), *supra* note 16, at 155.

88. General Orders (Sept. 13, 1777), *in* 11 WAR SERIES, *supra* note 3, at 211, 211-12.

89. 8 CONTINENTAL JOURNALS, *supra* note 38, at 733-34; *see also* 1 ANSON PHELPS STOKES, CHURCH AND STATE IN THE UNITED STATES 470-71 (1950).

90. More information on these events can be found at 1 STOKES, *supra* note 89, at 472-73; *see also* The Library of Congress, IV. Religion and the Congress of the Confederation, 1774-89 (Oct. 27, 2003), http://www.loc.gov/exhibits/religion/rel04. html.

91. Letter from George Washington to Reverend John Rodgers (June 11, 1783), *in* 27 WRITINGS, *supra* note 1, at 1, 1. Aitken suffered financial losses as a result of his project, and he later appealed to Washington for assistance. By then, Washington was serving as president. Tobias Lear responded on Washington's behalf, suggesting that the legislature, not the executive, was best equipped to help with Aitken's application. Letter from Tobias Lear to Robert Aitken (June 14, 1790), *in* 5 THE PAPERS OF GEORGE WASHINGTON: PRESIDENTIAL SERIES 495 n., 495 n. (Dorothy Twohig et al. eds., 1996).

92. *See* discussion *supra* Introduction, note 29 and accompanying text.

93. *E.g.*, Answer from George Washington to the Address of Congress (Mar. 21, 1782), *in* 24 WRITINGS, *supra* note 1, at 83, 83; General Orders (May 5, 1778), *supra* note 76, at 38; General Orders (Aug. 12, 1776), *supra* note 24, at 674; Address from George Washington to the Inhabitants of Canada (Sept. 14, 1775), *supra* note 3, at 461; *see also* Letter from George Washington to George Plater & Thomas Cockey Dey (Nov. 23, 1781), *in* 23 WRITINGS, *supra* note 1, at 358, 358; General Orders (Oct. 15, 1777), *in* 11 WAR SERIES, *supra* note 3, at 512, 512; General Orders (Feb. 27, 1776), *supra* note 18, at 380; General Orders (Nov. 28, 1775), *supra* note 85, at 443; Address from George Washington to the Inhabitants of Bermuda (Sept. 6, 1775), *supra* note 3, at 419; Letter from George Washington to Jonathan Trumbull, Sr. (July 18, 1775), *supra* note 14, at 131; Address from George Washington to the Massachusetts Provincial Congress (July 4, 1775), *in* 1 WAR SERIES, *supra* note 3, at 59, 60.

94. Michael Novak and Jana Novak also discuss Washington's use of nondenominational terminology. NOVAK & NOVAK, *supra* note 3, at 120-22, 243-45.

95. General Orders (Sept. 17, 1775), *in* 2 WAR SERIES, *supra* note 3, at 1, 1.

96. *See* BOLLER, *supra* note 41, at 126-27; 2 WAR SERIES, *supra* note 3, at 1 n.1; *cf.* HEN-RIQUES, *supra* note 27, at 176 (citing incident, but as evidence that Washington not "doctrinaire" when it came to matters of religion).

97. Letter from Major Christopher French to George Washington (Oct. 9, 1775), *in* 2 WAR SERIES, *supra* note 3, at 130, 131-32.

98. Letter from George Washington to Major Christopher French (Oct. 25, 1775), *in* 2 WAR SERIES, *supra* note 3, at 234, 234.

99. Letter from George Washington to Colonel Benedict Arnold (Sept. 14, 1775), *in* 1 WAR SERIES, *supra* note 3, at 455, 456.

100. *See also* BOLLER, *supra* note 41, at 125.

101. Instructions from George Washington to Colonel Benedict Arnold (Sept. 14, 1775), *supra* note 16, at 459.

102. *Id.*; *see also* BOLLER, *supra* note 41, at 124-25.

103. Pope's Day was comparable to Guy Fawkes' Day. The former was celebrated in the colonies, while the latter was celebrated in England. BOLLER, *supra* note 41, at 125.

104. General Orders (Nov. 5, 1775), *in* 2 WAR SERIES, *supra* note 3, at 300, 300.

105. *Id.*

106. *Id.*

107. BOLLER, *supra* note 41, at 125-26.

108. For a discussion of Washington and the Quakers during the Revolution, see *id.* at 129-37.

109. Washington denied their initial request to enter the city, on the grounds that no one was allowed to enter. However, he agreed to help them with a plan by which Boston Quakers would come out and meet the others, who would deliver the assistance. BOLLER, *supra* note 41, at 130; *see also* MARGARET HOPE BACON, THE QUIET REBELS: THE STORY OF THE QUAKERS IN AMERICA 74-75 (1985).

110. BOLLER, *supra* note 41, at 130.

111. For more information on the circumstances surrounding these arrests, see BACON, *supra* note 109, at 73; ISAAC SHARPLESS, THE QUAKERS IN THE REVOLUTION 151-68 (Univ. Press of the Pac. 2002) (1902); *see also* 14 WAR SERIES, *supra* note 3, at 372 n.1.

112. *See* Letter from George Washington to Thomas Wharton, Jr. (Apr. 6, 1778), *in* 14 WAR SERIES, *supra* note 3, at 416, 416-417; Letter from George Washington to Thomas Wharton, Jr. (Apr. 5, 1778), *in* 14 WAR SERIES, *supra* note 3, at 409, 409; *see also* SHARPLESS, *supra* note 111, at 167-68; 14 WAR SERIES, *supra* note 3, at 372 n.3, 417 nn.1-2.

113. Letter from George Washington to the Pennsylvania Council of Safety (Jan. 29, 1777), *in* 8 WAR SERIES, *supra* note 3, at 182, 182.

114. Letter from George Washington to the Pennsylvania Council of Safety (Jan. 19, 1777), *in* 8 WAR SERIES, *supra* note 3, at 107, 108; *see also* Vincent Phillip Muñoz, *Religion and the Common Good: George Washington on Church and State*, *in* THE FOUNDERS ON GOD AND GOVERNMENT 1, 14 (Daniel L. Dreisbach et al. eds., 2004).

115. Proclamation Concerning Persons Swearing British Allegiance (Jan. 25, 1777), *in* 8 WAR SERIES, *supra* note 3, at 152, 152.

116. BOLLER, *supra* note 41, at 132; Muñoz, *supra* note 114, at 14; SHARPLESS, *supra* note 111, at 168-69.

117. Letter from George Washington to William Livingston (May 11, 1777), *in* 9 WAR SERIES, *supra* note 3, at 387, 388; *see also* BOLLER, *supra* note 41, at 131.

118. BOLLER, *supra* note 41, at 131-32.

119. *See* Authority to Collect Clothing (Nov. 1777), *in* 12 WAR SERIES, *supra* note 3, at 76, 76; *see also* BOLLER, *supra* note 41, at 131; Muñoz, *supra* note 114, at 15; Letter from George Washington to Brigadier General John Lacey, Jr. (Mar. 20, 1778), *in* 14 WAR SERIES, *supra* note 3, at 238, 238; 13 WAR SERIES, *supra* note 3, at 373 n. (noting Washington's response to Letter from Colonel Walter Stewart to George Washington (Jan. 28, 1778), *in* 13 WAR SERIES, *supra* note 3, at 371, 372); 11 WAR SERIES, *supra* note 3, at 407 n.

120. *See* 8 WAR SERIES, *supra* note 3, at 431 n.1.

121. Letter from George Washington to Brigadier General John Lacey, Jr. (Mar. 20, 1778), *supra* note 119, at 238; *see also* BOLLER, *supra* note 41, at 132; SHARPLESS, *supra* note 111, at 183.

122. Letter from Brigadier General John Lacey, Jr. to George Washington (Mar. 21, 1778), *in* 14 WAR SERIES, *supra* note 3, at 251, 251.

123. Letter from George Washington to Brigadier General Lachlan McIntosh (Mar. 21, 1778), *in* 14 WAR SERIES, *supra* note 3, at 257, 257.

124. Muñoz, *supra* note 114, at 15.

125. *Id.*

126. BOLLER, *supra* note 41, at 136; *see also* BACON, *supra* note 109, at 71-72.

127. BOLLER, *supra* note 41, at 136. Following the Revolution, Washington's opinion of the Quakers apparently improved. He reportedly told one Frenchman that "'in the course of the war, he had entertained an ill opinion of this society . . . [and] he attributed to their political sentiments, the effect of their religious principles. . . . [but he had since] acquired an esteem for them.'" *Id.* at 137 (citation omitted).

128. General Orders (Aug. 1, 1776), *in* 5 WAR SERIES, *supra* note 3, at 534, 534.

129. *Id.*

130. 5 DOUGLAS SOUTHALL FREEMAN, GEORGE WASHINGTON, A BIOGRAPHY: VICTORY WITH THE HELP OF FRANCE 345-93 (1952).

131. The Treaty of Paris was signed on September 3, 1783, although preliminary articles of peace were signed in November 1782. *Id.* at 438, 455. Washington formally retired on December 23, 1783. *Id.* at 474-77.

132. Letter from George Washington to the Mayor, Aldermen, and Commonalty of Albany (Aug. 4, 1783), *in* 27 WRITINGS, *supra* note 1, at 78, 78. A few such letters were written before the preliminary articles of peace were signed in November 1782. This correspondence reflected on the need for providential help if the war was to be brought to a happy conclusion. Letter from George Washington to the Ministers, Elders, and Deacons of the Reformed Dutch Church of Schenectady (June 30, 1782), *in* 24 WRITINGS, *supra* note 1, at 390, 391; Letter from George Washington to the Magistrates and Military Officers of Schenectady (June 30, 1782), *in* 24 WRITINGS, *supra* note 1, at 390, 390; Letter from George Washington to George Plater & Thomas Cockey Dey (Nov. 23, 1781), *supra* note 93, at 358.

133. Letter from George Washington to the Legislature of New Jersey (Dec. 6, 1783), *in* 27 WRITINGS, *supra* note 1, at 260, 261; *see also* Letter from George Washington to the Learned Professions of Philadelphia (Dec. 13, 1783), *in* 27 WRITINGS, *supra* note 1, at 268, 269; Letter from George Washington to the Magistrates of the City and

County of Philadelphia (Dec. 13, 1783), *in* 27 WRITINGS, *supra* note 1, at 267, 267; Letter from George Washington to the General Assembly of Pennsylvania (Dec. 9, 1783), *in* 27 WRITINGS, *supra* note 1, at 264, 264; Letter from George Washington to the Minister, Elders, and Deacons of the Two United Dutch Reformed Churches of Hackensack and Schalenburgh and the Inhabitants of Hackensack (Nov. 10, 1783), *in* 27 WRITINGS, *supra* note 1, at 239, 239; Letter from George Washington to the Officers of the Somerset County Militia (Nov. 7, 1783), *supra* note 16, at 235; Letter from George Washington to the Magistrates and Inhabitants of the Borough of Elizabeth (Aug. 21, 1783), *in* 27 WRITINGS, *supra* note 1, at 113, 113; Letter from George Washington to Reverend William Gordon (July 8, 1783), *in* 27 WRITINGS, *supra* note 1, at 48, 50; Letter from George Washington to Reverend John Rodgers (June 11, 1783), *supra* note 91, at 1.

134. Letter from George Washington to the Massachusetts Senate and House of Representatives (Aug. 10, 1783), *in* 27 WRITINGS, *supra* note 1, at 93, 93; *see also* Letter from George Washington to the Mayor, Recorder, Aldermen, and Common Council of Annapolis (Dec. 22, 1783), *in* 27 WRITINGS, *supra* note 1, at 281, 281; Letter from George Washington to the Burgesses and Common Council of the Borough of Wilmington (Dec. 16, 1783), *in* 27 WRITINGS, *supra* note 1, at 276, 276; Letter from George Washington to the Militia Officers of Bergen County (Nov. 10, 1783), *in* 27 WRITINGS, *supra* note 1, at 240, 240; Address from George Washington to Congress (Aug. 26, 1783), *in* 27 WRITINGS, *supra* note 1, at 116, 117; Letter from George Washington to the Inhabitants of Princeton and Neighborhood, Together with the President and Faculty of the College (Aug. 25, 1783), *in* 27 WRITINGS, *supra* note 1, at 115, 116.

135. Letter from George Washington to the Ministers, Elders, and Deacons of the Reformed Dutch Church at Albany (June 28, 1782), *in* 24 WRITINGS, *supra* note 1, at 389, 390 (emphasis added); *see also* Letter from George Washington to the Militia Officers of the City and Liberties of Philadelphia (Dec. 12, 1783), *in* 27 WRITINGS, *supra* note 1, at 266, 266; Letter from George Washington to the Freeholders and Inhabitants of Kings County (Dec. 1, 1783), *in* 27 WRITINGS, *supra* note 1, at 252, 252-53; Letter from George Washington to the Magistrates and Supervisors of Tryon County (Aug. 1, 1783), *in* 27 WRITINGS, *supra* note 1, at 73, 73; Letter from George Washington to Major General Israel Putnam (June 2, 1783), *in* 26 WRITINGS, *supra* note 1, at 461, 463; Letter from George Washington to Major General Nathanael Greene (Mar. 31, 1783), *in* 26 WRITINGS, *supra* note 1, at 275, 275.

136. Letter from George Washington to the Ministers, Elders, Deacons, and Members of the Reformed German Congregation of New York (Nov. 27, 1783), *in* 27 WRITINGS, *supra* note 1, at 249, 249 (emphasis added).

137. Letter from George Washington to the Learned Professions of Philadelphia (Dec. 13, 1783), *supra* note 133, at 269 (emphasis added).

138. Farewell Orders to the Armies of the United States (Nov. 2, 1783), *in* 27 WRITINGS, *supra* note 1, at 222, 223.

139. *Id.*

140. Circular Letter from George Washington to the States (June 8, 1783), *in* 26 WRITINGS, *supra* note 1, at 483, 484.

141. *Id.* at 485.

142. *Id*. Washington also stated:

> The foundation of our Empire was not laid in the gloomy age of Ignorance and Superstition, but at an Epocha when the rights of mankind were better understood and more clearly defined, than at any former period ... [Among other factors], the pure and benign light of Revelation, [has] had a meliorating influence on mankind and increased the blessings of Society.

    Id. For an argument that Washington's audience would have known that "the benign light of Revelation" referred to the Bible, see Daniel L. Dreisbach, George Washington on Religion's Place in Public Life: Lessons from the Farewell Addresses, The Future of Religion in American Politics: Second Annual Symposium in Honor of Ronald Reagan, Robertson School of Government, Regent University (Feb. 2, 2007) (transcript on file with author).

143. Circular Letter from George Washington to the States (June 8, 1783), *supra* note 140, at 485.

144. *Id*. at 496. Dreisbach notes that Washington's text adapts a verse from the Bible: "[W]hat doth the Lord require of thee, but to do justly, and to love mercy, and to walk humbly with thy God?" *Micah* 6:8; *see also* Dreisbach, *supra* note 142. When used as "Washington's Prayer," the words "Almighty God" and a conclusion such as "Through Jesus Christ our Lord" are typically added. BOLLER, *supra* note 41, at 72; *see also, e.g.*, HENRIQUES, *supra* note 27, at 175; FRANKLIN STEINER, THE RELIGIOUS BELIEFS OF OUR PRESIDENTS: FROM WASHINGTON TO F.D.R. 19-20 (Prometheus Books 1995) (1936).

145. Circular Letter from George Washington to the States (June 8, 1783), *supra* note 140, at 496.

146. *Id*. at 487.

147. *See, e.g.*, BOLLER, *supra* note 41, at 72-74; *see also* HENRIQUES, *supra* note 27, at 175.

148. Address from George Washington to Congress on Resigning His Commission (Dec. 23, 1783), *in* 27 WRITINGS, *supra* note 1, at 284, 285.

149. Letter from George Washington to the Ministers, Elders, Deacons, and Members of the Reformed German Congregation of New York (Nov. 27, 1783), *supra* note 136, at 249; *see also* Letter from George Washington to the Minister, Elders, and Deacons of the Two United Dutch Reformed Churches of Hackensack and Schalenburgh and the Inhabitants of Hackensack (Nov. 10, 1783), *supra* note 133, at 239.

150. Letter from George Washington to the Minister, Elders, and Deacons of the Reformed Protestant Dutch Church in Kingston (Nov. 16, 1782), *in* 25 WRITINGS, *supra* note 1, at 346, 346-47; *see also* Letter from George Washington to the Ministers, Elders, and Deacons of the Reformed Dutch Church at Albany (June 28, 1782), *supra* note 135, at 390.

151. General Orders (Apr. 18, 1783), *supra* note 16, at 335.

152. *Id*. at 336.

FOUR

1.　Letter from George Washington to George Mason (Oct. 3, 1785), *in* 3 THE PAPERS OF GEORGE WASHINGTON: CONFEDERATION SERIES 292, 292-93 (W.W.

Abbot et al. eds., 1994) [the collection is hereinafter referred to as CONFEDERA-TION SERIES].

2. For descriptions of this period of Washington's life, see JOSEPH J. ELLIS, HIS EXCELLENCY: GEORGE WASHINGTON 147-71 (2004); JAMES THOMAS FLEXNER, WASHINGTON: THE INDISPENSABLE MAN 183-203 (Back Bay ed. 1974); 6 DOUG-LAS SOUTHALL FREEMAN, GEORGE WASHINGTON, A BIOGRAPHY: PATRIOT AND PRESIDENT 1-77 (1954); SHELBY LITTLE, GEORGE WASHINGTON 315-27 (1929).

3. Or, if he did, it was not recorded in his diary, according to Douglas Southall Freeman's review. *See* 6 FREEMAN, *supra* note 2, at 6.

4. For descriptions of the events discussed in these paragraphs, see Everson v. Bd. of Educ., 330 U.S. 1, 33-39 (1947) (Rutledge, J., dissenting); Thomas E. Buckley, S.J., *The Religious Rhetoric of Thomas Jefferson, in* THE FOUNDERS ON GOD AND GOVERNMENT 53, 59-67 (Daniel L. Dreisbach et al. eds., 2004); Daniel L. Dreis-bach, *George Mason's Pursuit of Religious Liberty in Revolutionary Virginia, in* THE FOUNDERS ON GOD AND GOVERNMENT, *supra,* at 207, 224-32; Arlin M. Adams & Charles J. Emmerich, *A Heritage of Religious Liberty,* 137 U. PA. L. REV. 1559, 1573-75 (1989); Daniel L. Dreisbach, *Thomas Jefferson and Bills Number 82-86 of the Revision of the Laws of Virginia, 1776-1786: New Light on the Jeffersonian Model of Church-State Relations,* 69 N.C. L. REV. 159, 163-70 (1990); Douglas Laycock, *A Survey of Religious Liberty in the United States,* 47 OHIO ST. L.J. 409, 410-11 (1986).

5. *Everson,* 330 U.S. at 74 (Rutledge, J., dissenting) (citation omitted).

6. Letter from George Mason to George Washington (Oct. 2, 1785), *in* 3 CONFED-ERATION SERIES, *supra* note 1, at 290, 290.

7. Letter from George Washington to George Mason (Oct. 3, 1785), *supra* note 1, at 292-93.

8. *Id.* at 293.

9. *Id.*

10. *Id.*

11. *Id.*

12. 2 CONFEDERATION SERIES, *supra* note 1, at 199-200; *see also* Lady Huntingdon's Plan for Settlement (Apr. 8, 1784), *in* 2 CONFEDERATION SERIES, *supra* note 1, at 211, 213-14.

13. 2 CONFEDERATION SERIES, *supra* note 1, at 199 (quoting a draft of the letter).

14. Letter from George Washington to the Countess of Huntingdon (Aug. 10, 1783), *in* 27 THE WRITINGS OF GEORGE WASHINGTON FROM THE ORIGINAL MANUSCRIPT SOURCES 1745-1799, at 87, 88 (John C. Fitzpatrick ed., 1938). Washington later com-mented to Richard Henry Lee that he did not take an "active or responsible part" in the project because it would "by no means comport with the plan of retirement I had promised myself." Letter from George Washington to Richard Henry Lee (Feb. 8, 1785), *in* 2 CONFEDERATION SERIES, *supra* note 1, at 330, 330.

15. Letter from George Washington to the Countess of Huntingdon (Aug. 10, 1783), *supra* note 14, at 88.

16. *See* 2 CONFEDERATION SERIES, *supra* note 1, at 199; *see also* Letter from James Jay to George Washington (Dec. 20, 1784), *in* 2 CONFEDERATION SERIES, *supra* note 1, at 200, 200-01.

17. Letter from George Washington to the Countess of Huntingdon (Feb. 27, 1785), *in* 2 CONFEDERATION SERIES, *supra* note 1, at 392, 392.

18. Letter from George Washington to James Jay (Jan. 25, 1785), *in* 2 CONFEDERATION SERIES, *supra* note 1, at 291, 291.

19. *See id.* at 291-92.
20. *See id.* at 293.
21. Letter from George Washington to Richard Henry Lee (Feb. 8, 1785), *supra* note 14, at 331.
22. Letter from Richard Henry Lee to George Washington (Feb. 27, 1785), *in* 2 CONFEDERATION SERIES, *supra* note 1, at 395, 395; *see also* Letter from George Washington to the Countess of Huntingdon (June 30, 1785), *in* 3 CONFEDERATION SERIES, *supra* note 1, at 92, 92-93; 2 CONFEDERATION SERIES, *supra* note 1, at 199-200.
23. Letter from George Washington to Richard Henry Lee (Feb. 8, 1785), *supra* note 14, at 331. Nevertheless, as Washington noted to Lee, potential dangers existed from allowing foreigners with "strong prejudices against us, and our forms of Government" to live close not only to Americans, but also to British Canada. *Id.* at 332.
24. *Id.* at 331.
25. *See generally* ARTICLES OF CONFEDERATION (1781); *see also* GORDON S. WOOD, THE CREATION OF THE AMERICAN REPUBLIC, 1776-1787, at 354-63 (W.W. Norton & Co. 1972) (1969).
26. THE FEDERALIST No. 40, at 244 (James Madison) (Clinton Rossiter ed., Signet Classic 2003) (1961); *see also* CAROL BERKIN, A BRILLIANT SOLUTION: INVENTING THE AMERICAN CONSTITUTION 11-29 (2002); CATHERINE DRINKER BOWEN, MIRACLE AT PHILADELPHIA: THE STORY OF THE CONSTITUTIONAL CONVENTION, MAY TO SEPTEMBER 1787, at 5-11 (2d prtg. 1986).
27. *E.g.*, Letter from George Washington to James Madison (Nov. 18, 1786), *in* 4 CONFEDERATION SERIES, *supra* note 1, at 382, 382-83; Letter from George Washington to Theodorick Bland (Nov. 18, 1786), *in* 4 CONFEDERATION SERIES, *supra* note 1, at 377, 378; *see also* ELLIS, *supra* note 2, at 173; 6 FREEMAN, *supra* note 2, at 75.
28. JAMES MACGREGOR BURNS & SUSAN DUNN, GEORGE WASHINGTON 36 (American Presidents Series, Arthur M. Schlesinger, Jr. ed., 2004); ELLIS, *supra* note 2, at 174; 6 FREEMAN, *supra* note 2, at 82.
29. *See, e.g.*, 6 FREEMAN, *supra* note 2, at 81-84.
30. BOWEN, *supra* note 26, at 17; 6 FREEMAN, *supra* note 2, at 88, 90; *see also* ROGER A. BRUNS, U.S. NAT'L ARCHIVES & RECORDS ADMIN., A MORE PERFECT UNION: THE CREATION OF THE U.S. CONSTITUTION, http://www.archives.gov/national-archives-experience/charters/constitution_history.html (last visited May 4, 2007).
31. JAMES MADISON, NOTES OF DEBATES IN THE FEDERAL CONVENTION OF 1787, at 23-24 (W.W. Norton & Co. 1987) (1893).
32. *Id.* at 24.
33. FLEXNER, *supra* note 2, at 207; 6 FREEMAN, *supra* note 2, at 97. On most issues, however, Washington voted with the Virginians. BOWEN, *supra* note 26, at 29; 6 FREEMAN, *supra* note 2, at 96-97.
34. 6 FREEMAN, *supra* note 2, at 107-08 n."A Constitution—Established in Convention"; *see also, e.g.*, ELLIS, *supra* note 2, at 177; FLEXNER, *supra* note 2, at 207; PAUL JOHNSON, GEORGE WASHINGTON: THE FOUNDING FATHER 89 (Eminent Lives Series, James Atlas ed., 2005).
35. BOWEN, *supra* note 26, at 29.
36. *Id.* at 29, 257; 6 FREEMAN, *supra* note 2, at 110-11; *see also* BERKIN, *supra* note 26, at 165; 5 CONFEDERATION SERIES, *supra* note 1, at 331 n.1.

37. 6 FREEMAN, *supra* note 2, at III; *see also* BOWEN, *supra* note 26, at 257.
38. Daniel L. Dreisbach, *In Search of a Christian Commonwealth: An Examination of Selected Nineteenth-Century Commentaries on References to God and the Christian Religion in the United States Constitution*, 48 BAYLOR L. REV. 927, 928 (1996) [hereinafter Dreisbach, *In Search of*]; *see also* I ANSON PHELPS STOKES, CHURCH AND STATE IN THE UNITED STATES 523 (1950).
39. Unless the concluding line with the date, "in the Year of our Lord," is included. U.S. CONST. art. VII; *see also* Dreisbach, *In Search of, supra* note 38, at 964-94.
40. *See* MADISON, *supra* note 31, at 560-61; *see also* Dreisbach, *In Search of, supra* note 38, at 949. For a discussion of the religious test oaths then included in the state constitutions, see Adams & Emmerich, *supra* note 4, at 1576-77; Gerard V. Bradley, *The No Religious Test Clause and the Constitution of Religious Liberty: A Machine that Has Gone of Itself*, 37 CASE W. RES. L. REV. 674, 681-87 (1987).
41. *See* MADISON, *supra* note 31, at 561.
42. Letter from George Washington to Annis Boudinot Stockton (Aug. 31, 1788), *in* 6 CONFEDERATION SERIES, *supra* note 1, at 496, 497; Letter from George Washington to William Tudor (Aug. 18, 1788), *in* 6 CONFEDERATION SERIES, *supra* note 1, at 465, 466; Letter from George Washington to Jonathan Trumbull, Jr. (July 20, 1788), *in* 6 CONFEDERATION SERIES, *supra* note 1, at 389, 390; Letter from George Washington to Benjamin Lincoln (June 29, 1788), *in* 6 CONFEDERATION SERIES, *supra* note 1, at 365, 365; Letter from George Washington to Lafayette (June 18, 1788), *in* 6 CONFEDERATION SERIES, *supra* note 1, at 335, 338; Letter from George Washington to Lafayette (May 28, 1788), *in* 6 CONFEDERATION SERIES, *supra* note 1, at 297, 299.
43. Letter from George Washington to Lafayette (Feb. 7, 1788), *in* 6 CONFEDERATION SERIES, *supra* note 1, at 95, 95.
44. Letter from George Washington to Benjamin Lincoln (Aug. 28, 1788), *in* 6 CONFEDERATION SERIES, *supra* note 1, at 482, 483; *see also* Letter from George Washington to Richard Peters (Sept. 7, 1788), *in* 6 CONFEDERATION SERIES, *supra* note 1, at 504, 506; Letter from George Washington to James McHenry (July 31, 1788), *in* 6 CONFEDERATION SERIES, *supra* note 1, at 409, 410; Letter from George Washington to Jonathan Trumbull, Jr. (July 20, 1788), *supra* note 42, at 390; Letter from George Washington to Benjamin Lincoln (June 29, 1788), *supra* note 42, at 365; Letter from George Washington to Charles Cotesworth Pinckney (June 28, 1788), *in* 6 CONFEDERATION SERIES, *supra* note 1, at 360, 361.
45. Letter from George Washington to Annis Boudinot Stockton (Aug. 31, 1788), *supra* note 42, at 497; Letter from George Washington to Lafayette (Feb. 7, 1788), *supra* note 43, at 96.
46. Letter from the Presbytery of the Eastward to George Washington (Oct. 28, 1789), *in* 4 THE PAPERS OF GEORGE WASHINGTON: PRESIDENTIAL SERIES 275 n.1, 275 n.1 (W.W. Abbot et al. eds., 1993) [the collection is hereinafter referred to as PRESIDENTIAL SERIES]; *see also* PAUL F. BOLLER, JR., GEORGE WASHINGTON & RELIGION 147-48 (1963).
47. Letter from George Washington to the Presbyterian Ministers of Massachusetts and New Hampshire (Nov. 2, 1789), *in* 4 PRESIDENTIAL SERIES, *supra* note 46, at 274, 274.
48. *Id.* (emphasis added).
49. *Id.*

50. Letter from the United Baptist Churches of Virginia to George Washington (May 8-10, 1789), *in* 2 PRESIDENTIAL SERIES, *supra* note 46, at 424 n.1, 425 n.1; *see also* BOLLER, *supra* note 46, at 141-44.
51. Letter from George Washington to the United Baptist Churches of Virginia (May 1789), *in* 2 PRESIDENTIAL SERIES, *supra* note 46, at 423, 424.
52. *Id.*
53. *See, e.g.,* Letter from George Washington to David Humphreys (Oct. 10, 1787), *in* 5 CONFEDERATION SERIES, *supra* note 1, at 365, 365; *see also* Letter from George Washington to Lafayette (Feb. 7, 1788), *supra* note 43, at 95-97; Letter from George Washington to Edmund Randolph (Jan. 8, 1788), *in* 6 CONFEDERATION SERIES, *supra* note 1, at 17, 17-18.
54. 1 STOKES, *supra* note 38, at 536-37.

FIVE

1. First Inaugural Address (Apr. 30, 1789), *in* 2 THE PAPERS OF GEORGE WASHINGTON: PRESIDENTIAL SERIES 173, 174 (W.W. Abbot et al. eds., 1987) [the collection is hereinafter referred to as PRESIDENTIAL SERIES].
2. CATHERINE DRINKER BOWEN, MIRACLE AT PHILADELPHIA: THE STORY OF THE CONSTITUTIONAL CONVENTION, MAY TO SEPTEMBER 1787, at 61 (2d prtg. 1986); *see also* JAMES THOMAS FLEXNER, WASHINGTON: THE INDISPENSABLE MAN 209 (Back Bay ed. 1974).
3. *See, e.g.,* 6 DOUGLAS SOUTHALL FREEMAN, GEORGE WASHINGTON, A BIOGRAPHY: PATRIOT AND PRESIDENT 117 & n.1 (1954).
4. *E.g., id.* at 140 (citing James Monroe); *see also* CAROL BERKIN, A BRILLIANT SOLUTION: INVENTING THE AMERICAN CONSTITUTION 178 (2002); FLEXNER, *supra* note 2, at 211.
5. Letter from George Washington to Alexander Hamilton (Aug. 28, 1788), *in* 6 THE PAPERS OF GEORGE WASHINGTON: CONFEDERATION SERIES 480, 481 (Dorothy Twohig et al. eds., 1997).
6. *E.g.,* Letter from Gouverneur Morris to George Washington (Dec. 6, 1788), *in* 1 PRESIDENTIAL SERIES, *supra* note 1, at 165, 165-66; Letter from Alexander Hamilton to George Washington (Sept. 1788), *in* 1 PRESIDENTIAL SERIES, *supra* note 1, at 23, 23-24; *see also, e.g.,* Letter from William Hartshorne to George Washington (Mar. 28, 1789), *in* 1 PRESIDENTIAL SERIES, *supra* note 1, at 458, 458; Letter from Benjamin Harrison to George Washington (Feb. 26, 1789), *in* 1 PRESIDENTIAL SERIES, *supra* note 1, at 345, 345; Letter from Lachlan McIntosh to George Washington (Feb. 14, 1789), *in* 1 PRESIDENTIAL SERIES, *supra* note 1, at 305, 306; Letter from Jonathan Trumbull, Jr. to George Washington (Oct. 28, 1788), *in* 1 PRESIDENTIAL SERIES, *supra* note 1, at 79, 80.
7. Letter from George Washington to Jonathan Trumbull, Jr. (Dec. 4, 1788), *in* 1 PRESIDENTIAL SERIES, *supra* note 1, at 158, 159; *see also* Letter from George Washington to Crèvecoeur (Apr. 10, 1789), *in* 2 PRESIDENTIAL SERIES, *supra* note 1, at 43, 44; Letter from George Washington to Benjamin Harrison (Mar. 9, 1789), *in* 1 PRESIDENTIAL SERIES, *supra* note 1, at 375, 376; Letter from George Washington to William Gordon (Dec. 23, 1788), *in* 1 PRESIDENTIAL SERIES, *supra* note 1, at 200, 200.
8. 6 FREEMAN, *supra* note 3, at 164.

9. Letter from George Washington to James Madison (May 5, 1789), *in* 2 PRESIDEN-
    TIAL SERIES, *supra* note 1, at 216, 216-17; *see also* DAVID P. CURRIE, THE CONSTITU-
    TION IN CONGRESS: THE FEDERALIST PERIOD, 1789—1801, at 4 & n.7 (1997).

10. For instance, when the new Bank of the United States was proposed, Washington
    solicited opinions from his cabinet as he sought to determine whether such a bank
    lies within the scope of federal power under the Constitution. *E.g.*, 6 FREEMAN,
    supra note 3, at 291-93. Later, when the House sought to obtain papers from the
    executive regarding treaty negotiations with Britain (thereby inserting itself into
    the treaty-making process), he responded in a similar manner and obtained opin-
    ions from his cabinet regarding the constitutionality of refusing the request from
    the House. JOHN ALEXANDER CARROLL & MARY WELLS ASHWORTH, GEORGE
    WASHINGTON: FIRST IN PEACE 353-55 (1957). Washington was prone to ask for
    opinions even on small matters, such as whether he could change the meeting
    place for Congress when an emergency occurred during a congressional recess. *See,
    e.g.*, CARROLL & ASHWORTH, *supra*, at 131-35; *see also* JAMES MACGREGOR BURNS
    & SUSAN DUNN, GEORGE WASHINGTON 53, 73-74 (American Presidents Series,
    Arthur M. Schlesinger, Jr. ed., 2004); PAUL JOHNSON, GEORGE WASHINGTON: THE
    FOUNDING FATHER 96 (Eminent Lives Series, James Atlas ed., 2005).

11. A story has been told that Washington was consulted regarding the creation of a
    Roman Catholic American episcopate during his early years as president. As this
    story goes, Pope Pius VI sent an emissary to talk to Benjamin Franklin, the U.S.
    Ambassador in Paris. The pope wanted to confer with the American government
    regarding the appointment of a Catholic bishop in America. Franklin reportedly
    corresponded with Washington, who responded that, in the new United States,
    the government would not be involved in such decisions. Opening Remarks of
    Ambassador Jim Nicholson at the 20th Anniversary Conference of the U.S. Em-
    bassy to the Holy See (Dec. 3, 2004), http://vatican.usembassy.gov/policy/topics/
    relfreedom/Religious%20Freedom.pdf. The story is not discussed in the text of
    this chapter because it is inaccurate. The real events occurred in 1783-84, before
    Washington was president. The then-governing Continental Congress agreed
    that decisions regarding Roman Catholic leadership were not the business of the
    new American government. *See, e.g.*, PETER GUILDAY, THE LIFE AND TIMES OF
    JOHN CARROLL 179-97 (1954); THOMAS T. MCAVOY, C.S.C., A HISTORY OF THE
    CATHOLIC CHURCH IN THE UNITED STATES 45-46 (1969); ANNABELLE M. MEL-
    VILLE, JOHN CARROLL OF BALTIMORE: FOUNDER OF THE AMERICAN CATHOLIC
    HIERARCHY 57-68 (1955); I ANSON PHELPS STOKES, CHURCH AND STATE IN THE
    UNITED STATES 477-80 (1950).

12. For instance, Washington was notified of an issue concerning certain Quakers,
    who refused to participate in American celebrations by lighting candles in their
    windows, as their neighbors did. On one occasion in October 1781, following the
    victory at Yorktown, an unruly mob sought out homes without lit candles in the
    windows. Rioters smashed the windows in these homes and destroyed the occu-
    pants' furniture. Letter from William Hartshorne to George Washington (Mar. 28,
    1789), *supra* note 6, at 459; *see also* I PRESIDENTIAL SERIES, *supra* note 1, at 459 n.2.
    The Quakers feared that their refusal to participate in celebrations of Washington's
    election would result in similar retaliation. Washington expressed concern, but also
    noted his lack of control over the matter. "Could any way be pointed out to me by
    which I might ward off the evil dreaded by the Quakers, I would, with peculiar

pleasure, take every proper step to prevent it," he wrote Hartshorne, "nothing would be more painful to me than to be the *innocent* cause of distress or injury to any individual of my Country." Letter from George Washington to William Hartshorne (Apr. 1, 1789), *in* 2 PRESIDENTIAL SERIES, *supra* note 1, at 1, 1-2.

13. Descriptions of the first inauguration day can be found at 6 FREEMAN, *supra* note 3, at 185-98; 2 PRESIDENTIAL SERIES, *supra* note 1, at 154-56; *see also New-York, May 1*, DAILY ADVERTISER (New York, NY), May 1, 1789, at 2.

14. U.S. CONST. art. II, § 1, cl. 8. Presidents may also "affirm," rather than "swear," but according to Douglas Southall Freeman, Washington chose to "swear." 6 FREEMAN, *supra* note 3, at 192.

15. 6 FREEMAN, *supra* note 3, at 192 (stating that Washington "*bent forward* as he spoke and . . . he kissed the book") (emphasis added). *But see* BURNS & DUNN, *supra* note 10, at 47 (stating that Washington "*lifted the Bible* to his lips") (emphasis added). For many years, historians and other scholars have reported that Washington also added the words "so help me God" to the inaugural oath. *E.g.*, 6 FREEMAN, *supra* note 3, at 192; JOHN C. MCCOLLISTER, PH.D., GOD AND THE OVAL OFFICE: THE RELIGIOUS FAITH OF OUR 43 PRESIDENTS 5-6 (2005); JOHN SUTHERLAND BONNELL, PRESIDENTIAL PROFILES: RELIGION IN THE LIFE OF AMERICAN PRESIDENTS 20 (1971). Recent research by the staff of Mount Vernon has shown that no contemporaneous evidence for this story exists. To be clear, Mount Vernon's staff does not claim that Washington definitely did *not* add the words "so help me, God" to his oath. Instead, staff members merely note that they cannot definitively prove it one way or another, as they once thought they could. Interview with Mary Thompson, Research Specialist, Mount Vernon, at Mount Vernon (Jan. 30, 2006).

16. 6 FREEMAN, *supra* note 3, at 195 & n.61; *see also* BURNS & DUNN, *supra* note 10, at 48; 2 PRESIDENTIAL SERIES, *supra* note 1, at 155.

17. 6 FREEMAN, *supra* note 3, at 196; 2 PRESIDENTIAL SERIES, *supra* note 1, at 155; 1 STOKES, *supra* note 11, at 484-86; *see also* 1 ANNALS OF CONG. 25-26, 241 (1789).

18. 1 STOKES, *supra* note 11, at 860.

19. *See* 1 ANNALS OF CONG. 25 (1789); *see also* 6 FREEMAN, *supra* note 3, at 186; 2 PRESIDENTIAL SERIES, *supra* note 1, at 154.

20. First Inaugural Address (Apr. 30, 1789), *supra* note 1, at 173-74.

21. *Id.* at 174 (emphasis added).

22. *Id.*

23. *Id.*

24. *Id.* at 175.

25. *Id.*

26. *Id.*

27. *Id.*

28. *Id.* For an argument that Heaven's "eternal rules" is a reference to the Ten Commandments, see PETER A. LILLBACK, GEORGE WASHINGTON'S SACRED FIRE 223-24 (2006).

29. First Inaugural Address (Apr. 30, 1789), *supra* note 1, at 176-77.

30. 1 ANNALS OF CONG. 949 (1789).

31. *Id.*

32. *Id.* at 949-50; *see also* PAUL F. BOLLER, JR., GEORGE WASHINGTON & RELIGION 63 (1963); 4 PRESIDENTIAL SERIES, *supra* note 1, at 129 n.1; 1 STOKES, *supra* note 11, at 486-87.

33. *See* 1 ANNALS OF CONG. 92 (1789).
34. U.S. CONST. amend. I. The House approved this language on Thursday, September 24, the day before the Day of Thanksgiving was proposed. *See* 1 ANNALS OF CONG. 948 (1789). The Senate approved the language on Friday, September 25. *Id.* at 90. It approved the resolution regarding a Day of Thanksgiving on Saturday, September 26. *Id.* at 92.
35. *E.g.*, NAT'L ARCHIVES & RECORDS ADMIN., BILL OF RIGHTS, http://www.archives. gov/national-archives-experience/charters/bill_of_rights_transcript.html (last visited May 7, 2007).
36. Others have made similar arguments. *See, e.g.*, ROBERT L. CORD, SEPARATION OF CHURCH AND STATE: HISTORICAL FACT AND CURRENT FICTION 27-29 (1982); CURRIE, *supra* note 9, at 12-13.
37. A constitutional amendment requires concurrence by 2/3 of each House of Congress and 3/4 of the states. (Alternatively, the legislatures of 2/3 of the states may call for a convention to propose amendments. Any resulting proposals must still be approved by 3/4 of the states.) U.S. CONST. art. V. The First Congress did not deem presidential approval to be a necessary part of the amendment process, despite the constitutional requirement that "Every Order, Resolution, or Vote to which the Concurrence of the Senate and House of Representatives may be necessary (except on a question of Adjournment) shall be presented to the President of the United States." *Id.* art. I, § 7, cl.3; *see also* CURRIE, *supra* note 9, at 115.
38. *See* 4 PRESIDENTIAL SERIES, *supra* note 1, at 129 n.1.
39. Thanksgiving Proclamation (Oct. 3, 1789), *in* 4 PRESIDENTIAL SERIES, *supra* note 1, at 131, 131-32.
40. *Id.* (emphasis added).
41. *Id.* at 132; *see also* MICHAEL NOVAK & JANA NOVAK, WASHINGTON'S GOD: RELIGION, LIBERTY, AND THE FATHER OF OUR COUNTRY 145-46 (2006).
42. Thanksgiving Proclamation (Oct. 3, 1789), *supra* note 39, at 132 (emphasis added).
43. *Id.*
44. *Id.*
45. Letter from George Washington to the Governor and Legislature of New Hampshire (Nov. 3, 1789), *in* 4 PRESIDENTIAL SERIES, *supra* note 1, at 277, 277.
46. Letter from George Washington to the Maryland Legislature (Jan. 20, 1790), *in* 5 PRESIDENTIAL SERIES, *supra* note 1, at 25, 25; *see also, e.g.*, Letter from George Washington to the Hebrew Congregations of Philadelphia, New York, Charleston, and Richmond (Dec. 13, 1790), *in* 7 PRESIDENTIAL SERIES, *supra* note 1, at 61, 62; Letter from George Washington to the Virginia Legislature (Apr. 27, 1790), *in* 5 PRESIDENTIAL SERIES, *supra* note 1, at 349, 349; Address from George Washington to the United States Senate and House of Representatives (Jan. 8, 1790), *in* 4 PRESIDENTIAL SERIES, *supra* note 1, at 543, 543; Letter from George Washington to the Georgia Legislature (Dec. 1789), *in* 4 PRESIDENTIAL SERIES, *supra* note 1, at 457, 457; Letter from George Washington to the Society of Quakers (Oct. 1789), *in* 4 PRESIDENTIAL SERIES, *supra* note 1, at 265, 265; Letter from George Washington to the Board of Trustees of Dartmouth College (Aug. 1789), *in* 3 PRESIDENTIAL SERIES, *supra* note 1, at 573, 573; Letter from George Washington to the Officials of Washington College (July 11, 1789), *in* 3 PRESIDENTIAL SERIES, *supra* note 1, at 177, 177; Letter from George Washington to the United Baptist Churches of Virginia (May 1789), *in* 2 PRESIDENTIAL SERIES, *supra* note 1, at 423, 423; Let-

ter from George Washington to the Mayor, Recorder, Aldermen, and Common Council of Philadelphia (Apr. 20, 1789), *in* 2 PRESIDENTIAL SERIES, *supra* note 1, at 83, 83.

47. Letter from George Washington to the Citizens of Portsmouth (Nov. 2, 1789), *in* 4 PRESIDENTIAL SERIES, *supra* note 1, at 272, 272; *see also* Letter from George Washington to the Inhabitants of Providence, Rhode Island (Aug. 19, 1790), *in* 6 PRESIDENTIAL SERIES, *supra* note 1, at 299, 300; Letter from George Washington to the Clergy of Newport, Rhode Island (Aug. 18, 1790), *in* 6 PRESIDENTIAL SE-RIES, *supra* note 1, at 279, 279; Letter from George Washington to the People of South Carolina (July 5, 1790), *in* 6 PRESIDENTIAL SERIES, *supra* note 1, at 16, 16; Letter from George Washington to the Synod of the Dutch Reformed Church in North America (Oct. 1789), *in* 4 PRESIDENTIAL SERIES, *supra* note 1, at 263, 263-64; Letter from George Washington to the Connecticut Legislature (Oct. 17, 1789), *in* 4 PRESIDENTIAL SERIES, *supra* note 1, at 202, 202; Letter from George Washington to the General Assembly of the Presbyterian Church (May 1789), *in* 2 PRESIDENTIAL SERIES, *supra* note 1, at 420, 420; Letter from George Washington to the Citizens of New York City (May 9, 1789), *in* 2 PRESIDENTIAL SERIES, *supra* note 1, at 242, 242-43; Letter from George Washington to the Pennsylvania Legislature (Apr. 21, 1789), *in* 2 PRESIDENTIAL SERIES, *supra* note 1, at 105, 105.

48. *See, e.g.*, Letter from George Washington to the Citizens of Portsmouth (Nov. 2, 1789), *supra* note 47, at 272-73; Letter from George Washington to the Connecticut Legislature (Oct. 17, 1789), *supra* note 47, at 202; Letter from George Washington to the Massachusetts Senate and House of Representatives (July 9, 1789), *in* 3 PRESIDENTIAL SERIES, *supra* note 1, at 165, 165-66; Letter from George Washington to the United States Senate (May 18, 1789), *in* 2 PRESIDENTIAL SERIES, *supra* note 1, at 324, 324; Letter from George Washington to the United States House of Representatives (May 8, 1789), *in* 2 PRESIDENTIAL SERIES, *supra* note 1, at 232, 232; Letter from George Washington to the German Lutherans of Philadelphia (Apr. 1789), *in* 2 PRESIDENTIAL SERIES, *supra* note 1, at 179, 180; Letter from George Washington to the Judges of the Pennsylvania Supreme Court (Apr. 20, 1789), *in* 2 PRESIDENTIAL SERIES, *supra* note 1, at 84, 84-85; Letter from George Washington to the Officials of Wilmington, Delaware (Apr. 19-20, 1789), *in* 2 PRESIDENTIAL SERIES, *supra* note 1, at 77, 77; *see also* Letter from George Washington to the Officials and Citizens of Richmond (Apr. 12, 1791), *in* 8 PRESIDENTIAL SERIES, *supra* note 1, at 86, 86; Letter from George Washington to the Governor and Council of North Carolina (Aug. 26, 1790), *in* 6 PRESIDENTIAL SERIES, *supra* note 1, at 327, 327; Letter from George Washington to the Hebrew Congregation in Newport, Rhode Island (Aug. 18, 1790), *in* 6 PRESIDENTIAL SERIES, *supra* note 1, at 284, 285; Letter from George Washington to the Savannah, Ga., Hebrew Congregation (May 1790), *in* 5 PRESIDENTIAL SERIES, *supra* note 1, at 448, 448-49; Letter from George Washington to Roman Catholics in America (Mar. 1790), *in* 5 PRESIDENTIAL SERIES, *supra* note 1, at 299, 299; Letter from George Washington to Charleston, S.C., Officials (Feb. 1790), *in* 5 PRESIDENTIAL SERIES, *supra* note 1, at 188, 189; Letter from George Washington to the Citizens of Marblehead (Nov. 2, 1789), *in* 4 PRESIDENTIAL SERIES, *supra* note 1, at 270, 271; Letter from George Washington to the Pennsylvania Legislature (Sept. 12, 1789), *in* 4 PRESIDENTIAL SERIES, *supra* note 1, at 23, 24; Letter from George Washington to the Governor and Council of North Carolina (June 19, 1789), *in* 3 PRESIDENTIAL SERIES, *supra*

note 1, at 47, 48; Letter from George Washington to the Pennsylvania Society of the Cincinnati (Apr. 20, 1789), *in* 2 PRESIDENTIAL SERIES, *supra* note 1, at 80, 80-81.

49. Letter from George Washington to the Mayor, Corporation, and Citizens of Alexandria (Apr. 16, 1789), *in* 2 PRESIDENTIAL SERIES, *supra* note 1, at 59, 60.

50. Letter from George Washington to the Citizens of Baltimore (Apr. 17, 1789), *in* 2 PRESIDENTIAL SERIES, *supra* note 1, at 62, 62.

51. Letter from George Washington to Arthur Fenner (June 4, 1790), *in* 5 PRESIDENTIAL SERIES, *supra* note 1, at 470, 470 (emphasis added).

52. U.S. CONST. art. 1, § 8, cl. 17.

53. Washington biographer Joseph Ellis discusses the debate and compromise at length. *See* JOSEPH J. ELLIS, FOUNDING BROTHERS: THE REVOLUTIONARY GENERATION 48-80 (2000).

54. Law of July 16, 1790, ch. 28, 1 Stat. 130; *see also* 6 FREEMAN, *supra* note 3, at 299.

55. *See, e.g.*, JEFFREY F. MEYER, MYTHS IN STONE: RELIGIOUS DIMENSIONS OF WASHINGTON, D.C. 21 (2001); RICHARD W. STEPHENSON, "A PLAN WHOL[L]Y NEW": PIERRE CHARLES L'ENFANT'S PLAN OF THE CITY OF WASHINGTON 14 (1993).

56. Letter from Pierre-Charles L'Enfant to George Washington (Aug. 19, 1791), *in* 8 PRESIDENTIAL SERIES, *supra* note 1, at 439, 441; *see also* 1 STOKES, *supra* note 11, at 493.

57. MEYER, *supra* note 55, at 79 (citing the legend on L'Enfant's map); *see also* 1 STOKES, *supra* note 11, at 493.

58. Letter from Pierre-Charles L'Enfant to George Washington (Aug. 19, 1791), *supra* note 56, at 444.

59. 1 STOKES, *supra* note 11, at 493.

60. *See* 6 FREEMAN, *supra* note 3, at 333.

61. *See* MEYER, *supra* note 55, at 79.

62. *See id.* at 76-79; *see also* WASHINGTON NATIONAL CATHEDRAL, A VOICE, A PLACE, A PEOPLE: HISTORY, http://www.cathedral.org/cathedral/discover/history.shtml (last visited May 8, 2007).

63. 6 FREEMAN, *supra* note 3, at 240 (citation omitted).

64. NOVAK & NOVAK, *supra* note 41, at 170.

65. Letter from the Society of Quakers to George Washington (Sept. 28-Oct. 3, 1789), *in* 4 PRESIDENTIAL SERIES, *supra* note 1, at 266 n.1, 267 n.1.

66. *Id.*

67. Letter from George Washington to the Society of Quakers (Oct. 1789), *supra* note 46, at 266.

68. *Id.*

69. *Id.*

70. Letter from the Hebrew Congregation in Newport, Rhode Island, to George Washington (Aug. 17, 1790), *in* 6 PRESIDENTIAL SERIES, *supra* note 1, at 286 n.1, 286 n.1.

71. *Id.*

72. *Id.*

73. Letter from George Washington to the Hebrew Congregation in Newport, Rhode Island (Aug. 18, 1790), *supra* note 48, at 285.

74. *Id.*; *see also* Letter from George Washington to the Savannah, Ga., Hebrew Congregation (May 1790), *supra* note 48, at 448.

75. *See also, e.g.*, Letter from George Washington to Roman Catholics in America (Mar. 1790), *supra* note 48, at 299; Letter from George Washington to the Society of Free Quakers (Mar. 1790), *in* 5 PRESIDENTIAL SERIES, *supra* note 1, at 296, 296-97; Letter from George Washington to the United Baptist Churches of Virginia (May 1789), *supra* note 46, at 424; Letter from George Washington to the Bishops of the Methodist Episcopal Church (May 29, 1789), *in* 2 PRESIDENTIAL SERIES, *supra* note 1, at 411, 411-12.

76. Letter from George Washington to the Hebrew Congregation in Newport, Rhode Island (Aug. 18, 1790), *supra* note 48, at 285.

77. *Id.* (emphasis added). Washington's contemporaneous writings to other churches echoed these dual expectations: Americans may have the right to religious liberty, but they also have the duty to be good citizens. *See, e.g.*, Letter from George Washington to Roman Catholics in America (Mar. 1790), *supra* note 48, at 299; Letter from George Washington to the United Baptist Churches of Virginia (May 1789), *supra* note 46, at 424; Letter from George Washington to the General Assembly of the Presbyterian Church (May 1789), *supra* note 47, at 420.

78. Letter from George Washington to the Protestant Episcopal Church (Aug. 19, 1789), *in* 3 PRESIDENTIAL SERIES, *supra* note 1, at 496, 497.

79. Letter from the Roman Catholics in America to George Washington (Mar. 15, 1790), *in* 5 PRESIDENTIAL SERIES, *supra* note 1, at 300 n., 300 n.

80. Letter from George Washington to Roman Catholics in America (Mar. 1790), *supra* note 48, at 299.

81. Letter from George Washington to the Bishops of the Methodist Episcopal Church (May 29, 1789), *supra* note 75, at 412.

82. *Id.* at 411-12.

83. Letter from George Washington to the Synod of the Dutch Reformed Church in North America (Oct. 1789), *supra* note 47, at 264.

84. Letter from George Washington to the German Reformed Congregations (June 1789), *in* 3 PRESIDENTIAL SERIES, *supra* note 1, at 92, 92-93.

85. Letter from George Washington to the Society of Quakers (Oct. 1789), *supra* note 46, at 266.

86. *Id.*

87. Letter from the General Assembly of the Presbyterian Church to George Washington (May 26, 1789), *in* 2 PRESIDENTIAL SERIES, *supra* note 1, at 421 n., 422 n.

88. Washington's letter did reference the Christian religion, but in a different context. He stated that no man "can possibly be a true Christian" if he is a "bad member of the civil community." Letter from George Washington to the General Assembly of the Presbyterian Church (May 1789), *supra* note 47, at 420.

89. *Id.*

90. *Id.*

91. Letter from the Congregational Ministers of New Haven to George Washington (Oct. 17, 1789), *in* 4 PRESIDENTIAL SERIES, *supra* note 1, at 199 n.1, 199 n.1.

92. Letter from George Washington to the Congregational Ministers of New Haven (Oct. 17, 1789), *in* 4 PRESIDENTIAL SERIES, *supra* note 1, at 198, 198.

93. *Id.*

94. Letter from George Washington to the Protestant Episcopal Church (Aug. 19, 1789), *supra* note 78, at 497.

95. Letter from George Washington to the Synod of the Dutch Reformed Church

in North America (Oct. 1789), *supra* note 47, at 264; *see also* Letter from George Washington to the Convention of the Universal Church (Aug. 9, 1790), *in* 6 PRESIDENTIAL SERIES, *supra* note 1, at 223, 223.

96. U.S. CONST. amend. I.

97. Washington did, however, see an early draft of the amendments in May 1789. He told Madison that he saw "nothing exceptionable in the proposed amendments. Some of them, in my opinion, are importantly necessary; others, though of themselves (in my conception) not very essential, are necessary to quiet the fears of some respectable characters and well meaning men. Upon the whole, therefore, not foreseeing any evil consequences that can result from their adoption, they have my wishes for a favourable reception in both houses." Letter from George Washington to James Madison (May 31, 1789), *in* 2 PRESIDENTIAL SERIES, note 1, at 419, 419.

98. *See* 6 FREEMAN, *supra* note 3, at 221; *see also* RICHARD NORTON SMITH, PATRIARCH: GEORGE WASHINGTON AND THE NEW AMERICAN NATION 22 (1993).

99. Others have noted the religious acts of the First Congress in their attempts to understand the meaning of the First Amendment. *See, e.g.*, GERARD V. BRADLEY, CHURCH-STATE RELATIONSHIPS IN AMERICA 97-98 (1987); CORD, *supra* note 36, at 23-29, 50-54; 1 STOKES, *supra* note 11, at 483-517; Kent Greenawalt, *Common Sense about Original and Subsequent Understandings of the Religion Clauses*, 8 U. PA. J. CONST. L. 479, 491, 497-504 (2006); Paul E. Salamanca, *The Role of Religion in Public Life and Official Pressure to Participate in Alcoholics Anonymous*, 65 U. CIN. L. REV. 1093, 1111-12 (1997).

100. 1 ANNALS OF CONG. 18 (1789).

101. *See id.* at 18-19, 24, 242; *see also* Rosenberger v. Rector & Visitors of the Univ. of Va., 515 U.S. 819, 858 (1995) (Thomas, J., concurring); MILDRED AMER, CONG. RESEARCH SERV., HOUSE AND SENATE CHAPLAINS (2007), http://www.senate.gov/reference/resources/pdf/RS20427.pdf.

102. *See* Law of Sept. 22, 1789, ch. 17, § 4, 1 Stat. 70, 71.

103. ASHBEL GREEN, THE LIFE OF ASHBEL GREEN, V.D.M. 263 (Joseph H. Jones ed., 1849).

104. *See, e.g.*, Letter from George Washington to John Adams (May 10, 1789), *in* 2 PRESIDENTIAL SERIES, *supra* note 1, at 245, 245-46; *see also* Letter from Alexander Hamilton to George Washington (May 5, 1789), *in* 2 PRESIDENTIAL SERIES, *supra* note 1, at 211, 211-14.

105. Law of Mar. 3, 1791, ch. 28, §§ 5-6, 1 Stat. 222, 222-23; *see also* CORD, *supra* note 36, at 54.

106. Law of Aug. 7, 1789, ch. 8, 1 Stat 50, 50-51; *see also* 1 ANNALS OF CONG. 57, 685, 702 (1789); CURRIE, *supra* note 9, at 103-07; 1 STOKES, *supra* note 11, at 480.

107. Law of Aug. 7, 1789, ch. 8, §§ 1-2, 1 Stat 50, 52-53.

108. *See id.*; *see also* CURRIE, *supra* note 9, at 106-07.

109. NORTHWEST ORDINANCE, § 14, art. 1 (1787).

110. *Id.* § 14, art. 3.

111. *See* CORD, *supra* note 36, at 61-62; 1 STOKES, *supra* note 11, at 481.

112. NORTHWEST ORDINANCE, § 14, art. 1.

113. Law of Sept. 24, 1789, ch. 20, 1 Stat 73.

114. *Id.* §§ 7-8, 27. An exception was made for those clerks opting for an affirmation, rather than an oath. *Id.* § 7.

115. Letter from George Washington to Gouverneur Morris (Oct. 13, 1789), *in* 4 PRESIDENTIAL SERIES, *supra* note 1, at 176, 176.
116. Law of Apr. 30, 1790, ch. 9, 1 Stat 112.
117. 1 STOKES, *supra* note 11, at 492.
118. Law of Apr. 30, 1790, ch. 9, § 31, 1 Stat 112, 119.
119. 1 STOKES, *supra* note 11, at 492.

SIX

1. The editors at *The Papers of George Washington* have not yet published the final volumes of their Presidential Series. The text of the Farewell Address, however, has been made available at http://gwpapers.virginia.edu/documents/farewell/transcript. html#top; *see also* Farewell Address (Sept. 19, 1796), *reprinted in* 35 THE WRITINGS OF GEORGE WASHINGTON FROM THE ORIGINAL MANUSCRIPT SOURCES 1745-1799, at 214, 229 (John C. Fitzpatrick ed., 1940) [the collection is hereinafter referred to as WRITINGS].

2. Madison's Conversations with Washington (May 5-25, 1792), *in* 10 THE PAPERS OF GEORGE WASHINGTON: PRESIDENTIAL SERIES 349, 351 (Philander D. Chase et al. eds., 2002) [the collection is hereinafter referred to as PRESIDENTIAL SERIES]; *see also* JAMES MACGREGOR BURNS & SUSAN DUNN, GEORGE WASHINGTON 93-95 (American Presidents Series, Arthur M. Schlesinger, Jr. ed., 2004).

3. Letter from George Washington to James Madison (May 20, 1792), *in* 10 PRESIDENTIAL SERIES, *supra* note 2, at 399, 400; *see also* 6 DOUGLAS SOUTHALL FREEMAN, GEORGE WASHINGTON, A BIOGRAPHY: PATRIOT AND PRESIDENT 356-58 (1954); RICHARD NORTON SMITH, PATRIARCH: GEORGE WASHINGTON AND THE NEW AMERICAN NATION 133-34 (1993).

4. Letter from George Washington to James Madison (May 20, 1792), *supra* note 3, at 400.

5. Letter from Thomas Jefferson to George Washington (May 23, 1792), *in* 10 PRESIDENTIAL SERIES, *supra* note 2, at 408, 412.

6. Thomas Jefferson's Conversation with Washington (Oct. 1, 1792), *in* 11 PRESIDENTIAL SERIES, *supra* note 2, at 182, 183.

7. Madison's Conversations with Washington (May 5-25, 1792), *supra* note 2, at 350; *see also* Letter from James Madison to George Washington (June 20, 1792), *in* 10 PRESIDENTIAL SERIES, *supra* note 2, at 478, 480.

8. Letter from Alexander Hamilton to George Washington (July 30-Aug. 3, 1792), *in* 10 PRESIDENTIAL SERIES, *supra* note 2, at 594, 594.

9. *E.g.*, BURNS & DUNN, *supra* note 2, at 95; 6 FREEMAN, *supra* note 3, at 383-84; SMITH, *supra* note 3, at 151-52.

10. By the President of the United States of America: A Proclamation (Jan. 1, 1795), *in* 1 A COMPILATION OF THE MESSAGES AND PAPERS OF THE PRESIDENTS: 1789-1897, at 179 (James D. Richardson ed., 1896) [hereinafter 1795 Thanksgiving Proclamation].

11. Proclamation (Sept. 25, 1794), *in* 33 WRITINGS, *supra* note 1, at 507, 508.

12. More information on the Whiskey Rebellion can be found at BURNS & DUNN, *supra* note 2, at 101-03; RICHARD BROOKHISER: ALEXANDER HAMILTON: AMERICAN 117-20 (1999); JOHN ALEXANDER CARROLL & MARY WELLS ASHWORTH, GEORGE WASHINGTON: FIRST IN PEACE 180-217 (1957); JOSEPH J. ELLIS, HIS EXCELLENCY:

GEORGE WASHINGTON 224-26 (2004); JAMES THOMAS FLEXNER, WASHINGTON: THE INDISPENSABLE MAN 312-20 (Back Bay ed. 1974); SMITH, *supra* note 3, at 210-23.

13. 1795 Thanksgiving Proclamation, *supra* note 10, at 180.
14. *Id.*
15. *Id.*
16. *Id.*
17. *Id.*
18. *Id.*
19. *Id.* (emphasis added).
20. *Id.* (emphasis added).
21. *Id.* (emphasis added).
22. *See* CHARLES H. CALLAHAN, WASHINGTON: THE MAN AND THE MASON 290-93 (1913); SMITH, *supra* note 3, at 182-83; MAJOR J. HUGO TATSCH, THE FACTS ABOUT GEORGE WASHINGTON AS A FREEMASON 24-27 (1931).
23. *See, e.g.*, Law of Mar. 10, 1796, ch. 4, § 3, 1 Stat. 448, 449; Law of Mar. 3, 1795, ch. 44, §§ 11-12, 1 Stat. 430, 431; Law of Mar. 27, 1794, ch. 11, §§ 2, 6, 1 Stat. 350, 350-51; Law of Mar. 5, 1792, ch. 9, § 7, 1 Stat. 241, 242.
24. Letter from George Washington to John Ettwein (May 2, 1788), *in* 6 THE PAPERS OF GEORGE WASHINGTON: CONFEDERATION SERIES 182 n.2, 182 n.2 (Dorothy Twohig et al. eds., 1997).
25. *Id.*
26. Message from George Washington to the Chiefs and Warriors of the Wabash and Illinois Indians (May 7, 1793), *in* 12 PRESIDENTIAL SERIES, *supra* note 2, at 551, 552; Message from George Washington to the Five Nations (Apr. 25, 1792), *in* 10 PRESIDENTIAL SERIES, *supra* note 2, at 316, 316; Address from George Washington to the Miami Indians (Mar. 11, 1791), *in* 7 PRESIDENTIAL SERIES, *supra* note 2, at 550, 551; *see also* 10 PRESIDENTIAL SERIES, *supra* note 2, at 187 n.2; 6 PRESIDENTIAL SERIES, *supra* note 2, at 249 n.; 3 PRESIDENTIAL SERIES, *supra* note 2, at 544 n.
27. Speech from George Washington to the Delaware Chiefs (May 12, 1779), *in* 15 WRITINGS, *supra* note 1, at 53, 55.
28. *Id.*
29. Letter from George Washington to Joseph Johnson (Feb. 20, 1776), *in* 3 THE PAPERS OF GEORGE WASHINGTON: REVOLUTIONARY WAR SERIES 349, 349 (W.W. Abbot et al. eds., 1988) [the collection is hereinafter referred to as WAR SERIES]; *see also* Letter from Eleazar Wheelock to George Washington (Jan. 26, 1776), *in* 3 WAR SERIES, *supra*, at 193, 193 (introducing Johnson).
30. Letter from George Washington to John Hancock (Sept. 30, 1775), *in* 2 WAR SERIES, *supra* note 29, at 70, 70. Kirkland also sought to attach the Six Nations to the American colonies, but with limited success. *See* 2 WAR SERIES, *supra* note 29, at 61 n.1.
31. 2 WAR SERIES, *supra* note 29, at 61 n.1.
32. Letter from George Washington to John Hancock (Sept. 30, 1775), *supra* note 30, at 70.
33. The funds supplemented an earlier appropriation. 2 WAR SERIES, *supra* note 29, at 71 n.1.
34. Instructions to the Commissioners for Treating with the Southern Indians (Aug. 29, 1789), *in* 1 AMERICAN STATE PAPERS: INDIAN AFFAIRS 65, 66 (1832).
35. *Id.* The American State papers are available on the website for the Library of Congress: http://memory.loc.gov/ammem/amlaw/lwsp.html.

36. Letter from John Christopher Kunze to George Washington (Jan. 7, 1790), *in* 4 PRESIDENTIAL SERIES, *supra* note 2, at 540, 541.
37. Letter from George Washington to John Christopher Kunze (Jan. 12, 1790), *in* 4 PRESIDENTIAL SERIES, *supra* note 2, at 542 n.2, 542 n.2.
38. Address from George Washington to the United States Senate and House of Representatives (Oct. 25, 1791), *in* 9 PRESIDENTIAL SERIES, *supra* note 2, at 110, 112.
39. Letter from John Carroll to George Washington (Mar. 20, 1792), *in* 10 PRESIDENTIAL SERIES, *supra* note 2, at 135, 135.
40. Letter from George Washington to John Carroll (Apr. 10, 1792), *in* 10 PRESIDENTIAL SERIES, *supra* note 2, at 242, 243.
41. *Id.* at 242.
42. *Id.* at 243. Washington also noted that the tribes of the Five Nations (another group of Indians) "are, in their religious concerns, under the immediate superintendance of the Revd Mr Kirkland." *Id.* at 242.
43. *Id.* at 243.
44. Letter from Henry Knox to George Washington (Mar. 12, 1793), *in* 12 PRESIDENTIAL SERIES, *supra* note 2, at 306, 306. The Quakers themselves also met with Washington to discuss the matter on a few occasions. 12 PRESIDENTIAL SERIES, *supra* note 2, at 355 n.6 & 417 n.2.
45. Letter from Henry Knox to George Washington (Mar. 12, 1793), *supra* note 44, at 307.
46. THE JOURNAL OF THE PROCEEDINGS OF THE PRESIDENT 1793-1797, at 87 (Dorothy Twohig ed., 1981).
47. Letter from George Washington to the Cabinet (Mar. 21, 1793), *in* 12 PRESIDENTIAL SERIES, *supra* note 2, at 354, 355.
48. *See* Instructions to Benjamin Lincoln, of Massachusetts, Beverley Randolph, of Virginia, and Timothy Pickering, of Pennsylvania, Commissioners Appointed for Treating with the Indians Northwest of the Ohio (Apr. 26, 1793), *in* 1 AMERICAN STATE PAPERS: INDIAN AFFAIRS 340, 341 (1832).
49. Treaty between the United States of America and the Oneida, Tuscarora, and Stockbridge Indians, Dwelling in the country of the Oneidas (Dec. 2, 1794), *in* 1 AMERICAN STATE PAPERS: INDIAN AFFAIRS 546, 546 (1832).
50. *Id.* at 546.
51. *See, e.g.*, ROBERT L. CORD, SEPARATION OF CHURCH AND STATE: HISTORICAL FACT AND CURRENT FICTION 58 (1982).
52. A provision in another treaty, the Treaty of Tripoli, is sometimes cited as evidence that Washington preferred a more complete separation between church and state. Article XI of the treaty provides, in relevant part, that the "government of the United States of America is not in any sense founded on the Christian religion." Treaty of Peace and Friendship Between the United States of America, and the Bey and Subjects of Tripoli, of Barbary, 8 Stat 154, 155 (1797). There is no reason, however, to consider this provision probative of Washington's views on church and state. The treaty was written in 1796, while Washington was still president, but there is no record of Washington requesting or approving the language quoted above. The treaty did not arrive in America for Senate ratification until after Washington's retirement. It was thus President John Adams who presented the treaty to the Senate for ratification. *See* Letter from John Adams to the United

States Senate (May 26, 1797), *in* 2 AMERICAN STATE PAPERS: FOREIGN RELATIONS 18 (1832); *see also* PAUL F. BOLLER, JR., GEORGE WASHINGTON & RELIGION 87-88 (1963); 1 ANSON PHELPS STOKES, CHURCH AND STATE IN THE UNITED STATES 497-98 (1950).

53. *See, e.g.*, GERARD V. BRADLEY, CHURCH-STATE RELATIONSHIPS IN AMERICA 100 (1987); CORD, *supra* note 51, at 41-44, 62.

54. The two provisions quoted in this sentence can be found at 28 JOURNALS OF THE CONTINENTAL CONGRESS, 1774-89, at 381 (John C. Fitzpatrick ed., Government Printing Office 1933); 33 *id.* at 430.

55. 34 *id.* at 486-87.

56. Law of June 1, 1796, ch. 46, 1 Stat. 490.

57. *Id.* §§ 2 & 5, 1 Stat. 491.

58. Letter from the Moravian Society for Propagating the Gospel to George Washington (July 10, 1789), *in* 3 PRESIDENTIAL SERIES, *supra* note 2, at 466 n.1, 466 n.1.

59. Letter from George Washington to the Moravian Society for Propagating the Gospel (Aug. 15, 1789), *in* 3 PRESIDENTIAL SERIES, *supra* note 2, at 466, 466.

60. Other scholars have recounted this aid in greater detail. *E.g.*, CORD, *supra* note 51, at 57-80.

61. Letter from George Washington to John Armstrong (Mar. 11, 1792), *in* 10 PRESIDENTIAL SERIES, *supra* note 2, at 85, 86; *see also* Letter from George Washington to Jonathan Williams (Mar. 2, 1795), *in* 34 WRITINGS, *supra* note 1, at 130, 130; Letter from George Washington to Alexander Hamilton (Aug. 26, 1792), *in* 11 PRESIDENTIAL SERIES, *supra* note 2, at 38, 39.

62. Letter from George Washington to the Members of the New Jerusalem Church of Baltimore (Jan. 27, 1793), *in* 12 PRESIDENTIAL SERIES, *supra* note 2, at 52, 52.

63. *Id.*

64. Letter from George Washington to the Inhabitants of Shepherds Town and Its Vicinity (Oct. 12, 1796), *in* 35 WRITINGS, *supra* note 1, at 242, 242; *see also* Letter from George Washington to the Inhabitants of the Borough of Carlisle (Oct. 6, 1794), *in* 33 WRITINGS, *supra* note 1, at 519, 519; Letter from George Washington to the Burgesses and the Citizens of Harrisburg (Oct. 4, 1794), *in* 33 WRITINGS, *supra* note 1, at 518, 518; Letter from George Washington to the Inhabitants of the City of New London (Sept. 2, 1793), *in* 33 WRITINGS, *supra* note 1, at 80, 80-81; Letter from George Washington to the Inhabitants of the City of Hartford (Aug. 4, 1793), *in* 33 WRITINGS, *supra* note 1, at 40, 40.

65. Letter from George Washington to Governor John Hawkins Stone (Dec. 23, 1796), *in* 35 WRITINGS, *supra* note 1, at 343, 344.

66. Seventh Annual Address from George Washington to Congress (Dec. 8, 1795), *in* 34 WRITINGS, *supra* note 1, at 386, 386; *see also* Eighth Annual Address from George Washington to Congress (Dec. 7, 1796), *in* 35 WRITINGS, *supra* note 1, at 310, 310-11.

67. Letter from George Washington to the Inhabitants of the City of Hartford (Aug. 4, 1793), *supra* note 64, at 40; *see also* Letter from George Washington to John Smith et al. (Nov. 28, 1796), *in* 35 WRITINGS, *supra* note 1, at 293, 294; Letter from George Washington to the Inhabitants of Shepherds Town and Its Vicinity (Oct. 12, 1796), *supra* note 64, at 242; Sixth Annual Address from George Washington to Congress (Nov. 19, 1794), *in* 34 WRITINGS, *supra* note 1, at 28, 37; Letter from George Washington to the Burgesses and the Citizens of Harrisburg (Oct. 4,

1794), *supra* note 64, at 518; Fifth Annual Address from George Washington to Congress (Dec. 3, 1793), *in* 33 WRITINGS, *supra* note 1, at 163, 164; Letter from George Washington to the Trustees of the Public School of Germantown (Nov. 6, 1793), *in* 33 WRITINGS, *supra* note 1, at 148, 149; Letter from George Washington to the House of Representatives (Nov. 12, 1792), *in* 11 PRESIDENTIAL SERIES, *supra* note 2, at 368 n., 368 n.; Address from George Washington to the United States Senate and House of Representatives (Nov. 6, 1792), *in* 11 PRESIDENTIAL SERIES, *supra* note 2, at 342, 347-48.

68. Letter from George Washington to the Inhabitants of Richmond (Aug. 28, 1793), *in* 33 WRITINGS, *supra* note 1, at 71, 72.

69. Letter from George Washington to the Inhabitants of the City of New London (Sept. 2, 1793), *supra* note 64, at 80-81.

70. Letter from George Washington to John Doughty (Sept. 23, 1793), *in* 33 WRITINGS, *supra* note 1, at 93, 93.

71. Letter from George Washington to Reverend James Madison (Sept. 23, 1793), *in* 33 WRITINGS, *supra* note 1, at 96, 97.

72. Letter from George Washington to the Inhabitants of the Borough of Carlisle (Oct. 6, 1794), *supra* note 64, at 519.

73. Letter from George Washington to the Citizens of Frederick County, Virginia (Dec. 16, 1795), *in* 34 WRITINGS, *supra* note 1, at 395, 395-96; *see also* Letter from George Washington to the Massachusetts Senators (Feb. 24, 1797), *in* 35 WRITINGS, *supra* note 1, at 397, 398; Letter from George Washington to the Pennsylvania House of Representatives (Feb. 17, 1797), *in* 35 WRITINGS, *supra* note 1, at 392, 393; Letter from George Washington to the Trustees of the Public School of Germantown (Nov. 6, 1793), *supra* note 67, at 149; Letter from George Washington to the Inhabitants of Richmond (Aug. 28, 1793), *supra* note 68, at 71-72; Letter from George Washington to the Inhabitants of the City of Hartford (Aug. 4, 1793), *supra* note 64, at 40.

74. Letter from George Washington to the Members of the New Jerusalem Church of Baltimore (Jan. 27, 1793), *supra* note 62, at 52-53.

75. Letter from George Washington to the Rector, Church Wardens, and Vestrymen of the United Episcopal Churches of Christ Church and St. Peter's (Mar. 2, 1797), *in* 35 WRITINGS, *supra* note 1, at 410, 411.

76. *Id.*

77. Letter from George Washington to the Clergy of Different Denominations Residing in and Near the City of Philadelphia (Mar. 3, 1797), *in* 35 WRITINGS, *supra* note 1, at 416, 416.

78. *Id.*

79. *E.g.*, CARROLL & ASHWORTH, *supra* note 12, at 381-82, 398-99; ELLIS, *supra* note 12, at 232-34; FLEXNER, *supra* note 12, at 347-49.

80. CARROLL & ASHWORTH, *supra* note 12, at 403.

81. *See, e.g.*, ELLIS, *supra* note 12, at 234; SMITH, *supra* note 3, at 278.

82. Farewell Address (Sept. 19, 1796), *supra* note 1, at http://gwpapers.virginia.edu/documents/farewell/transcript.html#top.

83. *Id.*

84. Letter from George Washington to James Madison (May 20, 1792), *supra* note 3, at 400-01.

85. First Inaugural Address (Apr. 30, 1789), *in* 2 PRESIDENTIAL SERIES, *supra* note 2, at 173, 174.
86. Farewell Address (Sept. 19, 1796), *supra* note 1, at http://gwpapers.virginia.edu/documents/farewell/transcript.html#top.
87. *Id.* Some people might argue, with reason, that Washington's statement is no longer true. Religious diversity has increased since the 1790s. On the other hand, even today most Americans share much common ground, even in their divergent religious beliefs. A large majority of Americans, whether they are Jewish, Christian, or Muslim, are monotheists who share a belief in a benevolent God who directs the course of human events. Indeed, these commonalities have driven such spiritual leaders as Pope John Paul II to argue for unity among these religious groups, focusing on their shared beliefs, rather than their theological differences. *See generally* HIS HOLINESS JOHN PAUL II, CROSSING THE THRESHOLD OF HOPE 77-104, 144-51 (1994).
88. Farewell Address (Sept. 19, 1796), *supra* note 1, at http://gwpapers.virginia.edu/documents/farewell/transcript.html#top (emphasis added).
89. *Id.*
90. *Id.*
91. *Id.*
92. *Id.*
93. *E.g.*, SMITH, *supra* note 3, at 278-79.
94. The bill was one for apportionment of congressional seats. The events surrounding the president's veto are discussed at 6 FREEMAN, *supra* note 3, at 343-47; 10 PRESIDENTIAL SERIES, *supra* note 2, at 195-214; *see also* Letter from George Washington to the United States House of Representatives (Apr. 5, 1792), *in* 10 PRESIDENTIAL SERIES, *supra* note 2, at 213, 213-14.
95. The House was debating Jay's Treaty and wanted certain papers related to the negotiations. CARROLL & ASHWORTH, *supra* note 12, at 347-59, 361-77; *see also* Letter from George Washington to the House of Representatives (Mar. 30, 1796), *in* 35 WRITINGS, *supra* note 1, at 2, 2-5.
96. Letter from George Washington to Doctor James Anderson (Dec. 24, 1795), *in* 34 WRITINGS, *supra* note 1, at 405, 407.

CONCLUSION

1. JOSEPH J. ELLIS, HIS EXCELLENCY: GEORGE WASHINGTON 12 (2004).
2. *See, e.g.*, Remarks (1787-88), *in* 5 THE PAPERS OF GEORGE WASHINGTON: CONFEDERATION SERIES 515, 515-26 (Dorothy Twohig et al. eds., 1997) [the collection is hereinafter referred to as CONFEDERATION SERIES]; *see also* PETER R. HENRIQUES, REALISTIC VISIONARY: A PORTRAIT OF GEORGE WASHINGTON 21-22 (2006).
3. Letter from George Washington to Edward Newenham (June 22, 1792), *in* 10 THE PAPERS OF GEORGE WASHINGTON: PRESIDENTIAL SERIES 493, 493 (Philander D. Chase et al. eds., 2002) [the collection is hereinafter referred to as PRESIDENTIAL SERIES]; *see also* Letter from George Washington to Edward Newenham (Oct. 20, 1792), *in* 11 PRESIDENTIAL SERIES, *supra*, at 246, 246.
4. Letter from George Washington to the Society of Quakers (Oct. 1789), *in* 4 PRESIDENTIAL SERIES, *supra* note 3, at 265, 266.

5. Letter from George Washington to the Hebrew Congregation in Newport, Rhode Island (Aug. 18, 1790), *in* 6 PRESIDENTIAL SERIES, *supra* note 3, at 284, 285.

6. Letter from George Washington to George Mason (Oct. 3, 1785), *in* 3 CONFEDERATION SERIES, *supra* note 2, at 292, 293.

7. Letter from George Washington to the Ministers, Elders, Deacons, and Members of the Reformed German Congregation of New York (Nov. 27, 1783), *in* 27 THE WRITINGS OF GEORGE WASHINGTON FROM THE ORIGINAL MANUSCRIPT SOURCES 1745-1799, at 249, 249 (John C. Fitzpatrick ed., 1938) [the collection is hereinafter referred to as WRITINGS].

8. Letter from George Washington to the Clergy of Different Denominations Residing in and Near the City of Philadelphia (Mar. 3, 1797), *in* 35 WRITINGS, *supra* note 7, at 416, 416.

9. *Id.*

EPILOGUE

1. Letter from Thomas Jefferson to the Danbury Baptist Association (Jan. 1, 1802), *in* DANIEL L. DREISBACH, THOMAS JEFFERSON AND THE WALL OF SEPARATION BETWEEN CHURCH AND STATE 148, 148 (2002).

2. Washington took his first oath of office in New York and his second oath in Philadelphia. 6 DOUGLAS SOUTHALL FREEMAN, GEORGE WASHINGTON, A BIOGRAPHY: PATRIOT AND PRESIDENT 185-98 (1954); JOHN ALEXANDER CARROLL & MARY WELLS ASHWORTH, GEORGE WASHINGTON: FIRST IN PEACE 7-9 (1957). Washington's successor, John Adams, took his first and only oath of office in Philadelphia. *E.g.*, DAVID MCCULLOUGH, JOHN ADAMS 467 (2001).

3. At the time, the party could be referred to as either "Republican" or "Democratic-Republican." However, this party is the forerunner of today's Democratic Party, rather than today's Republican Party. For ease of reference and to avoid confusion with modern-day political parties, this book will use the longer "Democratic-Republican" title when referring to the party during Jefferson's lifetime.

4. *E.g.*, MCCULLOUGH, *supra* note 2, at 564-66; *see also* BERNARD A. WEISBERGER, AMERICA AFIRE: JEFFERSON, ADAMS, AND THE FIRST CONTESTED ELECTION 1-3 (Perennial ed. 2001).

5. *See* JOSEPH J. ELLIS, FOUNDING BROTHERS: THE REVOLUTIONARY GENERATION 207 (2000); JOHN FERLING, ADAMS VS. JEFFERSON: THE TUMULTUOUS ELECTION OF 1800, at 18-35 (Pivotal Moments in American History Series, David Hackett Fischer & James M. McPherson eds., 2004).

6. The outcome was the result of the old Article II election process, used before the Twelfth Amendment was adopted. Under Article II, the first place winner in the Electoral College vote was elected president and the second place winner was elected vice president. U.S. CONST. art. II, § 1, cl. 3.

7. *See, e.g.*, MCCULLOUGH, *supra* note 2, at 475.

8. Joseph Ellis discusses the renewal of the Adams-Jefferson friendship at length in his book, *Founding Brothers*. ELLIS, *supra* note 5, at 206-48; *see also* MCCULLOUGH, *supra* note 2, at 603-08.

9. *See, e.g.*, PAUL F. BOLLER, JR., PRESIDENTIAL CAMPAIGNS 10-18 (rev. ed. 1996); *see also* FERLING, *supra* note 5, at 155-56.

10. *E.g.*, BOLLER, *supra* note 9, at 10-18; Thomas E. Buckley, S.J., *The Religious Rhetoric of Thomas Jefferson, in* THE FOUNDERS ON GOD AND GOVERNMENT 53, 69-70 (Daniel L. Dreisbach et al. eds., 2004); DREISBACH, *supra* note 1, at 18-20; FERLING, *supra* note 5, at 153-54; PHILIP HAMBURGER, SEPARATION OF CHURCH AND STATE 112-17 (4th prtg. 2002).

11. DREISBACH, *supra* note 1, at 18 (citation omitted); MICHAEL NOVAK & JANA NOVAK, WASHINGTON'S GOD: RELIGION, LIBERTY, AND THE FATHER OF OUR COUNTRY 162 (2006).

12. DREISBACH, *supra* note 1, at 20; HAMBURGER, *supra* note 10, at 117-20; *see also* Letter from Thomas Jefferson to De Witt Clinton (May 24, 1807), *in* 11 THE WRITINGS OF THOMAS JEFFERSON 208, 208 (Andrew A. Lipscomb & Albert Ellery Bergh eds., 1905).

13. *See, e.g.*, Buckley, *supra* note 10, at 69-70; DREISBACH, *supra* note 1, at 27-28.

14. *See, e.g.*, JOHN SUTHERLAND BONNELL, PRESIDENTIAL PROFILES: RELIGION IN THE LIFE OF AMERICAN PRESIDENTS 32-36 (1971); Buckley, *supra* note 10, at 53-56; ALF J. MAPP, JR., THE FAITHS OF OUR FATHERS: WHAT AMERICA'S FOUNDERS REALLY BELIEVED 6, 9-10 (2003); JOHN C. MCCOLLISTER, PH.D., GOD AND THE OVAL OFFICE: THE RELIGIOUS FAITH OF OUR 43 PRESIDENTS 17-20 (2005).

15. For a discussion of Jefferson's unorthodox religious beliefs, see *supra* note 14; *see also, e.g.*, MICHAEL NOVAK, ON TWO WINGS: HUMBLE FAITH AND COMMON SENSE AT THE AMERICAN FOUNDING 30-31, 129 (2002). Arguably, Jefferson's "less orthodox" views did not make him "less religious," so much as they made him religious in a different way. Peter Henriques seems to take this position when he argues that Jefferson may have been more religious than Washington in many respects. *See* PETER R. HENRIQUES, REALISTIC VISIONARY: A PORTRAIT OF GEORGE WASHINGTON 183-84 (2006).

16. *E.g.*, FERLING, *supra* note 5, at 201; 4 DUMAS MALONE, JEFFERSON AND HIS TIME: JEFFERSON THE PRESIDENT, FIRST TERM, 1801-1805, at 3 (1970); WEISBERGER, *supra* note 4, at 278.

17. *E.g.*, FERLING, *supra* note 5, at 201.

18. *E.g.*, *id.* at 201-02; 4 MALONE, *supra* note 16, at 29-32.

19. *See* DREISBACH, *supra* note 1, at 9-17; *see also* 4 MALONE, *supra* note 16, at 106-08.

20. *See* Address of the Danbury Baptist Association to Thomas Jefferson (Oct. 7, 1801), *in* DREISBACH, *supra* note 1, at 142, 142-44. Descriptions in this book of the circumstances surrounding Jefferson's letter to the Danbury Baptists rely heavily upon the excellent work of Daniel Dreisbach and Philip Hamburger. The professors' books are highly recommended for a more detailed discussion of these issues. *See generally* DREISBACH, *supra* note 1; HAMBURGER, *supra* note 10.

21. DREISBACH, *supra* note 1, at 32-33; *see also* ROBERT L. CORD, SEPARATION OF CHURCH AND STATE: HISTORICAL FACT AND CURRENT FICTION 4 (1982).

22. *See* Address of the Danbury Baptist Association to Thomas Jefferson (Oct. 7, 1801), *supra* note 20, at 142; *cf.* HAMBURGER, *supra* note 10, at 110 (describing early 19th-century Baptists as generally sympathetic to the Democratic-Republicans and distrustful of the Federalists).

23. *See* DREISBACH, *supra* note 1, at 25-26, 30; *see also* HAMBURGER, *supra* note 10, at 156.

24. Address of the Danbury Baptist Association to Thomas Jefferson (Oct. 7, 1801),

supra note 20, at 143.

25. DREISBACH, *supra* note 1, at 27, 34-47.

26. *Id.* at 27-30; HAMBURGER, *supra* note 10, at 6; *see also* Buckley, *supra* note 10, at 70-71.

27. *See* HAMBURGER, *supra* note 10, at 111, 147-62.

28. DREISBACH, *supra* note 1, at 21, 56; HAMBURGER, *supra* note 10, at 159, 174. Indeed, Jefferson's views on this issue so greatly differed from the public that he eventually dropped the one sentence on the issue of religious proclamations from his letter to the Danbury Baptists. *See* DREISBACH, *supra* note 1, at 39-40, 46; HAMBURGER, *supra* note 10, at 159-61.

29. Letter from Thomas Jefferson to Levi Lincoln (Jan. 1, 1802), *in* DREISBACH, *supra* note 1, at 146, 146; *see also* DREISBACH, *supra* note 1, at 25-26, 43-44; HAMBURGER, *supra* note 10, at 159.

30. DREISBACH, *supra* note 1, at 44.

31. Letter from Thomas Jefferson to the Danbury Baptist Association (Jan. 1, 1802), *supra* note 1, at 148 (second emphasis added).

32. *See* discussion *supra* Introduction, note 18 and accompanying text.

33. HAMBURGER, *supra* note 10, at 109-10, 144, 163-80.

34. DREISBACH, *supra* note 1, at 52-53; HAMBURGER, *supra* note 10, at 163-65.

35. Letter from Thomas Jefferson to the Danbury Baptist Association (Jan. 1, 1802), *supra* note 1, at 148.

36. DREISBACH, *supra* note 1, at 51-52; HAMBURGER, *supra* note 10, at 165, 180.

37. HAMBURGER, *supra* note 10, at 162 (citing James H. Hutson); *see also* DREISBACH, *supra* note 1, at 21-22; 1 ANSON PHELPS STOKES, CHURCH AND STATE IN THE UNITED STATES 499-501 (1950).

38. HAMBURGER, *supra* note 10, at 181.

39. *See* DREISBACH, *supra* note 1, at 57-58; David Barton, *The Image and the Reality: Thomas Jefferson and the First Amendment*, 17 NOTRE DAME J.L. ETHICS & PUB. POL'Y 399, 403-09 (2003); William F. Cox, Jr., *The Original Meaning of the Establishment Clause and Its Application to Education*, 13 REGENT U. L. REV. 111, 124 (2000/2001); Patrick M. Garry, *The Myth of Separation: America's Historical Experience with Church and State*, 33 HOFSTRA L. REV. 475, 498 (2004); *see also* Thomas Jefferson, Inauguration Address (Mar. 4, 1801), *in* THE LIFE AND SELECTED WRITINGS OF THOMAS JEFFERSON 321, 323 (Adrienne Koch & William Peden eds., reprtg. 1972).

40. *See* DREISBACH, *supra* note 1, at 55-70; Arlin M. Adams & Charles J. Emmerich, *A Heritage of Religious Liberty*, 137 U. PA. L. REV. 1559, 1585-86 (1989); Barton, *supra* note 39, at 406-09; Cox, *supra* note 39, at 140-41; Garry, *supra* note 39, at 497-98.

41. The legal history of "separation of church and state" is, by necessity, rather abbreviated in this section. An excellent and complete treatment of the subject can be found in a recent book by Philip Hamburger. *See generally* HAMBURGER, *supra* note 10.

42. 98 U.S. 145 (1879). Although the Court did not use the metaphor until 1879, a few legal scholars made occasional references to it. *See* DREISBACH, *supra* note 1, at 96-97.

43. Everson v. Bd. of Educ., 330 U.S. 1 (1947).

44. Jefferson's phrase is relied upon most heavily when the Court decides Establishment Clause cases. *See* discussion *supra* Introduction, note 4 and accompanying text.

45. *See generally Reynolds*, 98 U.S. at 145.
46. *Id*. at 161-62. *Reynolds* did not address the question of whether the First Amendment can be made applicable to the states, as *Everson* would. The case was before the Supreme Court because Reynolds lived in the terrorities, where he was subject to federal criminal laws. *See id*. at 162.
47. *Id*. at 162-67.
48. *Id*. at 163-64.
49. *Id*. at 164.
50. *Id*.
51. *Id*.
52. 330 U.S. 1 (1947). The concept was mentioned by dissenting judges in two cases shortly before *Everson*, however. *See* W. Va. State Bd. of Educ. v. Barnette, 319 U.S. 624, 654-60 (1943) (Frankfurter, J., dissenting); Murdock v. Pennsylvania, 319 U.S. 105, 130 (1943) (Reed, J., dissenting); *id*. at 140 (Frankfurter, J., dissenting). A 1908 case also made a brief reference to separationism. Ponce v. Roman Catholic Apostolic Church, 210 U.S. 296, 321 (1908) (discussing an action to quiet title on a church property in Puerto Rico and mentioning the "transfer of sovereignty from a regime of union of church and state to the American system of complete separation").
53. *Everson*, 330 U.S. at 18.
54. *Id*. at 16 (citing *Reynolds*, 98 U.S. at 164).
55. *Id*. at 18.
56. *See* HAMBURGER, *supra* note 10, at 3; Daniel L. Dreisbach, *A Lively and Fair Experiment: Religion and the American Constitutional Tradition*, 49 EMORY L.J. 223, 229-32 (2000); *see also* THE HERITAGE GUIDE TO THE CONSTITUTION 304 (David F. Forte & Matthew Spalding eds., 2005).
57. Letter from Thomas Jefferson to Levi Lincoln (Jan. 1, 1802), *supra* note 29, at 146; *see also* DREISBACH, *supra* note 1, at 25-26, 43-44, 100-02.
58. McCollum v. Bd. of Educ., 333 U.S. 203 (1948).
59. *Id*. at 205-09.
60. *See generally id*.
61. *Id*. at 212.
62. General Orders (Feb. 15, 1783), *in* 26 THE WRITINGS OF GEORGE WASHINGTON FROM THE ORIGINAL MANUSCRIPT SOURCES 1745-1799, at 135, 135 (John C. Fitzpatrick ed., 1938).
63. WILLIAM LOUGHTON SMITH, THE PRETENSIONS OF THOMAS JEFFERSON TO THE PRESIDENCY EXAMINED; AND THE CHARGES AGAINST JOHN ADAMS REFUTED 36-40 (United States, 1796); *see also* GEORGE C. ROGERS, JR., EVOLUTION OF A FEDERALIST: WILLIAM LOUGHTON SMITH OF CHARLESTON (1758-1812), at 292-93 (1962).
64. SMITH, *supra* note 63, at 39. In the quotation in the text, the long s, which resembles an f, has been updated.
65. *Id*. at 37.
66. Political Science (Mar. 4, 1825), *in* THE COMPLETE JEFFERSON 1112, 1112 (Saul K. Padover ed., 1943). The resolution named "text and documents" for use in the law school at the university. *Id*. The list was created by Jefferson, with the help of James Madison. Jefferson's original list did not include Washington's Farewell Address, but Madison suggested that it be added. Letter from James Madison

to Thomas Jefferson (Feb. 8, 1825), *in* 9 THE WRITINGS OF JAMES MADISON 218, 220-21 (Gaillard Hunt ed., 1910); *see also* 6 MALONE, *supra* note 16, at 417. Jefferson responded that he was "particularly pleased with your inclusion of Genl. Wash's addresses, which had not occurred to me or I should have referred to them also." Letter from Thomas Jefferson to James Madison (Feb. 12, 1825), http://memory. loc.gov/ammem/collections/jefferson_papers/mtjser1.html (last visited May 4, 2007).

67. The editors at *The Papers of George Washington* have not yet published the final volumes of their Presidential Series. The text of the Farewell Address, however, has been made available at http://gwpapers.virginia.edu/documents/farewell/transcript. html#top.

PART TWO

ONE

1. All writings in this section are reprinted from THE PAPERS OF GEORGE WASHINGTON: COLONIAL SERIES (W.W. Abbot et al. eds., 1983-1995).

TWO

1. Unless otherwise noted, all writings in this section are reprinted from THE PAPERS OF GEORGE WASHINGTON: REVOLUTIONARY WAR SERIES (W.W. Abbot et al. eds., 1985-2006).

2. The remainder of the writings in this section can be found in the Fitzpatrick collection of Washington's writings. THE WRITINGS OF GEORGE WASHINGTON FROM THE ORIGINAL MANUSCRIPT SOURCES 1745-1799 (John C. Fitzpatrick ed., 1931-44).

THREE

1. All writings in this section are reprinted from THE PAPERS OF GEORGE WASHINGTON: CONFEDERATION SERIES (W.W. Abbot et al. eds., 1992-1997).

FOUR

1. All writings in this section are reprinted from THE PAPERS OF GEORGE WASHINGTON: PRESIDENTIAL SERIES (W.W. Abbot et al. eds., 1987-2005).

FIVE

1. Unless otherwise noted, all writings in this section are reprinted from THE PAPERS OF GEORGE WASHINGTON: PRESIDENTIAL SERIES (W.W. Abbot et al. eds., 1987-2005).

2. The remainder of the writings in this section, with the exception of Washington's 1795 Thanksgiving Proclamation, can be found in the Fitzpatrick collection of Washington's writings. THE WRITINGS OF GEORGE WASHINGTON FROM THE ORIGINAL MANUSCRIPT SOURCES 1745-1799 (John C. Fitzpatrick ed., 1931-44).

3. By the President of the United States of America: A Proclamation (Jan. 1, 1795), *in* 1 A COMPILATION OF THE MESSAGES AND PAPERS OF THE PRESIDENTS: 1789-1897, at 179 (James D. Richardson ed., 1896).

4. The editors at *The Papers of George Washington* have not yet published the final volumes of their Presidential Series. The text of the Farewell Address, however, has been made available at http://gwpapers.virginia.edu/documents/farewell/transcript.html#top. The transcript can also be found in Fitzpatrick's collection of Washington's writings. *See* Farewell Address (Sept. 19, 1796), *reprinted in* 35 WRITINGS, *supra* note 2, at 214, 214-38.

Index